Thank You

~~~~~~~~~~~~~~~~~

'When opportunity knocks, a man still has to walk through the door'

Thank you to Pete Townsend, Clive Banks, and Dave Clogg for inspiring and encouraging me to write this book.

Thank you to my ghostwriter, Matthew Huggins, who helped me put this story into words and shared the journey of the last year with me.

Thank you to my editor, David Ethier, for his guidance and effort.

Thank you to my wee blue-nose friend Derek who helped with the name of the book, and Scottish Charlie for his ongoing support and our nutty banter

Thank you to my beautiful girlfriend Laurie for all her love and support.

There are many other friends I would like to thank. These friends have helped me in so many ways throughout my ongoing recovery journey – as well as the people that made this book possible. These people know who they are, because I have told them, and I thank you all for everything that you have done for me and with me.

I would not wish to take away your spiritual gift by mentioning each of your names.

Publishers Note

This is a true story.

However, some of the names, locations,
and character descriptions have been altered
to protect people's safety and identity.

*One evening an old Cherokee told his grandson
about a battle that goes on inside people.*

———————————

He said, 'My son, the battle is between
two "wolves" inside us all.

One is Evil. It is anger, envy, jealousy, sorrow, regret,
greed, arrogance, self-pity, guilt, resentment,
inferiority, lies, false pride, superiority, and ego.

The other is Good. It is joy, peace, love, hope,
serenity, humility, kindness, benevolence, empathy,
generosity, truth, compassion, and faith.'

The grandson thought about it for a minute and then
asked his grandfather: 'Which wolf wins?'

The old Cherokee simply replied, 'The one you feed.'

- Cherokee Fable

Prologue

I arrived at Lima airport, in Peru, close to midnight. The Peruvian man I had been sitting next to on the plane was checking the credentials of the taxi driver.

'You need to be careful,' he warned. 'There are lots of slums here. People will rob you. You need to go to your hotel and stay there at night.'

I hadn't booked accommodation. I had travelled the world without much of a plan and always managed to find a place to stay – whether an Indian drug dealer's hut in the middle of the Himalayas or a Spanish prison, I had always had a bed to sleep in. The Peruvian man was surprised about my lack of planning. I didn't even have a guidebook. He wrote down the name of a hotel.

'This is a safe area to go,' he said as he handed me the paper and ushered me into the taxi. 'Be careful of people.' I thanked him for the advice, but I didn't need it. I had smuggled drugs across borders with the threat of death penalties and begged in the slums of India. I could handle myself.

The taxi driver took me to a hotel. The next morning, I spoke with some tourists over breakfast. They were full of doom and gloom predictions as well.

'You have to be careful of the streets,' they warned. 'There are robbers with guns and knives. Stay close to the centre. The farther away you get, the less police there are. Don't trust the taxis.'

I thought: This might be dangerous for you, but I was once a big time drug dealer.

I didn't say it, though. I thanked them for the advice that I didn't need. I had carried around tens of thousands of pounds in the back streets of Brixton and never been robbed.

I got the bus to Cuzco. As the bus left Lima it bumped its way past the slums – lines of slanted and battered shacks. The people who were milling around were wearing dirty and tattered clothes. I had seen that kind of poverty before. I had lived on the streets, without even a shack to my name.

I ignored the advice I had been given and went to a nightclub outside the town centre. I stayed for a few hours. I wasn't drinking alcohol, so the club became boring after a while. It was one thirty in the morning when I left. I walked down the back streets, en route to my hotel. The streets were asleep – houses had their shutters closed and there were very few lights offering safety. In the darkness, across the back street, I saw three men coming towards me. They were small, but menacing in their walk. I looked at them as they got closer, and smiled.

I know what you're up to. Don't mess with me – I was like you once. I know what you're going to try to do to me.

I turned right to avoid having to tell them to fuck off. I knew that I could kick-box them if I had to. I was becoming an expert at kick-boxing with all the training I had been doing back in London. I didn't want the bother of having to take all three of them down, though.

I picked up my pace. They turned right, just as I had done, but a street ahead of me. I knew that they were pacing the other street to meet me at the end.

A taxi appeared. I knew getting in the taxi was the right thing to do, I just didn't want to waste the money. I was battling with the idea of risking a fight and walking back to the hotel. I still had the panicky tourist's voice in my head, warning me of robbers with guns and knives.

I got into the taxi and reached forward to tell the driver where to take me. Before I could get the words out, the three men were upon the car and getting through the doors. The taxi driver was shouting for them to get out, as if he had nothing to do with it. I knew that it was a set-up and that he was part of the gang trying to mug me.

I kicked at one of them as he opened the door. Another grabbed me from the side. I turned towards him to punch him back out of the car. That's when I saw the knife. It was a big kitchen knife. I froze as he put his arms around me and held the blade point to my neck. They shouted in Spanish. I sat back and they got in the car. The car drove off but I didn't know where it was going.

With the knife at my throat, I thought about what to do.

I had a money bag with four hundred dollars in it. I offered them twenty dollars, in the hope that I wouldn't have to hand over the lot. They shouted in Spanish and jabbed the blade against my skin.

We stopped at some traffic lights. There were people outside on the street partying and the window was slightly open. I shouted as loud as I could that I was being robbed. My travel companions shouted in Spanish and jabbed the blade harder against my skin. The car sped off.

I knew that fighting was not going to get me out of this situation. They were going to take everything I had and then kill me.

The car stopped in desolate land. There were a few wooden houses, but no lights were on. The ground was hard and dusty. They searched me and took my money, my camera, the belt from my waist, my watch, my earring – everything but my trousers and shirt. They even took my passport.

'Not my passport, please.' It would be a hassle to get a new passport. I had spent a lot of my time travelling in embassies trying to get a new passport. The men didn't care. They shouted in Spanish and pushed me to my knees. One of them got behind me and put his arms around my neck. He started to squeeze hard.

Fuck. I am going to die.

All I could think about was how fucked up this was. I had been close to death many times in my life. I had often wished myself dead. Yet, now, at five years clean from drugs and alcohol, I found myself on my knees being strangled to death.

They say your life flashes before your eyes when you die. It didn't for me. I thought about how much of life I had yet to live. I thought about my mum – that she would finally get the news she always feared: that I was found dead in a ditch.

I thought that this shouldn't be happening at five years clean.

I thought about what would be left of me.

That nobody would know what had happened to me.

That nobody would know my story.

As I fell into unconsciousness, I wondered whether I would ever get to finish this story.

For me, the story of my life had only just begun.

PART ONE

Chapter 1

Everybody else's mum on our estate did the cooking, the cleaning, and the mothering. My mum did the cooking, the cleaning, the mothering, and everything else. My dad worked occasionally and spent the rest of his time drinking and trying to kill himself, which was a complete pain in the arse for Mum and me.

That wasn't his plan. Nobody ever plans to make a career out of drinking and trying to kill themselves. It's a bit like that old saying about eating an elephant. How do you become an alcoholic? One drink at a time. Of course, for my dad it was one bottle at a time. Then another. And another.

When he did stop drinking it wouldn't be long before he was sick again. One minute he would be pacing the room, dripping sweat from his face, and the next shaking on the floor. Mum said it was the drink that made him see spiders, snakes, and things that were not there. I would be in the corner watching him shout and curse while Mum ran for the sick bowl. She would get back just in time to catch the vomit.

'Okay, Eddie, get it all out,' Mum would soothe. Then he would shake.

Is his heart going to go pop? Is he going to die? Please don't die, Dad, please don't die.

I had never seen anybody die. I was only seven.

Then he would see snakes, spiders, and dead Grandma.

'Your mother. It's your mother. She's watching me, she's here. Get away from me, stay away…' More sick.

'There's nothing here, Eddie, everything's okay,' Mum would stroke his hair.

Why aren't you scared, Mum? Why can't we see what Dad can see?

It would be hours like this. Dad sicking and screaming, seeing spiders, snakes, and dead Grandma. Mum calmly wiping away the sweat from his brow and the vomit from his chin. Eventually the screaming would stop and the shaking would turn into spasms, like the last attempts of a strangled dog trying to breathe. The sounds of sicking and screaming were then replaced with snoring.

It was the delirium tremens, Mum said. I knew what delirium tremens was before I kissed a girl, even before I could spell the words. Dad drank so many bottles that when he stopped his body would go into a shaking frenzy. That was why Dad could see things that were not there, but I still couldn't understand why he saw Grandma. Grandma had smoked herself to death with the cancer before I could remember anything about her. She must have been telling Dad off. She never liked him.

'You cannot marry that man, Anne,' she had told Mum. 'He's a drinker and a thief. He's not good enough for you. You think we sent you off to a good Catholic school in France for you to get pregnant the first chance with a drinker – and a murderer? Don't think I don't know what he done.'

She was talking about the 'accident'. He had been drunk that night. That wasn't a big deal. It was the late fifties and Friday and Saturday nights were spent dancing down at the Barrowland. He was only twenty and all his friends got drunk on the weekend. He hadn't wanted to drive that night but his friend had badgered him to go dancing. Dad never liked saying no to his friends. The pole that hit the van went straight through the middle and took his friend's arm

19

off. Dad flew through the windscreen and didn't die. His friend did.

It was all over the papers:

Man, 20, kills friend drunk driving; drunk driving man charged with manslaughter.

He was definitely going to prison – a man died. But Old Man Trammy was a top lawyer in Scotland and told the judge that Dad was going to live for the rest of his life with the shame of what he had done - that every time he looked in the mirror and saw the scars on his face, Dad would see his dead friend. The judge agreed and gave Dad a suspended sentence, hefty fine, and a long driving ban. He escaped a prison sentence, but Old Man Trammy was right: Dad had to live with the guilt for the rest of his life.

If it hadn't been for the accident, Dad and Mum probably wouldn't have met, and I wouldn't have been born. He wouldn't have looked at her twice before the accident, Mum said. Dad was a ladies' man and had been too busy charming his way through the women of Glasgow. After the accident his face was scarred and he wasn't a ladies' man any more. He could still use the charm, though. He sweet-talked my mum at the place they both worked at – a clothing store called Susie Stewarts. He winked at her in the morning and told her she was looking pretty fine. He sidled up to her at lunch and asked about her morning. Dad listened and smiled and Mum blushed.

Mum was head over heels for Dad. The scars didn't bother her. She could always see the best in people, and what she saw in my dad was a man who was trying as best he could to get on with life, despite the accident. She hadn't had a boyfriend before, and had never had sex. She had been sheltered from the rough streets of Glasgow in a Catholic convent in France and was oblivious to the ways of the Glaswegian working-class man. She took the winks and smiles and compliments as a sign of true love. She didn't know that's what a Glasgow boy does to every girl he wants to get into bed. Dad hadn't had the education and life Mum had got in France. While

20

she was being taught the difference between mortal and venial sins in the catechism of Catholicism, Dad was busy watching his dad hoodwink everybody out of a few pounds to gamble on the horses. Dad knew how to charm people *and* get what he wanted and Mum knew how to love.

Dad used his powers of charm to convince Mum to come to a party at his friend's flat. She was charmed enough to go and then discovered that nobody else was there. It was just her and Dad. As soon as she got to the flat, Dad didn't waste any time. A man who lacked experience of wooing or romancing, he pushed and she resisted until she didn't resist and he didn't need to push. And then she was pregnant. I couldn't really blame Grandma for not liking him.

But Mum didn't care. She loved him.

'Of course you love him. You're having his baby! But you don't even know him. You can't trust a drinker.'

Mum came from a family of drinkers. Her dad drank and her brothers drank. Her mother didn't want that life for her, and had hoped that sending her to a French Catholic school would mean she would know that being drunk was a sin. Mum knew that, but she also knew that sex out of marriage was as mortal a sin as drunkenness. What else could she do but get married? Abortion was out of the question. That was a mortal sin too. That's why Grandma didn't like Dad. She blamed him for leading her daughter into sin and having me born out of that sin. Mum was too scared to tell Grandma that anger, quarrelling and divorce were just as mortal a sin – Grandma was always angry with Mum or Dad about something and had been divorced for years.

So Mum and Dad got married. That's how I came into the world, and that's how Mum and Dad's life started together. No doubt with a bottle to celebrate. Then another. And another.

Granddad didn't share Grandma's dislike for Dad. He was a drinker too, and at some point they both must have thought that drinking was the only thing they were good at because they decided to run a pub in

Nottingham. I spent my time climbing the trees in Sherwood Forest just as Robin Hood would have done. Or maybe, as I was only three, I just clawed at the base of the trunks. As Robin Hood took from the rich to give to the poor, Dad and Granddad took so much drink from the pub that they became poor in the process.

We lived above the pub and I remember the smell. It was the smell of wood fire and barley beer, pipe smoke and peanuts. Even the jukebox shooting out the sounds of the Beatles, Buddy Holly, and the Stones had a smell to it. It was the smell of warmth and the smell of laughter. It was the smell of drinkers who didn't sick and shake and see spiders, snakes, and dead Grandma. I would ride around the pub in my toy car, with Mum serving the customers and Granddad and Dad playing cards and joking around.

Granddad's belly hung out over his trousers and no amount of buttons made a difference. He drank so much that it was a struggle for him to get dressed properly in the morning. He would roll out of bed, moaning and groaning about the morning, and fix his smile on just in time to open the doors to the first drinkers of the day. He was Mum's dad, but would have been better as Dad's with their love of the drink. They were great friends, but bad business partners. With the whole pub drunk, we went back to Scotland as poor as we had left. Granddad disappeared from memory.

We lived in the poor part of Partick, which was once a village settlement with no more than a few hundred residents, west of Glasgow. Several hundred years later, when we lived there, Partick was many villages, separated by invisible boundaries. The boundaries were set by how much money you had, which was determined by how big your house was and how many people you had to fit into it. The closest I got to the rich was the girl in school who had two names instead of one. My village consisted of three types of family: those who were poorer than my family, those who were richer than my family – and my family.

Although there were those that were richer and those that were poorer, we were all still working class in our village. I didn't know any other class existed. Upper class were the English lords, kings and queens in fairy tales and the middle class were over the border in that place most Scottish people loved to hate and blame for everything. In truth, they were just south of Dunbarton Road - no more than a mile away - but I only saw Partick and Glasgow through the families that were around me.

The poorer families had more children than they could feed with three or more to a bed. They wore second-hand clothes that had been second-hand for the last three families that had them. The kids had grimy, snotty faces and a stench of shit. It was a musty, stale smell of an arse not fully wiped, probably through lack of toilet paper. Those were the families that rarely got richer. The parents didn't work and their parents didn't work and *their* parents bypassed the Victorian workhouse for the poorhouse. The money they had came from the welfare.

The families that were richer than me were better off, but only just. Those kids wore Levi's and Wranglers, clean T-shirts, not a trace of shit, and enough toilet paper to keep a completely snot-free nose.

And then there was my family. Not far above the poorest, but nowhere near the richest and not much chance of ever getting there. The only reason we never hit the bottom was because Mum worked and Dad was so busy drinking he didn't have time to produce another kid. That kept me in cheap, but shit-free jeans. We had a small flat with one bedroom and a place for me to sleep, separated from the kitchen by a curtain.

Sixties Glasgow was a depressing place, however poor you were. The city was once a hub of trade and manufacturing – producing and exporting cloths, garments and locomotives across the empire. But the empire was breaking up. Products were becoming cheaper to manufacture in other countries. In the face of this onslaught of change, Glasgow continued to do what it had always done: build more. Only a decade earlier there were still plenty of jobs in the shipbuilding and engineering companies. Even a lot of the factories and mills survived for a while after the war finished. But, by the time I arrived, things had changed. At the end of the last century, Glasgow had half of the country's shipbuilding and supplied trains to the rest of the world. As I entered the world, we were lucky to afford a journey on a train, let alone get work building one.

Even the rich, who acquired their money from owning shipyards, refineries, forgeries, and factories, were losing their businesses. Most of them still had their money, though. It was the poor who worked for them that lost their jobs. They didn't have savings or assets to fall back on. The lucky ones went to work on the North Sea oil rigs, which paid well for dangerous work, and the rest tried to make ends meet with the jobs that were left. Glasgow was now littered with washed-out shipyards, broken factories and silent mills. All that was left was the dirt and grime of centuries-old smoke. Everything was caked in black.

Glasgow people had a history of fighting. Any time outsiders or the ruling classes threatened our way of life, we would rise up. Whatever the injustice from the authorities, we could down tools in protest. But now, with no tools to down, all that was left was to drink and try to forget it all. Therefore, everybody drank.

Friends and community would gather at the weekends to sing and laugh and dance and forget. They'd forget the slog of the week, forget the lack of money, forget the bills that mounted, and forget that their children had a worse future than they had, their parents had got and their parents before that had got.

If they didn't work, then they drank to forget they didn't work. They drank to turn off the rain and the misery of the cold. They drank to blur out the masses of black-stained, chipped, battered stone of the tenement homes. They drank to brighten the prospects from nothing to something, if only for a night, and they drank to express their melancholy, to ease the suffering of what they shared: hopelessness. Whatever reason, they just drank.

Those Friday and Saturday night gatherings, where the working week was washed away with beer, whiskey and singing and dancing, had the warmth of the pub, my first home. It had the laughter, the people chatting, people singing, people drinking. There was nothing depressing I could see in that. I would sneak in the room and watch from Mum's legs when she was too happy, too merry to care, and everybody else too drunk to notice me. Just like back in the Nottingham pub, everybody would drink until they were singing, arms draped around each other and swaying in time with the melody:

Ali bali, al bali bee, Sitting on yer daddy's knee, Waiting for a wee bobbie, Taie buy some cooters candy.

Then the laughter would turn to crying as they sang 'Nobody's Child':

I'm nobody's child, Just like a flower I'm growing wild, No mama's arms to hold me, No daddy's smile, Nobody wants me, I'm nobody's child.

The song made them sad. They sang and sang, then cried and cried, and then laughter turned to tears that turned to hugs – that ended in fights and shouting and slamming of doors. They came together to share their hopelessness and to forget, to wash away the blackness of their lives – but no matter how much they drank to forget, in the end, they still remembered and cried.

Dad was different, though. He always managed to drink enough to forget because he never cried. I never told anybody about Dad seeing spiders, snakes, and dead Grandma. It was a secret, Mum said. To us, Dad was sick. To everybody else Dad was a 'heavy drinker'. They just saw that he was like them. Their parents had been heavy drinkers and their parents before that had been heavy drinkers. The bosses of the factories and shipyards had been so worried about everybody being heavy drinkers and not turning up for work that they banned pubs in the tenement parts of town. Now, with most of the jobs gone, there was no need for a ban. Heavy drinkers were better than angry rioters.

I knew Dad was more than a heavy drinker because he couldn't stop even when he had a good reason to. He couldn't even take time off to stop when I had meningitis. Mum was fuming with me dying in the hospital bed, doctors fussing, and Dad leaving to go dance up at the Barrowland. Drinking came first. It even came before work. When he did get a job it wasn't for long. Mum would have to phone the boss and apologise for Dad being sick until they were fed up and gave the job to someone who was just a heavy drinker. Dad's job became drinking at the pub.

I got to walk with him to work when I was too young to do anything else. I liked the walk and hoped he would take me in the pub with him. It was the only time he was happy, in the pub with a pint in his hand and whiskey shot sitting ready, chewing the fat with his friends. I couldn't wait to sit by him and watch my dad be king of his own castle.

'Just be a minute, son, wait here and be a good boy,' he would say.

I was too young to come in the pub and too young to have any friends to play with, so all I could do was watch through the window. I'd spy the men drinking and smoking and chatting and laughing. There were no mums in the pubs. Women had been banned from the pubs for years. Of course, they were allowed by law, but the men still didn't like it. Besides, they were too busy at home cooking and cleaning and mothering.

I desperately wanted to be in the pub. I wanted to sit and laugh and chat. I wanted to watch and listen to my dad while he made them all laugh and bang the table.

Please, Dad, let me in the pub. How long do I have to wait out here? Please, Dad. Why am I standing out here? Why do I have to wait in the cold while you're in there, all warm and happy?

I couldn't say any of that, so I'd just stand and watch and eat my Golden Wonders.

I didn't give up hope that one day he would let me in the pub. I thought that maybe he was preparing me - that it was a test. If

I walked with him and waited patiently and watched, he would eventually open the door and welcome me in. It never happened. I would wait outside, whatever the weather. I broke my toe once, but still had to walk with Dad to the pub - although he walked and I limped.

He must let me in the pub now, with a broken toe.

He didn't. Even with a broken toe I did nothing outside except watch and wait for Dad.

On the way back home he would wobble from side to side and slur as he spoke.

'Now listen, son, don't tell your mother I had a drink, will you? She doesn't need to worry.'

He was always saying 'don't tell your mum' this or that. It was hard keeping all these secrets – I couldn't tell people about my dad seeing spiders, snakes, and dead Grandma, and I couldn't tell Mum about Dad drinking in the pub and keeping me waiting outside. I was torn. I wanted to keep Dad's secret. I thought that maybe he would let me in the pub if I didn't tell Mum. Maybe it was just part of the test before he could trust me to be on the inside. But Mum was always nice to me and always told me the truth. I didn't want to keep secrets from Mum. I didn't know what to do. I held out as long as I could in case it was a test. Eventually I gave up any hope of sitting with Dad in the pub and told Mum whenever he drank. After that, I told her everything.

Mum was like everybody else's mum in our town – they did the cooking, the cleaning, the mothering. The dads worked and taught their kids the things mums couldn't. They taught the sons how to be men. Men were warriors like John Wayne and Muhammad Ali. Men went to football. Getting to know whether your dad supported Celtic or Rangers would avoid getting into some tricky bar brawls. Dads taught kids to fight, in case they stumbled into a pub full of Rangers supporters wearing a Celtic scarf and hat. They taught them to talk and think like a man, not to cry but to 'stand up for

27

yourself, son'. Not to run, but to punch - especially when you're faced with a Rangers supporter.

The dads would take sons for their first pint - with much chatter amongst the other dads in the pub, reminiscing how they felt like a man when they cleared the glass. First pints for sons was a community event for dads in the pub, like the induction of a new gang member. Dads would make sure their son knew how to treat a lady – 'listen to your mother, don't talk back to her'.

My dad was too busy for football and it would be years before Mum would let me have my first pint. He did try to be a dad, but when he tried I was left confused.

I learnt how to steal from my dad. I knew that he liked it when I brought back milk bottles I had stolen from other people's doorsteps. Nothing would be said, but I could see the look of pride in his eyes. Dad had stolen cars. I had known they were stolen, because they were always different cars. Me and my friend were outside a chip shop one day, when Dad went past in a car that wasn't his. Later, the police came knocking. Another time he stole me a toy gun from the toy shop as I looked on.

This wasn't the only confusing message I got from my dad: 'Don't lie to your mother,' he would say. Then the next day: 'Don't tell your mother about this, son.'

'Go and play, son,' he would say. 'Can we play the Scalextric, Dad,' I would ask. It had been in the box since he bought it for me, from Christmas. 'Another time son, stop bothering me – I'm busy,' he would slur.

He was always talking back to Mum, too, telling her to mind her own business and get off his back. I felt sad for Mum, because she was just trying to do her job and on top of it all she had his job to do too. She only got a break from his job when drink couldn't be drunk or he was trying a new way of life. When he didn't drink, he worked and did the dad stuff with me - and even some of Mum's jobs as well.

We had a great time setting up the Scalextric set when he gave up the drink. Out of the box, around the bedroom we laid it. I pressed the trigger on the remote to set the cars off. They didn't go. Dad shouted at the cars, shouted at me to stop pressing the trigger, shouted at Mum to mind her own business, and then drank himself to sleep. Mum packed the Scalextric away and it was never seen again.

I always wondered: *Why don't you like me, Dad? What's wrong with me?*

Mum must have known what I was thinking because she loved me extra to make up the difference. She told me, 'I love you, son', and I told her 'I love you, Mum'. I followed her around seeking warm hugs and did what she said and I told her everything, even though Dad told me not to.

'Oh, you go running to your mum like you always do, you spoilt bastard,' he would hiss. 'You're spoilt by your mum, you need a firm hand.'

He thought I was a cry-baby. I could hear him when I'd wake them up with my tossing and turning, screams and cries.

'That son of yours needs to learn to be tougher. He's always crying; it's not right for a boy.'

I couldn't help the nightmares and I couldn't help crying. I didn't remember what I dreamt about, but I knew it was enough to cry. Mum would hold me, rocking me back to peace, and Dad would tut and huff and hash.

Mum rarely shouted at me or Dad, but kept her hugs and smiles for me. Everything felt easy around her – when she was in the room I could relax. All she had to do was be there and when she smiled at me I knew my world was okay. She only lost her temper with me once:

I smelt it before I felt it – it was a Dad smell. It was the smell of whiskey, beer, and cigarettes. Then I felt it.

WHACK.

I screamed.

Mum shouted.

WHACK.

29

Dad pleaded, 'Okay, Anne, that's enough. The boy's had enough.'

Mum whacked and whacked and whacked and I screamed and cried and cried.

'Okay, Anne. Okay, Anne, stop,' Dad said. 'STOP,' he shouted. Then she stopped.

She knelt beside me, her head rested on my hair, and my face wet from her tears. I didn't know what I did to make her so mad. I think she just lost it. She didn't have it easy, I knew that, because my Uncle Bobby used to come round and give her money and say to her, 'You've got a hard life there, Anne, with that wee boy to take care of and a husband who drinks.'

Uncle Bobby was right. Mum did have a hard life.

Chapter 2

I never wanted to go to big school. Everybody would be looking at me and they would know.

Look, there's that Dempster boy - his dad's a murderer, a drunk.

They would point and laugh and beat me up. I didn't know why I had to go to school. I was happy going to nursery in the morning and then to work with Mum for the rest of the day. She worked in Susie Stewarts, a dress and coat shop for women. I would sit and read *The Beano* and *The Dandy* with Mum smiling over me. 'You're a good lad there, aren't you, Mark', she would say and then present me to her customers. She would get me to sing Donny and Jimmy Osmond songs. I hated singing, especially in front of people, but I loved the attention it got me. They would smile and tell her what a nice lad she had. I wanted to be at work with Mum where she could show me off and let me read comics instead of going to school where everybody would point and laugh and beat me up.

'I'm sorry, Mark. I can't let you stay with me all the time. I have to go to work and you have to go to school,' she said.

I couldn't believe what I was hearing.

How can you leave me here? Leave me here where I don't have any friends and everybody is going to hate me?

All I could do was cry. I couldn't stop crying. I shook from crying.

'Oh there, there, Mark.' She hugged me tight, stroked her fingers through my hair, and then patted it back in place with a kiss. 'Look, you're a good boy. You go to school and you'll make friends. Just be yourself. Just be yourself, Mark, that's all you can ever be in life.'

I didn't have a clue what she was talking about. I didn't know how to be *myself*. What was *myself*? Mum was the only one that seemed to love me, but that was her job.

If I could just be like Dad in the pub.

Telling jokes, making the guys laugh, and getting slaps on the back. Then I'd make friends.

But I don't know any jokes.

I just want to stay here with Mum.

'Mark, please give it a try. I'll be here at the end of the day,' Mum said.

I didn't want to make her cry, and the teachers were coaxing me towards the door with all kinds of promises: the return of Mum, lots of games and fun. The teachers were right. I got to play games and have fun and Mum did come back. She took me to school in the morning and picked me up at the end of the day. I still got to go to work with her after school and read *The Beano* and *The Dandy* while she showed me off, but now I got a hamburger after she finished work as well. Life was better with a hamburger thrown in to the day.

The other kids didn't laugh and point and beat me up. As soon as I entered the class I looked around and found the roughest kids in the school. They were sitting at the back of the class. These kids looked like me. They had messy hair and scruffy clothes. Their faces were clean, but that was probably because they had been scrubbed from head to toe by their mums for the first day of term, just like my mum had done to me. I could see they were itching to dirty it. There was something else about these kids. They looked like they didn't care about anything. I was looking at them, but they weren't interested in me.

That's how I want to be. Without a care of what anybody thinks.

32

So I sat with the rough kids at the back of the class. It didn't take long for me to look like I didn't care. We were good at it. We didn't even care about getting told off, and we got told off a lot.

'You boys, stop whatever you're doing,' the teachers would say. We weren't always doing something wrong, but that didn't seem to matter. The teachers knew that we would be doing something wrong sometime soon.

'Stop whatever you are about to do. Don't think I can't see what you're up to,' they would say.

That always made us laugh. Laughing was the thing the teachers knew we were about to do because we would get told off for that as well.

Being with the rough kids was the most comfortable place for me. I was at home with them. They stole, and some of them were so poor they didn't wash. I didn't steal and Mum made me wash all the time, but I couldn't hang around with the good kids. Those kids thought they were better than I was. They sat at the front of the class where the girl with the two names sat. I wasn't as good as the kids at the front but I wasn't as bad as the kids at the back – so I was happy being King Rough.

John was the roughest of them all. He smelt of stale shit and piss and all the teachers would whisper about it loudly. With four brothers, he probably couldn't get his clothes washed much. That's a lot of clothes to keep washing when you have no money. He was one of the boys that stole from other people's coat pockets.

'Hey, Demmy, let's go and explore,' John would say, an explorer of all things nature, including people's pockets. 'I've seen these water rats, GIANT water rats, man. Let's go and see the water rats.'

Water rats beat a burger after school with Mum. We spent our time exploring up and down the Clyde and into the streets of river flowing through Glasgow and under Kelvin Bridge.

Mum was hysterical when I disappeared with John.

'Where in God's name have you been, Mark?'

33

Mum's hysteria peaked when I told her, 'Looking for water rats, Mum.' Where else did she think I was? She didn't like John or any of the rough kids that were my friends. I wasn't supposed to be hanging around with the boys that smelt of shit and piss, didn't wash their clothes, and spent their time stealing out of people's pockets. She wanted me to be up at the front of the class, learning as much as I could. But she'd told me to just be myself and that was what I was doing. I was being rough.

I was free with my new friends. Free from Dad seeing snakes, spiders, and dead Grandma, and free from having to worry about saying something that would make him angry. We spent our freedom exploring. Everything was an adventure. The blackened, cold, stone jungle we lived in was full of bins to climb and jump from one to the other. It was the winter of discontent, with everybody striking, but we didn't feel any discontent as we jumped the piles of rotting rubbish. I cleared a four or five foot drop every time, which was a rush for lads that were nearly ten years old.

Every time I took a run and jump, my heart would pound and the blood would rush from my head to my legs. Each time I cleared a bigger drop I would seek out the next challenging jump. The lads would cheer and clap and pat me on the back. I only fell once. I was mid-air, so didn't know anything until I was through the roof of an old, disused factory. It took hours for the rescue services to find me all cut and bruised and bloodied. I sat in the eerie dark, on the damp factory floor, shaking it was so cold. I thought I was dead. Then my eyes adjusted and I realised I wasn't dead. I was just going to die down there and get eaten by the rats. I forgot about all that when I was carried out to claps and cheers and hugs from Mum. It made the papers, with all the fire trucks and police it took to get me out:

Small boy falls through roof. Mother hysterical.

I was very lucky. When I fell through the roof, I narrowly missed being impaled on a forklift truck fork. I was famous, and the fact that I almost died went from my head. We dared each other to greater jumps and played kick the can and made tommyhawks. There were lots of games to play when you had friends, not like waiting outside the pub for Dad. I didn't even think about Dad seeing snakes, spiders, and dead Grandma when I was out with my pals exploring our freedom.

Every freedom has its price, though, and mine was the Partick Two. Tony and Chris were terrorists to my freedom and terrorised me and most of my friends. They were a few years older and wore Wrangler jeans. I couldn't understand why the kids with more money than us would want to beat us up. I did my best to avoid capture, but never knew where they were hiding, ready to pounce.

'Dempster, we see you. Fucking stop there, you wee fanny,' they would shout.

I ran, but my little legs couldn't carry me as fast as their slightly larger legs could. Trying to run was worse than staying and facing punishment – I got hit for running, hit for crying, and hit for not doing what they told me to do. I even got hit when I didn't run, didn't cry, and did exactly what they told me.

They forced me to eat the chicken giblets out of the bins and jump greater heights. I could jump the heights. I liked jumping the heights. Then they got angry at me for not falling to my death, so presented the giblets, hoping those would kill me instead. The giblets were full of guts and heart and mould and blood and puss. They smelt of dead water rats, rotting by the river, infested with maggots eating their way through the carcass. I wouldn't digest them. I couldn't, I would die for sure. I wanted to cry, but crying was a strategy I surrendered when I realised it got more laughs, more hits, and more giblets. If I could help it, I was never going to cry again.

Every time I went out I had to be on the lookout for Tony and Chris. I never got chased when I was with my friends, but most of them didn't live near me. I had to walk to go and meet them. I started to stay at home more. There was no freedom at home, with Dad always drinking and Mum working and looking after him. I was trapped, but it was still better than being beaten and forced to eat giblets.

I wish I could box them and beat them to the ground. I wish I wasn't a fanny.

Dad noticed I was keener to stay in the house than get out and explore and play games. He interrogated me and extracted their names. I don't know what he did, but one day he told me to go out and play, that nobody was going to be bothering me. After that, whenever I saw them, they just looked the other way. I felt like saying, *'Yeah, you look the other way or you'll get a punch in the face,'* but I just walked on. I was free again, free to explore and play, and that was enough. But I knew that if I wanted to stay free I had to become a fighter like Muhammad Ali.

Ali doesn't have to try to run away and eat giblets.

Dad had saved me this time, but maybe he was just having a good day. I couldn't rely on him being awake long enough to save me next time. I needed to learn how to look after myself.

I need to be like Ali and fight.

I didn't learn much in Catholic school except how to be a Catholic and that was easy but boring. You just had to remember you were bad and did lots of sin. Everything was a sin. Sex was a sin, kissing was a sin – even looking up Elaine's skirt was a sin. I couldn't understand it because the 'virgin' Mary must have had sex. The teachers said she didn't, the Bible said she didn't, but, even though I didn't know what sex was, I knew that babies didn't just appear. I asked how she got pregnant if she didn't have sex, but that was a stupid question apparently. God gave Mary the child, the Immaculate Conception, they said. Bullocks, I said.

Apparently it was all Eve's fault. She tempted Adam with an apple and there was a snake involved somewhere. I couldn't make sense of it all, but I could tell by the giggles from everyone around me and by the way the teacher was saying it that the apple and snake meant sex. I could understand it being Eve's fault, because it was always the girls that made me think sinful things, not the boys.

Dad didn't believe any of it either. 'A load of made up rubbish,' he said. Although he believed in aliens and all that stuff, which sounded as crazy as Mary having been a virgin, at least aliens were interesting. No aliens ever told me what to do, what to say, what to think. No aliens ever told me I was bad all the time and needed to confess and repent. No aliens made me go to chapel every week, like Mum did.

'Mark, get yourself washed and dressed. Put your safari jacket on,' she would say.

Not the bloody safari jacket, Mum.

You had to be smart for church and my safari jacket was the only smart thing I had. Nobody ever wore a suit unless they were in trouble with the police and had to see the judge. There's nothing worse than having to look smart. I was looking my best all ruffled and dirty and rough, but Jesus didn't like that in his church. We had to sit for hours listening to boring songs and stories that I thought weren't true. The only bit I liked was the Communion but that was only because there was enough distraction for me to talk to my friends.

Dad didn't have to go. Mum was the religious one, and she was worried that if she didn't pass it on she'd be the only one in Heaven from our family. Her mum would be there too, but me, Dad, Granddad and everyone else would be in Hell and Mum would be bored stiff in Heaven with her mum for eternity.

If my thoughts were a sin and each one was a black mark on my soul, then it couldn't have got any blacker. I tried to clean it by confessing to the Father every week. I would sit outside the confessional box waiting and stressing about what to say. I couldn't tell him most things, because I didn't know who was listening the other side of the cloth. But I knew I had to confess enough to keep myself out of Hell, and, since anything to do with sex or girls was a sin, I would make sure there was one of those thrown in, whether it had happened or not. I'd say I looked up Elaine's skirt even though I hadn't.

37

I would confess and get the hell out of there as fast as I could. Whatever sin it was, the Father would just tell me to say my Hail Marys. The number I said depended on the sin. I wished I knew what number there was for each sin as it took forever, no matter how fast I said them. I think the Father was pleased to get through it quickly anyway, with so many other kids who had black souls that needed cleaning in our school.

I didn't believe all those stories and I wasn't too sure about God. There must be something, I thought. The Earth, the trees, the water rats, Mum and Dad – they can't all just have appeared. If there was a God, he wasn't a very good one with Dad seeing snakes, spiders, and dead Grandma, and everybody in Glasgow not being able to get a job. I definitely believed there was a Devil and that there was a Hell. I knew with what I got up to I was definitely going to Hell if I didn't confess and say my Hail Marys. It always seemed a fair deal – confess and you don't go to Hell. Nobody ever said I needed to stop sinning! So I didn't. I didn't want to, either. Everybody was lying and cheating and I'd stand out if I didn't. The ones who didn't sin were altar boys and had to dress really smart for church and arrive early, which sounded like Hell on Earth. I was getting nowhere near an altar boy. They didn't see me and I didn't see them and that was fine by me.

Dad always went on at Mum for making me go to church.

Eventually she just gave in and said I didn't have to go any more. I started to believe there was a God I was so happy. I'm not sure Mum really wanted to go to church anyway because she stopped going soon after that. I think she was going because that's what her parents did and their parents did. She was just trying to carry it on, like her mother had wanted her to.

Chapter 3

I didn't know how to become hard. Not hard enough to fight like Ali and get everyone to fear me. Nobody messed with Ali, but everybody loved him. I'd watch John Wayne westerns with Dad and could see he was rougher than rough, harder than hard. He had those eyes that showed he was hard, those eyes that said to anybody who was looking, 'I'm hard, I'm fucking hard'. If I could squeeze them shut a little and purse my lips without pouting I would get it just right. It worked in the mirror and just in time to impress my future girlfriend.

Elaine Slaven was a Celtic princess without the clothes or the grace. She was a Celtic princess from a poor family that had seven kids in a small flat. *But, God, her red hair.* I'd melt the minute I saw it come glowing down the street. I loved Elaine Slaven; I was going to kiss Elaine Slaven. Elaine didn't know that, and she had standards. A hard man, a rough man was one of her standards - and with my eyes I was almost there.

On the weekend community drink we would be put together in a room. I would look at my future wife. I couldn't talk to her and she couldn't talk to me because she was shy and I was scared. But when I squeezed the eyes, pursed the lips…

The eyes said: *'I'm fucking hard. Look at me being all hard. Don't I just look fucking hard?'*

'Mark, what are you doing with your eyes?'

'What do you mean, what am I doing with my eyes? This is how I look.'

She started rolling about the floor, laughing, which crushed me. Then she delivered the final blow: 'You look like you're trying to go to the toilet.'

She laughed some more. God, I hated Elaine Slaven.

My dad was hard. Nobody messed with him and I could tell they all liked him by the way they patted him on the back and laughed at his jokes in the pub. I looked hard and walked hard just by standing next to him. We passed the kids playing, the neighbours chatting, the builders building - me with my chest puffed out as if I'm gearing up for high noon, *first one to draw*, squeezing my eyes, and pursing my lips.

'Mark, what are you doing with your eyes, son?'

God, Dad, this is how I look. This is how John Wayne looked; this is how a hard man looks; this is how you look.

'Mark, stop doing that with your eyes, you look like you're trying to take a shit.'

It was a lot of work trying to look hard and rough with everybody saying I looked like I was trying to go to the toilet, trying to take a shit. I don't know why I bothered. No matter how much I tried, I failed. Mum would say, 'Put your safari jacket on, Mark, you can't go out with nothing to keep you warm.' The safari jacket was the last straw. Nobody can look hard in a safari jacket, John Wayne eyes or not.

You had to look after yourself in Glasgow. Everybody was angry where I lived. The police weren't much help. Nobody ever bothered calling the police. That would make you a grass. I could see, even before I had to lick the giblets, that being hard, being a fighter would keep me safe. I could see that from watching my dad. Whether drunk or sober, he always knew how to stick up for himself, even stick up for me. He would never ask for help from anybody.

It was like that when someone stole my bike. Mum wanted to tell the police, but Dad was having none of it. He wanted to go round and sort it out with his fists. Mum's voice lost and Dad went round to get it back.

'I've come for my son's bike,' he said.

'No, man, this is my son's bike. I bought it,' the guy said.

'Fucking hand the bike over or else, you wee prick,' Dad said.

'What you gonna do? It's my son's bike, so get away from my house,' the guy said.

'Okay,' my dad said. 'I'll wait until tomorrow night. If you don't come by with the bike, there'll be trouble.'

My uncle, who was even harder than Dad, waited with him while me and Mum hid at the neighbour's. No doubt with a bottle. And another. And another. It was exactly like a John Wayne western: who's going to draw first. The guy turned up with his friend and they both took one look at my uncle, harder than all of them, and then another look at my dad, who was probably making the eyes.

'The bike will be back in the morning,' they said.

No, the eyes were not enough. I could see I had to fight hard to make people fear me like they feared my dad. If I was going to look after myself then I had to fight like Ali and my dad.

Gary was the best fighter in school. It was the only hierarchy we had: the best fighter, the second best fighter, and so on. I was only interested in those two spots. What's the point in being third in anything? Second was something to console myself with, if I had to. But first place - that was the gold I was going for. If I could be the first best fighter then nobody would mess with me. I wouldn't need to make eyes to look hard; I wouldn't even need my dad to protect me. Everybody would just know you don't mess with that Demmy, the first best fighter in school.

But Gary was my friend, so I couldn't fight him. Friends were never my friends for long – they always used to get other friends and I couldn't understand it.

Who the fuck do you think you are getting another friend?

41

I was so jealous I could explode. You could only be friends with me, not having other friends willy-nilly.

Gary started to get friendly with another boy, talking to him and spending less and less time with me.

Without me! Who does he think he is going off talking to another boy?

I couldn't say that. Gary would think I was nuts. So I just mocked him for looking like Donny Osmond.

'You look like a fucking fanny, Gary. Who you trying to be?' I said it in front of the other kids, especially my replacement.

'Dempster, you're getting it, you fanny,' Gary said.

'Who you calling a fucking fanny, Gary? You just watch yourself with those fanny shoes and shiny new clothes. You don't want to get them dirty.'

'Dempster. I'm gonna boot your balls.'

'Ah, you think you're cool with those shoes and those jeans and your new wee friend. I can batter you in a fight, Gary, let's do it.'

'Right, okay, Dempster, I fucking warned you. At break time, I'm gonna boot your balls.'

At break time, he booted me in the balls.

'Now, I told you I was gonna boot your balls, Dempster, you fucking fanny.'

As I lay there on the ground, I realised I was not the best fighter in school. Gary was.

I didn't miss Gary. I still had John, Peter, and Jamie. They were better than Gary. We built huts at the back of the tenements with old bits of wood, metal, and car seats. We could make a good hut out of anything. Some of the huts would be lavish with carpets and doors, but others would do with just a car seat. Our chief hut was a concrete box no bigger than a toilet. That was where I first had sex. At least, I thought it was sex.

We were ten and none of us knew anything much about sex. We knew about Adam and Eve and that sex was a sin, but that didn't help me know what to do. I used to rub against Mum sometimes, but that wasn't sex. I just had this good feeling inside when I did it. Not much happened *down there*. I was always rubbing against this or that. Whether a table leg or Mother's leg, it felt good. There was the woman who lived next door who wore a mini skirt. I'd get excited after seeing her and slide up and down the bannister, rubbing myself silly, but that wasn't sex. The only thing I knew about sex was that you got on top and bounced up and down, in and out, and groaned. Just as I was watching Peter do to Theresa right in front of me.

Up and down Peter bounced, in and out of Theresa, flat on her back with her legs up in the air.

'Ah, ah, ah,' she screamed.

'Go on, Peter, give it to her good,' we egged him on. What he was giving to her exactly I wasn't sure, but the others were shouting it so I did too. God, I wanted to bounce up and down, in and out of Theresa. I couldn't, though. Only Peter got to bounce up and down, in and out of Theresa.

Peter jumped off. I couldn't control myself. I jumped on, laughing with madness.

I'm gonna have sex, I'm gonna have sex.

I was laughing and trying to get it in.

I've got to get it in; where do I get it in? I hope I can get it in. God, please, help me get it in.

The guys were jumping up and down shouting.

'Stick your dick in her fanny.' That would have been helpful if I knew where the fanny was or even what it looked like. Theresa was lying there, but she wasn't moaning any more. She was getting pissed off.

'Fuck off,' she was shouting.

I'm pleading for more time, 'It's going in, it's going in,' whether it was going in or not.

'Fucking hurry up then, just do it,' she begged. Then I thought I'd got it in, but it might have just been rubbing against the seat. Theresa started going 'ah, ah, ah' so it didn't matter.

I thought I had had sex. And I was only ten.

I've got to do this all the time.

I tried to do it all the time, but Peter was selfish. He was always on top of Theresa, never giving us a go. We would play down the allotments, eating raw turnips, still caked in dirt. All of a sudden Peter would announce, 'I'm gonna have sex with Theresa,' and then just jump on her. I don't think she wanted to have sex at all because she told him he better hurry up. Whether she wanted to or not she always spread her legs and said, 'Ah, ah, ah.'

When she couldn't be bothered to lie down she would just tug him off. Sometimes she would tug me off, tugging as fast as she could. 'Are you finished yet?' she would moan, but I didn't know if I was finished. It felt good and I would have been happy for her to tug me all day long. I knew something else should be happening, that something should be coming out at some point, but I wasn't sure what it was supposed to be. I could feel something wanted to come out, but it never happened no matter how much she tugged.

I didn't like boys like I liked girls, but I liked tugging as much as John, Peter, and Jamie so sometimes we just tugged each other off. We spent all our time hanging out together, building huts, eating turnips from the allotment, and tugging each other – I never wanted it to end. But my friends always left and these guys were no different. I couldn't understand it. John, the two-timing bastard, got a new friend. Some wee fanny who thought he could do a better job as a friend than me. I was fuming, strutting up and down, huffing and puffing.

I'm gonna beat that wee fanny up. I'm gonna show him he can't be stealing my friends willy-nilly.

I had seen the wee fanny at the old railway. It was a ghost railway from a past time, overgrown with weeds and grass, with trees watching from above. I was told this was the railway where Bible John had killed all those prostitutes, leaving a Bible next to every dead body. Everybody knew Bible John, but nobody had seen him. All the mums would say, 'Don't be going far; Bible John could get

44

you,' and, 'Don't go down to the old railway; Bible John is well known for going to the old railway.' 'Bullocks,' I said. Why would Bible John go down to an old railway?

I went down there and sat by the tracks, watching and waiting for the wee fanny. I skulked between the trees, wolf-like, ready to pounce. Then he was there, skipping and jumping up the railway. I couldn't understand how this wee fanny, with his skipping and jumping, could replace me, the hardest boy in school. Not harder than Gary, but the second hardest boy for sure.

I leapt from behind the rock and stood facing him.

He stood facing me.

We faced each other for a while.

I tilted my head to the side, squeezed my eyes and pursed my lips, ready to draw my weapon, ready to shoot this wee fanny dead. *'Go on, make my day,'* I wanted to say.

Instead, I said: 'You're a wee fucking fanny. I'm gonna boot your balls. You better not run, you wee fanny.'

He looked around and I stayed staring. You had to stare to freak them out. I was too busy staring to notice the wee fanny charging towards me, and before I could skip or jump or even run away I was on the floor, hunched like a cat, with the wee fanny above me growling like a rabid dog.

WHACK, he hit.

WHACK, WHACK, WHACK.

I tried to claw him off, but we just ended up hugging. I squeezed as hard as I could to make it less of a hug and we rolled and rolled and I tried to punch and he tried to punch, but neither of us landed the punch on the other, just hitting the air and rolling and rolling and rolling, then lying flat on the ground, huffing and puffing and panting.

I don't know who won that fight, but it seemed to me that every time I had a fight I lost. This one I was going to call a draw - we both beat each other, no winner - and I was still the second best fighter in my school, with Gary the first and this wee fanny just having a lucky day.

Peter was next, the two-timing bastard. I went round to his house to have it out with him and, when he opened the door, I did the eyes.

'You fucking two-timing bastard,' I said.

'What are you talking about, Dempster, don't be calling me a bastard, you bastard.'

'No, Peter, don't deny it, you're a two-timing bastard and your mum's a cow. An old cow. And she fucking takes it up the arse.'

'Fuck you, you bastard, don't be calling my mum a cow, you're just a fanny.'

'I'm not a fanny, your mum's a fanny.' Then I told him, 'I'm gonna boot your balls.'

I put my fists up and made a face. *I'm mental,* my face said, *fucking mental and I'm gonna box you to the ground.*

Then he punched my mental face and I could feel my mental eye turn black.

'You fucking fanny,' he said and shut the door.

Now Peter was the second best fighter and I didn't know if that made me the third or the fourth, but I knew it meant I had no friends left.

What is wrong with me? Why can't I keep any friends?

All I wanted to do was play out with my friends. I wanted to do it all the time. First opportunity I got to get out of the house, I would be banging on one of their doors and pleading with them to come out and play: 'Stop your excuses,' I would say. 'Who needs to eat dinner anyway?'

I had to do something different to keep my friends.

If I get any friends again.

Dad had lots of friends, but I hated them. I watched him whenever he was with them and all they seemed to do was drink. He only ever laughed and smiled when he was drinking with them. Still, his friends never left him and they always laughed at his jokes. Graham

46

was Dad's best friend. He was the one I hated the most. I had to go to Graham's flat when his mum had died. People drank to forget their mum had died and they couldn't drink alone, so Dad took a carrier bag of beers and half a bottle of whiskey. I had to wait in Graham's bedroom to let them drink and laugh and sing alone.

'Go and play,' Dad said, but the room was completely bare, with nothing except a plastic chair. Graham told me to stop my moaning and be grateful for a chair. At least waiting for Dad outside the pub, I had my Golden Wonders to eat and I could spy through the window. All I could do in Graham's room was sit on the plastic chair, cursing Dad for having friends who had no furniture or toys or anything to play with.

Dad couldn't rely on Graham either, but he was always too drunk to see that. I could see it. I caught Graham looking at Mum's legs and thought: *You prick, you fucking prick.* I hated anybody looking at Mum that way. It felt like he was licking his lips as his eyes went up and down.

I'm gonna fucking box you, Graham. Get your eyes off my mum's legs.

I wanted to say something. I wanted to protect Mum from Graham's eyes and licked lips. I wanted to defend Dad - he was down the pub, too drunk to defend himself. Granddad saw him too, and stepped in to defend his son's honour.

'You fucking behave yourself, Graham,' he said.

'What you talking about, Bobby?'

'You know what I'm fucking talking about, Graham, you sneaky bastard. Watch yourself with those eyes.'

Even though Dad's friends laughed at his jokes and drank with him until there was no more drink to be drunk, he couldn't trust any of them. If Dad couldn't rely on his friends, what chance did I have?

When Dad tried to stop drinking, his friends would disappear. There was a brief moment of happiness a few days after he put down the bottle. He could laugh with me and Mum. He could go to work and help out around the house. He didn't need Graham or his friends down the pub to laugh at his jokes to make him happy. But it would never last.

His happiness would turn to sadness and then to anger. The bottles and cans would return, Graham would be staring at Mum's legs again, and his friends would be laughing at his jokes and slapping him on the back down the pub like he was king of his own castle. After that, it would be back to pacing up and down, seeing spiders, snakes, and dead Grandma all over again. The transition from Dr Jekyll to Mr Hyde would get quicker and quicker until it looked like Dr Jekyll was dead forever.

I always knew when he was drinking again. I could feel it the minute I came into the room. Mum would be manically cleaning, trying to keep herself busy and out of the way. Dad would be in front of the TV half asleep. I could see that change: his face sweaty with a big red nose and bloodshot eyes. I could smell the change: stale beer and fear in the air.

Got to keep quiet; he's going to drink; he's drunk; he's going to be sick; he's going to be pacing up and down; he's going to be seeing spiders, snakes, and dead Grandma.

One day he put his head in the oven. It had got too much for him. He had had enough of all the trying to stop drinking and then snakes, spiders, and dead Grandma. But he couldn't even kill himself properly, so he spent a few months in the nut hospital. When he came out he told me he was going to be a different man.

'I'm never drinking again, son. I promise,' he said.

I had never seen him look so determined. In just a few days he was happy again, he was working again, and he would laugh at the TV shows and I would laugh with him. I didn't need to know what we were laughing at. My dad was laughing and that was enough.

This time his old friends were replaced with new ones. His new friend Bill used to drink but had stopped years ago. I would walk with Dad and Bill to the church hall and they would disappear inside longer than Dad would stay in the pub. There were lots of friends of Bill and Dad in the hall. I would wait for Dad to come out again and I didn't mind that it was a long time or that I couldn't spy them through the window. I didn't even have a plastic chair to sit on. It didn't matter. Every time Dad came out of the hall surrounded by his new friends laughing and joking and shaking hands, I had a strange feeling inside. It was something I hadn't experienced before. It was a feeling of complete calm. A feeling of *everything is all right.*

I would listen as Bill talked to Dad on the way home in a soft voice, like Mum talked to me.

'You can do this,' Bill would say. 'But I think you should get out of Partick. Start afresh somewhere new. You will be drinking in no time with all your friends around here.'

Bill was right. Most of Dad's uncles drank and all of his friends drank. They were gone for now, but they would be back. They always came back and, with them, so did the drink.

'You're right, Bill,' Dad said.

So we left my two-timing friends, we left Dad's drunk friends who stared at Mum's legs, and we moved twenty miles to Helensbrough for a fresh start for Dad, a fresh start for Mum, and a fresh start for me.

'This time things are gonna be different, son,' Dad said.

This time I believed him.

Chapter 4

Helensbrough may have only been twenty miles from Partick, but it was like another country to me. The blackened, wind-battered stone merged into waving trees and green fields. People in Glasgow said Helensbrough folk were country people, soft people.

'Sheep shaggers, the lot of 'em, and so dim they wouldn't know the difference between shagging a sheep or shagging their own mum.'

People from Helensbrough said Glasgow folk were tough, so I didn't need to look to find the rough kids in my new school. They found me. The first boy I met was born in Glasgow, and had spent most of his life there before moving to Helensbrough. He was a bit rough and mean. Matthew wanted to be my friend, but I was only interested in finding out the pecking order of fighters.

'Who's the best fighter in the school?' I asked.

I wasn't going to be the second best fighter in this school. Being anything but the first best fighter was hard work. This time I was going to be the number one, the Muhammad Ali, the champion nobody dared mess with, certainly not someone replaced by a new wee fanny friend. If I could sort this out on day one - show everybody I was the best fighter - then my life at this school was going to be great.

Matthew said the best fighter was Dods and pointed him out to me. I eyed him up and down.

I can beat him. He might get a few punches in. It will be tough, but I can boot his balls until he's begging for surrender.

'Hey, Dods,' I shouted so that everybody could hear. There was a sudden hush from everybody around us. I did the eyes. 'You think you're the best fighter in school? Well, now I'm the best fighter.'

Dods eyed me up and down. Matthew looked from me to Dods and then from Dods to me.

'I don't think so,' Dods shouted back. 'Glasgow boys are poofs.'

Everybody's watching. Got to see this through. If I beat him then I'm king of the school and I never have to worry about my friends leaving me again.

'Okay, Dods, let's iron this all out – at break time we're gonna have a fight and we'll see who's the best fighter in this school.'

The hush from the other kids spread to whispers and then chatter. Across the school word had spread that Dods was going to beat up the new kid from Glasgow.

Can't back out now.

Matthew sat at my side all morning. I wasn't sure if I liked him, but, with everybody chatting about how Dods was going to be beating me up, it gave me an ally. I was pretty confident I could beat Dods, but, now that everybody knew about the fight, I started to worry about what would happen if I lost to Dods. The voice egging me on was now expressing caution.

Maybe this isn't such a good idea. What am I doing, challenging the best fighter in school on day one? I could still back out. I don't have to do this.

The voices were battling.

I do have to do it. If I don't, everybody will think I'm a fanny and beat me up all the time. My friends will keep leaving me, and everywhere I go the kids will laugh and point at me.

I wasn't going to back out of this. At break time we marched to the shelter and everybody came to watch the new kid from Glasgow get beaten up by Dods. I looked around us at the circle of Dods' supporters. I looked over at Matthew – the only boy rooting for me.

I'll show these kids who I am.

51

I looked back at Dods, put my fists up, puffed my chest out, and shook my head like I was mental, fucking mad. I made the eyes and circled him. Dods looked scared. Helensbrough kids didn't fight like this, with the mental face and the John Wayne eyes. I was scared too. I didn't know whether to run or punch. I knew from the fights in Partick that the first one to punch wins, so I lunged and punched as fast and hard as I could.

I must have closed my eyes because I hit the well - its aluminium ring. A sharp pain shot from my fist to the top of my arm and I stumbled back. I steadied my feet and looked around for Dods. He was already in the distance, running off. Everybody else was silent and staring at the well. Matthew was in the corner with his mouth open. He ran towards me, pointing at the dent in the well - a dent my fist couldn't have made. The dent was too big.

'Fucking hell,' Matthew said. 'You punched a massive dent right in that well. You are the best fighter in school.'

Nobody needs to know I didn't dent the well. I'm the best fighter in this school now.

All around the school the news spread and they heard it:

The new kid from Glasgow, he's fucking mental. Got such a good right hand and, Jesus, he put a big dent in the well.

I'd won the lottery. Before, I'd had to fight and fight and had often lost; but denting a well – I didn't need to fight ever again. Dods decided it was a good idea to be friends with the best fighter in the school, Matthew thought I was a gift from God, and I got another friend called Roddy who was just another one of my gang. These were friends that I owned - friends who couldn't replace me even if they wanted to. If they did, I could dent them too.

In Partick there were just the bins, the tenements, and our huts where we could play. In Helensbrough, we had endless fields and forests to explore. My new friends and I would weave in and out of the trees like Robin Hood and his merry men. Robin Hood only ever had a bow and arrow. I had something much better – a BSA

Meteor air rifle. It only had pellets, not real bullets, but you could still shoot at rabbits and birds and it made a *pip* sound like a bang.

'I'm the best shot with this air rifle. I could shoot and hit a blade of grass with this thing. I bet I could shoot so close to your hand you'd feel the air brush past,' I said to Dods as we stopped for breath on an adventure through the woods.

Dods didn't look like he wanted to find out. Nobody wants to be the boy that you prove you're the best shot against. I had already reduced him to the second best fighter in school on day one.

'Come on, Dods, just put your hand up on that tree and I'll show you.'

Because I dented the well everybody was scared of the mad boy from Glasgow, so he put his hand up. I took aim and PIP. Dods started screaming. Blood was dripping from his hand. The pellet was lodged in his middle finger.

'Ahhhhhhhh,' Dod's screamed like a baby.

'I'm sorry, Dods. I don't know what happened. It must've been the wind.' I went to help him. Then I remembered that Dods has brothers - big brothers, lots of brothers, brothers that wouldn't think twice of booting my balls. I had no chance against them. I looked at Dods and held up my fist.

'Listen, Dods, you better not fucking tell anybody about this. Better not tell your brothers, or I'll beat you up, I will, I'll fucking boot your balls.'

He nodded and I pulled the pellet from his hand. It was the least I could do.

Matthew had won the lottery too. Being friends with the best fighter in school, a rough and mean kid from Glasgow, made him more popular than he had ever been. He followed me around like a dog follows his master. Everything I did, he did. Everything I liked, he liked. He wanted to see my house. I didn't mind. I could take Matthew back home. I could take anybody home, because we were in a new place where nobody knew about my dad being a heavy drinker. Besides, we had lived in Helensbrough for a month and he was still sober.

As soon as I opened the door and me and Matthew walked in I could smell something was wrong. It was the smell of stale beer.

Maybe it's the next-door neighbours. Dad doesn't drink any more. It can't be him.

Mum said hello to Matthew. I could see something was different about her. She looked tired. Her eyes were red. She was cleaning.

Maybe she's got a cold. She has to clean the house. It's her job: the cooking, the cleaning, and the mothering. Dad doesn't drink any more. It can't be because of him.

Dad came out and smiled at Matthew.

'Hello there, son, now what's your wee name there?'

Now I could smell and see it clearly. Dad stank of beer and whiskey. He still looked happy, but slurred his words. He was drunk.

I don't understand. How could he drink when the reason we came here was to be away from his uncles and everyone who drank?

I looked at him. I wanted to punch him.

You fucking bastard. You said it was going to be different this time.

Matthew started to talk to Dad. I could see he liked Dad, but he didn't know what was coming - he didn't know that the smiles and laughter would become pacing and shaking and sweating and sicking and seeing spiders, snakes and dead Grandma. I knew it. I wanted to get Matthew out of there as soon as possible. I wanted to punch Dad for being drunk, but I couldn't. I went to bed and hoped that in the morning Dad would be sober again.

Dad was sober in the morning. After a few days of being scared to come home and seeing him drunk, I began to relax. It didn't happen again. In fact, it didn't happen for an entire year and a half. He got another friend called Bill and went to the local church hall with him every week. He worked for the council and was out of the house from first thing in the morning until late at night. He spent more time away from home than when he was drinking. At least this time he was getting paid for his time away from home. It still made him grumpy, though. We spent some more time together, but not much. He helped me with my maths, which was something I was good at. I was good at swimming as well, but he wasn't interested in that so didn't bother much with it.

After that year and a half he went to fewer and fewer meetings with Bill down the church hall, until Bill was never around. Then he was off to Glasgow to get a bike for my thirteenth birthday. But Dad's uncles and Dad's friends were in Glasgow. Instead of Dad returning with the bike, Mum and me went down to Southern General Hospital. Dad had tubes hanging out of his body, his brain swamped in blood. He had gone to get my bike, but had met up with some old friends on the way. He must have forgotten that Bill was his friend too, because he only met up with the friends that drank. He drank so much he fell down the stairs. He would have bled to death, but a little girl had found him lying in a pool of his own blood pouring out of his fractured skull. The doctors were fighting to stop the blood clots and drain the bleeding when we got to the hospital.

'Expect the worst, Mrs Dempster, this is very bad. He may not live,' the doctors said.

Then, when he lived, they changed the news from very bad to just bad.

'Mrs Dempster, he won't be the same. He will have brain damage – not much left to walk and talk and do what he did before. He won't be able to work.'

They didn't know much. He didn't work when he drank anyway. But I still wanted him to walk and talk. What was I supposed to do with a dad who couldn't walk and talk?

He had been in hospital before, but that had been the nut hospital. It was all too much for him back then, Mum had said - the pacing, the shaking, the sweating, seeing spiders, snakes, and dead Grandma. Too much for him that sticking his head in the oven had seemed like the only thing to do. I was only eight then, and all I knew was that my dad was in hospital trying to get better. Like the time he was in jail, I never saw him. We just told people he was away working, away on the oil rigs. I didn't go to the hospital or the jail and I didn't want to. I was happy at home with Mum. But now I was in the hospital seeing Dad, asleep, with tubes winding out of his body. Mum was crying, and the nurses were stroking her back and giving her tissues and cups of tea. I just sat and watched everything go on around me.

What is he gonna be like when he wakes up if he can't walk and talk?

He didn't know who I was when he woke up. He had forgotten he had a son. That was normal, the doctors said. He would remember soon enough. The doctors were right. Soon enough he walked a bit and talked a bit. He started to remember me, remember I was his wee boy and, even though he couldn't walk and talk properly, it was better than before because he didn't remember he drank. Nobody bothers to drink when they forget they need to. Step by step, word by word, he got better, although he never could speak properly again.

I felt sad for him. I knew he had that crash where his friend was killed and he had lost his good looks with the scars on his face. Now he had a friend who died, lost his good looks, hated life so much he'd put his head in an oven, been to jail, lost lots of jobs, seen spiders, snakes and dead Grandma, and, to top it all - couldn't walk or talk properly. It was amazing he was still alive, but he wasn't any help to me or Mum any more. Not that he had ever been much help. There was just always the hope – the promise – that one day he would be. Now there wasn't even that.

Dad walked and talked enough to get a job for a while and, because he forgot he needed to drink, Mum didn't have to lie to them about not being able to get to work. One day somebody gave him a pint and he must have remembered he liked it because he had another, and another, and another - until he forgot he couldn't drink and was drunk all over again. This time he just kept forgetting he got drunk the day before, forgetting it made him sick, and each

56

drink was like the first, way back when he was young, when the drink made life better.

I'd stand by the door, watching him drinking his Special Brew and laughing at the stupid TV programme.

What have you got to laugh about, you fucking bastard?

I'd find myself saying out loud: 'You're a fucking bastard,' then I'd run for my life. He would chase me and it became the only time we hung out together - me calling Dad a fucking bastard and him chasing me to teach me a lesson. I was scared being chased by Dad, knowing that if he caught me I would get a beating that would hurt for days. But I started to love the rush more than I feared the pain of the beating. Each time I would leave it a little closer between me calling him a fucking bastard and him chasing me out of the door until one day he got me and hit me and would have killed me if the neighbour hadn't disturbed us.

I was now the man of the house, my mum was everything else, and my dad was just someone who lived with us. At some point it just became the way it was. Neither good nor bad. Just my dad. My family. My life.

* * *

'Ahhh, no, Mark, I don't want to box.'

'Don't be such a fanny, just put your hands up and box.' Dods knew he would get beat. He couldn't box, but I needed somebody to try out my new punch.

'Ahhhh,' he screamed.

What a baby! I didn't punch him that hard.

I boxed Matthew too. Every day I would be back at their doors and I could see the look on their faces. They didn't want me boxing them, but they never dared not to come out. They were too scared of what I would do to them.

Matthew's mum complained to my mum.

57

'Mark, why do you keep boxing your friends?' Mum asked. 'It's not a nice thing to do to people. I expect more of you than that.'

What a baby! What a fanny, crying to his mother.

'I'm just playing around, Mum. It's all pretend boxing. They like it,' I said.

'Nobody likes getting boxed, Mark. Why are you so angry all the time that you need to box your friends?'

I didn't know why I was angry. I didn't think I was angry, but I knew I must be with all the boxing and shooting air rifles at people.

'Be nice to Matthew and stop boxing him,' Mum said.

I stopped boxing Matthew. I started boxing Roddy, but his dad told Mum, and she said, 'Stop boxing Roddy.' I stopped boxing Roddy. Then I boxed Dods again, and he told his brothers who didn't bother telling Mum. They just burned me with hot knives to teach me a lesson. It did teach me a lesson. I needed to make sure Dods never told his brothers again.

If I was angry, I didn't know what about or who at. I just had this feeling – like an ache in the stomach – that vanished when I boxed one of my friends. The few moments before and after the moment of impact between my fist and their bodies, I felt a rush - a spurt of energy - running from the hairs on my head to the tips of my toes. It relieved the ache in the stomach, and then put me on top of the world.

I'm in control now. I am the power.

I had to keep doing it, though. I had to keep boxing friends, keep fighting people to feel that relief, that rush. The relief lasted only a few moments and got less and less each time.

The problem with being the power is that someone always wants to bring you down to size. Until secondary school there was nobody with the guts to do it. Secondary school was about five times the size of junior school and there were lots of fighters. These fighters were really mad. It was a rough school with riots. They smashed windows and started fires. They threw desks around and shouted and swore at the teachers. Nobody did any praying in this school even though they all committed many more sins than we had back in Partick. The train to school was chaos, and it took forever with everyone pulling alarm chains. I didn't know how I was supposed to stay the best fighter in this school.

I found Barney on the first day: bulldog face and built like a rhino. I looked at him and he looked at me.

This guy could just sit on me and beat me without even laying a punch.

I turned to Matthew.

'I'm the second best fighter in the class,' I said. Barney must have known about the dent in the well because he was happy not to have to defend his title. He told people, 'Mark's the second best fighter in this class.'

I was happy with second best fighter. It was a big enough school where second best was as good as first in my last school. But McNeil wasn't happy. We played on the rugby team together, and I always had a suspicion he didn't like me. He never said it - it was just the way he looked at me.

'You were fucking shit with that try,' he said after the game one day.

I knew he didn't like me.

'Who you calling shit, you fanny?' I asked. Then he punched me. I couldn't believe it. Nobody punches the second best fighter in school unless you're the first best fighter. I couldn't just punch him back right then, though. It was a long time since I'd had to fight anybody who would punch back.

'Fucking dick, you wait till I get changed – I'm gonna boot your balls when we get out of here,' I said, buying some time to plan my attack.

Fighting had evolved since the battles with friends in Partick and the denting of the well. The John Wayne eyes, the mad face, the putting up of fists and the circling were redundant. Now I had to grab their hair and pull it until they fell down, then kick and kick and punch and punch. If they didn't have enough hair, I could just headbutt them in the face.

So I pulled his hair and kicked and punched. I was kicking and kicking and punching and punching until I was huffing and puffing and out of kicks, out of punches, and out of fight. I bent down to breathe, and then WHACK, WHACK - two punches to the face and I was beat.

'Okay, okay, I give in, I give in,' I said. McNeil didn't hear, or didn't care, and just carried on punching and kicking until I was on the floor, sure I was dead. This was the worst thing that could have happened to me. Now I wasn't even the second best fighter, and McNeil would slap me every time I saw him just in case I forgot. The only thing that kept me safe, the only thing that kept my friends from replacing me, was fighting. But McNeil had put enough of a dent in me that nobody was scared any more. I had lost my ace card. I hated secondary school and I hated my life.

Mum could see I wasn't happy. She decided to find me a new school where I could have a fresh start.

'You have got to get your head down and learn as much as you can, Mark. You can make something of yourself if you try.'

Maybe Mum's right. I could try to study this time. It's got to be better than always fighting and losing.

I knew things had to be different. I just didn't know how I was going to make them different.

Chapter 5

I started drinking Special Brew when I was thirteen. Mum would be in bed, Dad would be passed out, and I would be sitting by the window, sipping on some of the strong beer Dad had forgotten to finish. Dad was drunk all the time and it always got him into trouble. But Dad was sick. Everybody else drank and they didn't do things that got them into trouble.

What's the harm in me taking a few sips? I'm not sick like Dad.

I got a buzz with each sip. It was the same buzz I got from jumping the bins back in Partick, clearing four or five foot drops. It was the same buzz from bouncing up and down, in and out of Theresa, from boxing my friends, and from swearing at my dad. After a few sips of Special Brew everything went away. My dad with his spiders, snakes, and dead Grandma, my mum with her cooking and cleaning, mothering, and nobody to talk to, my friends who always replaced me and the constant battle - the tiring endless tussle of making sure I was the best fighter. I was the only friend to have. A few sips and I was free.

If only my friends could see me now, drinking Special Brew. Drinking at this age! They would all know I was cool. They would all know I was hard.

I looked out of the window, hoping someone would come up the road and see me looking drunk and cool. I would hear the high heels clock-clocking and remember the stories of the women who lived at the submarine base. Loose women, they said, loose and pretty and coming home from the disco clubs drunk. There I was – young, drunk, and horny – with no girlfriend, but ready to kiss them, bounce up and down, in and out, and anything else they wanted.

They swayed from side to side past the window in their short skirts, made up like dolls, in twos and threes, and sometimes completely on their own. I imagined myself kissing them, touching their breasts, and finding their fanny. But, no matter how much Special Brew I sipped, I still couldn't jump out of the window and chase them down the street. I could get Mum's clothes catalogue and have a good wank looking at the older women in their bras and knickers. So I did that. But – still - nothing came out.

I was a paperboy for the *Glasgow Evening Times* when I had my first proper drink about a year after my first sips of Special Brew. Almost every fourteen-year-old had a part-time job to get a bit of sweet money. I didn't need to buy sweets because the shelves in the shop were stacked with them. There were so many sweets that nobody noticed when some of them went missing. Then a few more. Then some more. Until, before anybody could notice, boxes of the sweets were leaving the shop under my coat. I was making more money a few yards up from the school tuck shop, selling them for half price. Word got around and I become the school black market for cheap chocolate.

What harm am I doing selling a few sweets? They pay me almost nothing for all the work I do delivering papers.

Saturday night was the sports edition and the best place to sell that paper was to the drinkers in the pubs. That's where I met John Brett. He was a proper man of eighteen, a leader of his own clan of Bretts. They were all dressed in a uniform of hippy hair with beads around their necks and an array of multi-coloured garments from head to toe. I stopped my paper selling just to watch them for a while.

These guys are cool, hanging out together with their long hippy hair, laughing and chatting and playing pool.

John must have seen me watching them. He was watching me note down every one of their actions and mannerisms for some future version of myself.

'Hey, guys, look what we have here: a young head in our presence.'

Was he talking to me? He's looking at me! He called me a young head.

'What's your name, lad?'

He called me lad! He looked at me, right in my eyes with his long, cool, hippy hair and called me lad.

'M...m...m...Mark,' I said, or stuttered, or maybe just sang from the top of my voice I was so happy with the recognition from this god. He smiled wide, slapped my back, and nudged me forward to the rest of the guys as if presenting me on his stage.

'Guys, this is Mark. I like this young head.' Some of the clan smiled. Some of them looked at each other and laughed. The others just carried on, too cool to stop what they were doing. I didn't care. John Brett, clan chief, said he liked me.

I am officially a cool lad.

I was sitting in the middle of the clan with John hunched over me. All eyes were split between me and the half pint that sat there, waiting to be drunk.

My first half pint. This is it. The big time. This is what the cool guys do.

I took a sip. Then another. And another. Then I was slamming the glass down on the table, every drop drained, making an *Ahhhhh* sound, and licking my lips just like I had seen Dad and his friends do hundreds of times before.

I looked around and saw the guys, my guys.

I love you guys.

They were all looking at me with admiration. I was grinning from ear to ear, tingles starting in my toes and weaving up my legs. The tingles shot to my stomach, to my neck, then up my throat to my mouth. Everything was brighter, the guys were cooler, John's hair was more colourful. Then the tingle went to my ears, making the music louder. It went to my head and the tingles started spinning like a pinball stuck in a loop to loop and shooting right down to my feet with such speed they wanted to dance, do the shake and shake it all out.

'I want another one,' I said to John.

He laughed, 'I think you've had enough, son.'

I couldn't wait until the next Saturday. Every week I would down my half pint and, sometimes, a whiskey to wash it down, which was even better than the half pint. I could talk to anybody after half a pint *and* a whiskey. I was just one of them now. Not fourteen, but eighteen. I could talk to anybody about anything. They would talk about football and I would suddenly know everything about football. They would listen and laugh at everything I said, never laughing at me. Nobody laughs at you when you've had half a pint and a whiskey and are talking about football.

They would talk about women and I would suddenly know everything about women. It didn't matter that I had only had sex with Theresa and probably didn't even get it in. It didn't matter that I wanked myself silly to photos of old women in bras and nothing ever came out. It didn't matter that Elaine Slaven had laughed at my eyes and thought I was trying to go to the toilet. It didn't matter because I was now a man.

I never have to worry about friends again. If I drink like this, I'm the king of my own castle.

And there it was. That was the moment. For others it was the first time they scored a goal and thought: *I'm gonna be a footballer.* It was when they saw a plane in the sky and thought: *I'm gonna fly one of those some day.* For me it was sitting with the clan, John Brett's arm hooked around my neck like a big brother, and the guys laughing and talking and nodding at me like I was something. It was with my whiskey glass in one hand, cigarette in the other. That was the moment I decided: *I've got to be like this all the time.*

I didn't want to be the best fighter any more. I didn't need to be

64

the best fighter. All I wanted was to be popular like these guys. And these guys drank.

Mum didn't know about my drinking. It turned out that I didn't need to tell her everything. She let me have 'just the one' on New Year's Eve. It was a big party and all the neighbours had come round to our flat to sing and dance and be happy. Mum was so happy, she didn't notice that just the one became another, then another, and another, and another, and…

Is that Susan over there? My God, Susan's looking fine tonight.

Susan was looking juicy, whatever juicy was. Red lipstick, short skirt, and killer legs. Susan and Donald lived next door. She was probably about forty years old, but to me she was whiskey pretty and *who the hell is Donald, anyway?* The room parted as I glided over to her with my chest puffed out, hair patted down, eyebrows licked to the sides, and John Wayne eyes.

'Hey, Susan.'

She looked down and I didn't notice she needed to bend to ruffle my hair to the side. I just felt her hand.

Yeah, that's what I'm talking about, Susan.

At some point I must have tried to kiss her because Mum was in front of me.

'Mark, what did you think you were doing to Susan?' she asked.

'Don't worry, Anne. The wee lads drunk, there's no harm done,' Donald said.

Shut up, Donald.

I was shit sick, too sick to feel anything but my bed. I sank into it and slept until the next day. I had no idea why my head was beating like a band of military drums. Mum told me about the dancing round the room, the strutting, the sidling up to Susan, the hand on her leg, the *'I love you, Susan,'* and then my lips missing hers completely and headbutting the couch. I couldn't remember any of it.

Oh God, oh dear God, I can never ever see Susan again.

A few weeks after the Susan mishap, I was looking out of my

window with my can of Special Brew. I could see my new friends coming up the road laughing and drinking. With my parents in bed, I sneaked out with my can and hobbled over. I was dragging my legs like I was drunk, drunker than I was because I was stone cold sober. I wanted them to see me drunk because they would tell everybody in school and I would be a hero because of drunkenness.

'What's going on, lads, 'cause I'm fucking pissed,' I slurred.

They pointed and laughed, but nobody was laughing at me.

'Fucking hell, Dempster's pissed.' They were cheering, so I tagged along to the party, and spent the whole night with my can pretending I was pissed. I went home buzzing from the fact I had fooled them. Tomorrow at school they would spread the news that Dempster was a drunken, Dempster was a pisshead.

The whole school is going to love me for this.

Next day I was ready for the praise, ready for admiration, and ready for looks and whispers.

'That's Dempster, he's a pisshead, the coolest guy in school,' the whisperers would say.

When I bowled through the school gates, some kids were pointing and laughing. Something was different this time, though. They weren't laughing with me, they were definitely laughing at me.

'That's Dempster, gets pissed on only one can,' the whisperers shouted.

'Hey, Dempster, One Can Man, how's your head?' someone asked. I didn't even know the guy who asked it.

One Can Man? This wasn't what was supposed to happen.

Some kids were shouting to other kids.

The boy who gets pissed on one can, can't handle his drink.

It's not so bad not being the best fighter in school, but getting pissed on one can was the worst thing that could have happened to me. I hadn't even been pissed, but I couldn't tell everyone I had faked it. That would be worse.

66

The only thing I could do was jump into every fight that happened. If I went crazy, *fucking crazy*, and kicked and punched and spat and gouged at every opportunity that came up then they would forget about the One Can Man tag they had for me. They did. Instead of the One Can Man tag, they started calling me Psycho Dempster. I was okay with that. If I was going to be anything I would rather be Psycho than One Can Man.

My new reputation as a psycho got me my first girlfriend – Dawn Davis. There were only two girls that had big tits in our school and Dawn was one of them. So when her friend told me that Dawn fancied me I was ready to go over and snog her in front of everybody right then. Instead I waited for two weeks, worrying and planning.

There was so much to think about before I went over to ask Dawn out on a date. If I asked her in front of everybody would she laugh at me? Was it a trick to get me to go psycho again? I watched her in class for a few days to see if she looked back at me.

If she looks, I'll ask her out.

She looked.

If she looks again, I'll ask her out.

She looked again.

If she looks again and smiles, I'll ask her out.

She looked again and smiled, but I still couldn't go over there and ask her. If it weren't for her big breasts I would have given up on the whole thing. Every night I would wank myself to sleep thinking about Dawn's breasts and what I would do to her on our date.

I'm going to snog her with my tongue. Kiss those breasts, suck those nipples. I'm going to stick my dick in her fanny. I'm going to get in there as fast as I can, bounce up and down, in and out, and stuff is going to come out all inside you, Dawn, and over your big breasts... Dawn... Dawn...

Stuff came out that time. All because Dawn Davis, the girl with the biggest breasts in school - not the first biggest, but definitely the second biggest - fancied me. I was definitely going to ask Dawn out.

She was sitting near the front of the class, which meant I had to walk at least five desks to get to her. She was with all her friends.

I don't have to do this. I can still go back.

Her friends were looking over at me and smiling. They were whispering to each other.

Still time to back out of this. Just walk to the door and run. I could just pretend I'm going to the toilet.

I was in front of her. My hand was shaking. Everybody in the class was looking at me.

They're all watching me, waiting for me to get laughed at so they can laugh at me too.

Dawn looked up at me and smiled.

Look at those breasts. Fuck it. Just do it.

'Hey, Dawn, I heard you fancy me.'

She said nothing.

'Well, if you did, I mean, you know, we could, I don't know if you're free, but maybe you could…'

Just get on with it. You sound like a freak.

'Do you want to go out with me?'

More silence. This was torture.

I knew she didn't fancy me.

'Yeah, okay,' she said.

I was in lust before, but now I was in love. I was going to marry Dawn as soon as possible. First, we had to get our date out of the way, which was to be Saturday - a full four days from now. I didn't know what I was supposed to do until the first date. I saw her in every class, at the break times and in the corridor.

Should I ignore her? Should I say hello? Do I talk to her?

I didn't know if we were boyfriend and girlfriend before the date. There should be rules about these things, a handbook printed up and given to you after you ask a girl out on a first date. I didn't need to worry because Dawn took care of what needed to be done. She came over and talked to me and we hung out together all week. By the first date we were snogging for hours at the back of the cinema, my hand trying to cop a good feel of her big tits.

I was the happiest boy in school until somebody told me Gareth had already had sex with her. I couldn't believe it. Not only was Gareth the second best fighter (I was only the third) but he had a massive dick. I would sneak a look at it in the changing rooms, just to compare and see what I was up against.

Bloody hell. He has loads more hairs than me all over his balls.

I couldn't stand it. He'd had sex with Dawn with that massive thing covered in hair.

Look at his smug face. I'm not having him even look at Dawn any more.

'Hey, Gareth, don't go anywhere near my girlfriend!'

Before he could answer, or I could remember that he was the second best fighter in school, I tried to head butt him and completely missed.

'Okay, Dempster, you want to fight? Three thirty, by the boilers.'

I forgot that you had to make an appointment for a fight. It was all so much more sophisticated now. We even had a referee to make sure things were fair, but mostly to look out for the teachers. Surrounded by cheering, most of them for Gareth, I kicked and punched and got a few in before he thumped me to the floor. The referee jumped in to warn about the teacher coming.

'Fancy a rematch tomorrow, Dempster?' he asked.

I would have. I should have. But I was already black and blue and I couldn't go through the shame of it again.

'No, no – you win,' I panted in shame.

The fight was over and the crowd dispersed, leaving me to lick my wounds. Then Chris, the fourth best fighter in school, came up to me. He had a look of hope in his eyes.

'Hey, Dempster, I watched you lose that fight. I reckon I could beat you.' There was no way I was surrendering third place to go to fourth or fifth. It was bad enough that Gareth had had sex with my girlfriend and beaten me to a pulp in front of everybody.

'If you want a smack in the mouth, let's take it up, Chris.'

He could see I wasn't messing and gave up before we started. He was just trying his luck, trying to get me in a moment of weakness. I could understand it. Being the fourth best fighter in school didn't even get you a nod from the guys at the cool table.

It wasn't just Gareth that got me wound up about Dawn. I was obsessed with her. I wanted to be with her all of the time, and I couldn't stand anybody else talking to her or looking at her. If it was another boy talking to her, I thought they were trying to chat her up. If it was another girl talking to her, especially if it was one of her friends, I thought they were telling her I was no good. If it was the teachers talking to her, I thought they were marking her schoolwork down because she was dating me.

It was just as bad when we weren't together. I would obsess about what she might be doing, who might be talking to her as well as making up in my head what they might be saying. I was worried mostly about her cheating on me with someone else. Maybe going back to Gareth. I knew she wanted to have sex, but I couldn't. As much as I wanted to, as much as I had planned it over and over in my head, I kept thinking I wasn't going to be able to find the fanny. All I could think about was the size of my willy compared to Gareth's. It just didn't measure up.

I couldn't tell Dawn any of this. She would think I was nuts. Instead, she just thought I was an obsessive, jealous, and possessive boyfriend. She didn't need that hassle, so sent the same girl who had informed me that Dawn fancied me over to tell me Dawn had dumped me. I was smashed – heartbroken – and I didn't think I would ever get over it. I would soon find something to replace her, to wash away those feelings, and it wasn't another girl or drink. It was drugs, and I found them exactly when I needed them.

I used to look at the stoners and think: *That's stupid, why take drugs? Why do something that makes you sleepy?* My dad never took drugs and none of his friends did. If drink made me feel like king of my own castle, then why would I ever need anything else? Davey would sit next to me in class, stinking and steaming of hash. The smell was sweet, but he looked sour.

He would look at me and I would get paranoid. Finally it got to me, so I asked him directly.

'What you looking at, Davey?'

'Oh, nothing, man, everything's cool.'

He said it slow and deep like he was half asleep. He seemed different to the rest of us, like he floated through corridors, breezed through classes, and nothing bothered him. Amongst the chaos, Davey was at peace.

Maybe I should give this hash thing a try.

My head kept telling me I should give it a try, but I still had Dad's words in my head telling me, 'Only idiots take drugs. Can't stand a drug addict.' He would slur the words he'd be so drunk.

Most of my friends were starting to puff. I smelt the sweet grass on everyone. A couple of friends offered me a smoke on their bong, and it didn't take much to ask myself: *Why not try it once? What have I got to lose?*

They passed it to me, watching as eagerly as the clan had watched me drink my first half pint. I smoked some but I didn't see the big deal. It didn't do anything.

Maybe I'm doing it wrong. I'll try it again, just to see if I did it right.

I tried it again at a house party. It wasn't much of a party - just a bunch of stoners swaying their heads to chilled music and passing around bongs. I could barely make out the faces through the smoke. Most of them were older than me and some of the girls were oozing sex they were so hot. I watched them for instruction, determined to do it the right way this time. I held my head back and took the smoke in. I could feel it running down my throat and into my stomach and then my head...went...slower. My legs were funny, sinking into the ground, and my whole body was numb and soft and chewy all at the same time. I didn't care what time it was or what I had to do or what I was supposed to do. I had completely forgotten about Dawn.

71

Hash is much better than a half pint and a whiskey.

With a half pint and a whiskey I could talk all night about anything, whether I knew it or not. I could look at women and imagine touching them, kissing them, wanking until I was red raw. I could do anything and everything I wanted to even if it was just in my head. With hash I was free – completely free. I could just lie back and float away.

I'm not sure how I got home or how long it took. There was so much to see as I walked home. I was a child seeing everything for the first time. The houses were grand, the sky was bright and the air was warm. The world was a much better place stoned. I got home and felt like a bite to eat, so I got the cheese and bread from the fridge, just a little – then some more and then everything in the fridge was in my belly.

Mum said, 'Mark, you're a hungry one tonight, aren't you? You been playing rugby today?'

I said, 'Yeah,' but it felt like I'd said it so slowly and so loud that she must know. I ate as quietly as I could, but every chew sounded like it was in stereo, so loud I was sure the neighbours would come knocking. Mum and Dad kept looking and it felt like Mum was staring at me and saying with her eyes, *'I know what you've been up to, Mark.'* I went to my room and passed out. I don't remember anything else other than the most peaceful sleep I had ever had. I woke up the next day with no headache, no sickness – just one thought:

I've got to do this all the time.

When I'd first changed schools I'd tried to apply myself for a while – until the drinking and the obsession with Dawn took over. Now, with the hash and the parties, I spent less time studying. I had other things to do and I couldn't help feeling that I was learning everything I needed to learn hanging out with other people, drinking and smoking. When I wasn't smoking, I was trying to get my hand down the knickers of the other girls asleep at the parties. Each time I got just under the waistband they would tell me to chill and go back to sleep. 'I'm really sorry, just mashed up,' I would say, only to repeat it again about ten minutes later, always with the same result. I didn't get my hand anywhere near a fanny, no matter how much I tried. I didn't get any praise for my three O level passes either.

Mum was upset. She'd wanted me to do well at school. I could see that. But she and Dad were getting divorced, so she had other things to worry about. She had had enough of Dad drinking and seeing snakes, spiders, and dead Grandma. Mostly, she was worried what I might do to my dad. I was now old enough to fight him and I told her many times that I would stab him if he carried on hitting me and drinking. The fact that I was old enough to do what I wanted gave Mum the permission she needed to leave Dad and start afresh with somebody new. Not that I cared about any of that.

I had learnt what I needed to from my childhood. How to fight, how to jump bins, how to have sex (I think), and how to drink. I learnt that I never needed to feel shit about anything with a drink and hash. I didn't realise I had crossed a line, and I couldn't say when I crossed it. Maybe it was when I took those first few sips of Special Brew, maybe with my first half pint. It might have even happened when I got the rush from jumping the bins and boxing my friends. I don't think it was Dad's fault and I know it wasn't Mum's. It wasn't even as if I look back at my childhood and think it was bad. How could it have been bad if it had been all I knew, and everybody else's life resembled mine? At some point I just crossed the imaginary line, with no warning, no worry, no prophecy of some future locked up in jail or needles sticking out of my arm, dying. But that's where I was heading, and there was nothing I could do about it.

I was dead already; I just didn't know it.

PART TWO

Chapter 6

I'm eighteen, in jail, and lying against a thin, soft mat. The cold hard concrete is seeping through, claiming my back. I'm staring at the ceiling with so many names and dates scrawled across it that I can hardly see the piss white colour. I can smell the cement, bleach, and dirt. I can hear the slamming of metal into walls, the sound of a bolt click, the click of the lock saying to me:

Mark, you're fucked.

They had caught me with the scales in the bag, and nobody carried scales for anything other than weighing drugs in Glasgow. I wasn't wearing chef whites coming back from cooking class. I couldn't sell drugs with no scales – a little over and I'm out of pocket, a little under they're likely to glass me for it. I was stinking and steaming of weed because, by the time I got to Davey's, it was past midnight. I had to smoke a few joints to settle down for the night. It had been a heavy day.

I had trekked to the Vale for four ounces of hash and then back to mine to weigh it out. The scales were broken, so I went to Davey's to borrow his, and, to top it all off, I'd been working all day at the base.

If only the police had minded their own business. Now I'm in this poxy jail cell, probably going to prison. I'm definitely going to lose my job.

Losing my job wouldn't have been that bad. I could have focused on my dealing business. It wasn't difficult to sell weed to the hippies and dope heads of Glasgow, and I was getting more and more customers. The day job had become a bit of a distraction. But Mum had got me the job and I didn't want to upset her. She had written to the nuclear base in Fasland. As her dad had worked for the Ministry of Defence - she pleaded - could they give her hard-working, honest son an apprenticeship? They did.

I spent two years at college learning about electricity and wiring. I even passed the exams, which was a miracle with all the hash I was smoking. It would be a job for life, a good job with money and a career. All the kids leaving my school wanted an apprenticeship at the base. Their parents would have killed to get them the gig. My mum just used her dad's name. She would be distraught if I lost that.

How the fuck did I get here?

It was the peace camp that distracted me from the plans that Mum had for me. As the bus grumbled us into the base, we passed the peace camp. The side of the road was littered with caravans, tarpaulins, and a big tepee marked with a CND sign. CND meant Campaign for Nuclear Disarmament, but I didn't care about the planet being blown to pieces. The sign said freedom to me. I could see they were free by the way they lived on the camp. Amongst the trees, the hippies surrounded the campfires. They were dressed in multi-coloured jumpers, woolly hats, and were studded and tattooed all over. The dogs roamed about them while they smoked joints and chanted. They didn't shout. They weren't smashing things up. Just smoking and chanting. The hippies were at peace.

They reminded me of John Brett and the clan. The clan of Brett's thought that they were hippies. I thought I was a hippy. But the hippies at the peace camp weren't glassing people in pubs like I had seen the clan do - one minute loving, the next killing. They weren't beating their friends up and shooting air rifles. As I passed the camp I resented the life I had more and more. I didn't want to have to go to work every day in a job I hated doing. I didn't want to battle to

77

be the most popular guy in town. I wanted to be a free, peace-loving hippy. Being a drug dealer was my best route to that.

It wasn't an overnight decision to become a drug dealer. I had learnt that crime was an acceptable way of life from watching my dad. I had learnt as much as I could about the dealing way of life from hanging out with Walshy and the guys after I had left school. I had met Walshy playing football with Dods, back when I was still shooting air rifles. Walshy was depressing. He was always whingeing about something, and I wanted to beat him up for it. But he had brothers who were bigger than I was, so I just smoked hash with him instead.

Walshy became a butcher's apprentice, but much preferred his old part-time job cleaning the slates in the betting shop. He had a taste for gambling and *claimed* he knew what he was doing, but never made any money doing it. His mum would gossip with my mum outside the church when we were young, but since Mum had left the church Walshy's mum was left alone to do God's work. While his dad was watching football and his mum out, we would get high in his room and talk about a future of travelling and adventure together.

'They're all doing it, Walshy. Off to India on a spiritual journey – learning how to live, man,' I said.

'I don't see why you have to go to the other side of the world to learn to live. A lot of money and hassle for nothing,' he moaned.

'Think about it, Walshy. Smoking hash out in the streets, where nobody is going to arrest you for it. Trekking through the Himalayas…'

'What if you get lost?' Walshy had a way of finding the thing that is least likely to happen and making it sound like it is definitely going to happen.

'Lost?'

'Yeah, man. You're walking through the mountains, stoned, and then you lose your way. You're going to die up there, Mark.'

With all his worrying he was going grey already. There was

something about Walshy worrying, though, that was endearing to me. He was part of our group of friends and I couldn't imagine us being a group of friends without him. Ronnie, Davey, Walshy, and me smoked hash and dreamt about a different life to the one we had. When we smoked and got high we were free. But when we weren't high, we were just like our parents, and their parents, and their parents before that: stuck amongst the blackened, cold, dirty stone of our tenement homes, with miserable weather and jobs we hated.

On the weekends we did what our parents had done to wash away the working week and the misery of life. We drank. But this was the eighties so we tripped on LSD and magic mushrooms too. Friday night I'd down half a bottle of cheap wine and a flagon of cider. That would send me jumping over hedges and getting into scraps. I'd wake up the next day wondering why I was covered in scratches and bits of leaves in my hair. I would look in the mirror and find black eyes from the scraps the night before, but have no recollection of anything happening.

I was sixteen when I took my first trip. Ronnie, Walshy, Davey, and I all sat around brewing the mushrooms in hot water. I didn't see what was magic about them. They just looked like mushrooms in hot water. They tasted bitter. Nothing like mushrooms. Walshy was worried about everything, yet he didn't waste any time sipping on the mushroom tea.

I sipped a little. They sipped a little.

I sipped some more. They sipped some more.

Then I downed the cup.

'Calm down, man,' Ronnie said. 'You don't want a bad trip your first time.'

Ronnie knew more about tripping than all of us. He was almost twenty and already had several years of dealing and using drugs under his belt. He was our dealer. I wondered why Ronnie wanted to hang around with guys who were several years his junior. We had nothing like the experience and street credibility he had. He was

79

a pioneer in the dealing world of Glasgow. Ronnie was the first to supply LSD in town. Whatever new batch of hash or LSD, he was the first to sell it in our town. Pioneers rarely prosper, and Ronnie was no different. He was always getting busted. He had an Australian girlfriend whom he smuggled hash to. He posted the drugs to her, stuffed in shoes. The shoes got busted by the Australian customs and she did six months in jail. The people who do business with pioneers rarely prosper either.

It's the people who follow after the pioneers that prosper. Watching Ronnie work and listening to the way he thought about things inspired me. For one thing, I thought I could do it better. I wasn't going to make the same mistakes he was making. I wasn't going to be getting caught and others caught with me. But I still thought I had a lot to learn from Ronnie. Maybe that's why he hung around with us. Us looking up to him probably boosted his ego. I wasn't going to let him know that. He already had a big enough ego. I ignored his mushroom tea advice and downed another cup. Then another. And another.

'Right. Let's get down the pub,' I said.

'No, Mark. What are you talking about? We're tripping. You don't want to be tripping down the pub,' Walshy moaned.

'Bullocks!' I said. 'I want to check out the girls.'

'Yeah, that sounds like a plan,' Ronnie said.

Ronnie was good with the girls and always had an attractive girlfriend. Or two. That pissed me off, because he was tough to compete against when chatting up the girls. I was always ready to take up the challenge, though, and, if I didn't succeed, try it on with some of Ronnie's cast-offs. The problem was, when we got to the pub, I could see the girls, but I couldn't move my head or any other part of my body. I had my pint in my hand, frozen in time. My whole body was numb. Except, I could still think.

Why can't I fucking move?

Nobody around me seemed to notice me sitting with my arm

80

held out, frozen, grasping my pint. Walshy was sitting next to me, looking miserable. Davey and Ronnie were chatting to girls. I was stuck in time, left with my thoughts.

Fuck. This is it. I'm frozen. It's finally happened. I'm frozen here forever. They're going to have to nut me off and lock me up and then I'll just be like this for another fifty years until I die of old age.

At some point I just became unfrozen, and my body went back to normal. I got back to drinking my pint like nothing had ever happened and never even bothered telling the lads. Tripping was like that. One minute my life was in mortal danger, the next I'm having the most pleasant few moments of my life. After that first time, we tripped every weekend. Our routine was smoke, smoke, smoke, smoke during the week; drink, drink, drink on Friday; trip on Saturday; and then sleep most of Sunday.

I was happy with that weekly routine. I didn't like going to work every day, but the drinking, the smoking, and the tripping made it bearable. I didn't look at my life and think it needed a girlfriend. Of course, I always looked at it and knew it needed more sex. Or at least some sex. Any sex, actually. The guys were great for chatting and getting high with, but we were too old to be tugging each other off. I was beyond desperation to have sex by the time I met Clare. I was seventeen, and the closest I had got to having sex was fingering the drunk girls at Ronnie's house parties. By this age I knew enough to know fingering wasn't sex.

I met Clare on a campsite in France. I helped her put up her tent in the hope that she would let me sleep with her. She didn't. But she did let me stay in her tent that night and we talked into the early hours. She was an attractive blonde with long hair. I thought she was voluptuous, curvaceous. Whenever a really attractive girl seemed to like me, I could never quite believe it. I never thought I was attractive. I was too awkward in my seventeen-year-old body. When I had to leave the next day, and Clare agreed to give me her address, I congratulated my character - my charm - for doing a good job on convincing her I was worthy. I was even more surprised when I saw the address – St Paul's and Mary's University in Cheltenham. She was studying English literature.

This girl is out of my league.

Clare and I were from opposite worlds. She was from the posh end of Middlesex and I was from the back dens of Glasgow. Our families couldn't have been more different. I would visit her at her mother's house. I never got used to sitting around the table for a dinner of three courses. Her mother was a medium – a good medium too, because she had me pegged down from day one.

'Mark, I am sensing an aura about you. Some dark energy,' she said.

'What dark energy?' I asked. I was a big fan of all things dark at that age. Alistair Crowley was my hero at the time.

'The dark energy. It is a really strong influence on you, Mark. Very strong. You are going to have a difficult life. You are going to have real difficulties, turmoil, and futility.' She looked at me seriously and solemnly after she'd finished. Clare looked worried too. I wasn't. I thought this was the best news ever.

'Cool,' I said.

Clare didn't seem to mind about me having all this dark energy. She didn't know about my plans to become a drug dealer, but she knew I smoked hash and tripped with the guys. We smoked weed together sometimes, but she didn't smoke much. Given the difference in our backgrounds I think I was her *bit of rough*. She didn't need to try to fit into my world either. She could always just settle into any new group. When she visited me in Glasgow she was happy to sit and talk with my mum. She didn't mind our small flat. Mum liked her too – liked her enough to offer up her own bed.

'Oh, you don't need to sleep in with Mark tonight, Clare. You can have my bed,' Mum said.

'No, Mrs Dempster, I don't mind. I want to stay with Mark.'

I wanted Clare to stay with me too. She had already had sex before. She had dated another Scottish boy for several months and was a lot more experienced with sex than I was. I didn't feel as threatened as I had with Gareth and Dawn. I didn't know Clare's Scottish ex, so didn't have to compare myself to him. Besides, by this point in my life I was chomping at the bit for sex.

It wasn't like the time with Theresa in the concrete hut, when I was ten. There was nobody watching this time. I was going to take it slow and make our first time together special.

'When we make love, I want it to mean something, Mark,' she had said. I had never heard it called that before.

Making love.

Sex. Shagging. Fucking. Doing it. But never making love. She bought some sexy stockings and knickers for the love-making. It was my job to put the music on, light the candles, and kiss her softly. I started slowly, kissing her lips, kissing her neck, touching her breasts. I kept touching her breasts for the next five minutes. Then, with the foreplay completed, I put myself inside Clare, pushed several times, and then came.

'Don't worry, Mark,' she soothed.

Don't worry about what?

'Was it okay for you?' I asked.

'Yes, yes, it was lovely. We just need to go a little slower next time,' she said. Clare had had good sex and she had had bad sex. She was trying her best to steer me towards good sex. I knew I could do better. I just couldn't stop myself from finishing so quickly.

The next week she bought me a book – *A Guide to Love-Making.*

There is no way I am reading that.

It turned out there was fun to be had in reading it, though. Clare wanted to practise what I had learnt from the book – so the more I read, the more I learnt, and the more we practised. The more we practised love making, the more I fell in love with Clare. She had plans for her future and she had plans for my future, too. I always thought that I wasn't good enough for her – that she would probably be better off with somebody who spoke and thought like her. I just couldn't let her go off and find that person. Within a few days of being together I told her, *'I love you, Clare,'* and she told me, *'I love you, Mark.'*

There was a honeymoon period between Clare and me that lasted at least three months. She never questioned me smoking weed and tripping with the guys. But the more I visited at her home in Bath and the more she visited me in Glasgow, I was starting to worry her.

'Don't you have plans, Mark?' she would ask.

Yes. I want to be a big time drug dealer.

'Yes. I've got the job at the base. I'm at college,' I would say.

'But you smoke dope all the time with your friends. They're not exactly the best influence, are they?'

I couldn't stand it when she bad-mouthed my friends.

'It's hash, Clare. Hash is a spiritual drug.'

'I'm just saying, Mark. You can do better for yourself.'

Her parents would tell me the same thing. They would ask questions about what my plans were for my life. I always felt out of place around their dinner table, talking life plans and having 'family' conversation. It was alien to me. The only way I would cope was to go off into the woods and smoke a joint. I thought nobody could tell I was stoned. Maybe the dark energy Clare's mother saw in me was really just the smell of hash lingering on my clothes.

Clare would smoke hash with me too – but she never smoked much, and, when she did, it just made her paranoid. She wasn't any fun when she was like that. She always got jealous when I talked to other girls. She even got jealous when I talked to my cousin at a family wedding. Sure, she was attractive, but she was my cousin. Clare got so jealous she threw an ashtray out of the window. That was the first time we tripped together. I thought that doing some superman LSD would be the best way to diffuse things. But, even when high, she turned the conversation around to my plans for the future. I knew that she wanted to have children and settle down. I loved Clare, but settling down was not one of my immediate plans.

84

Clare couldn't see that I already had a career and I was already studying. I had been watching Ronnie and learning everything I could from him. He had a book that he kept reading. It was called *The Great Book of Hashish*. When I read it, a whole world of opportunity opened up before my eyes. The book was full of pictures of hash from Lebanon, Morocco, and India. The hash looked like blocks of chocolate and sticks of gold, hand rolled in the mountains. The life portrayed in *The Great Book* looked serene: get up in the morning to the sound of bells rung by monks, smoke hash for breakfast looking out over the mountains, and then spend the day rolling hash. It was the most romantic thing I had seen.

I want to travel to where the hash looks like sticks of chocolate and gold.

There was just no way that I could tell Clare that. She wouldn't have understood.

Clare wasn't around lots of hippies and travellers at her posh university. I was around them all the time in Glasgow. So many people around me were adopting the hippy lifestyle. A lot of the older hippies had already taken the pilgrimage to the Hash Mountains in India. I could spot the ones who had been to India. They wore beads around their necks.

Maru considered himself a spiritual guru. He wore beads around his neck that had a picture of the Indian spiritual guru Bhagwan Rajneesh dangling from them. He sat in the pub, drinking with the rest of us. Yet he looked different from the rest of us. Maru was well known in town. He was a good fighter and people were scared of him. But he was also clever. I was fascinated with him and begged him to tell me about the guru and the spiritual way of life. He sat in his purple clothes, telling me and the lads about Bhagwan. In the middle of one of his passionate descriptions of a spiritual way of life I witnessed somebody challenge him to a fight. He stopped to headbutt him and then returned to his spiritual lecture about love and peace, his opponent out cold on the floor next to us.

It was the hippies at the CND camp who inspired me to seek a peaceful and carefree way of life. It was Maru who inspired me to seek a *spiritual* way of life. It was Ronnie who inspired me to deal drugs. All three inspirations seemed a compatible way of life. Maru said that hash was a big part of the spirituality of Indian life; so, in dealing hash, I would be dealing spirituality.

That's how I ended up in the jail cell.

I knew that if I was to make the transition to big time dealer, the man who gets you the hash, then I would need to have more of it. I got introduced to a man who sold hash to dealers and within weeks I was buying four or five ounces at a time. My list of customers included half the apprentices at the base.

Fuck. If I lose this job I lose half my customer base. I really don't want to lose this job.

The click of the lock and the jail cell door was open. A police officer was standing to the side in full uniform and another man walked in. He didn't have a uniform – just a suit the colour of shit. The names and dates on the ceiling were etched into his face, each wrinkle representing one of the names.

I'll be there soon, etched on to his face, like a prize trophy, another one locked up, rotting away in jail for the rest of my life.

I knew what happened to people he put away. Dad had been in prison, my uncles had been in prison, even cousin Bobby got put away. People in prison got glassed in the face, stabbed, and raped. People died in prison. The youth prisons were just as bad. Kids from my school disappeared to those places and were never seen or heard of again.

The guy with the shit-coloured suit and the prize trophy wrinkles leant back against the wall with his hands in his pockets.

'Well, Dempster, in a bit of a fucking pickle, aren't ye?'

I didn't reply, didn't even acknowledge he was there. It was all a game from then on.

Don't talk to the detectives and don't give anything away. They'll twist it against me.

'Not talking, are we? That's fine. You see, Dempster, you little shit, we got what we need. You're fucked and you better get used to these four walls, 'cause drug dealing is a big fucking crime.'

'You got NOTHING.'

'So you do talk. I'll tell you exactly what we've got.' He began to pace, his head rocking as he talked, hands sewn into his pockets. 'We've got some weighing scales concealed from my officers, we've got you telling them it was a tape recorder – A FUCKING TAPE RECORDER – and we've got you on possession. Not the first time is it, Dempster? You've been cautioned before for possession.' He stopped talking, turned to me, and waited for an answer. He wanted some look of defeat, some recognition that I was as fucked as he said I was. I didn't give him even a flicker of the eyelid and that frustrated him.

'Why is it you kids never learn? Got everything to play for, got a good job, a good future, and you fuck it all up trying to be the big man, trying to be the hard man. Everybody wants to be a dealer, eh? Well, NOT ON MY PATCH.'

'I'm not saying anything.'

He leant against the wall again and smiled. I was wondering what he was smiling about.

Don't ask. Don't say anything to the detectives.

'We don't need you to say anything.' He pulled out a piece of paper and waved it in the air. 'I've got a search warrant for your house.' Then he turned on his heels and walked out of the door. It felt like he was running with the speed the door shut. I was on my feet hitting the wall.

Fuck, fuck, fuck.

They searched my house and found the coke, the hash, the money, and the names. I was pacing and sweating and thinking about the names. It was a book containing a list of my customers – nicknames, mostly. Some of them would knife me in the stomach if they thought I had grassed them. The names were my biggest worry. The coke

87

was only a gram - nothing they could pin on me for intent to supply. Not that it mattered. They had enough to charge me with the hash, the scales, and the wads of cash.

The cash. They've taken my fucking money.

Each time my head uncovered another mistake, something else that was going to trap me with a jail sentence or a blade to the stomach, it bitched at me. My head spun, tripping through fear and doom, beating me, bitching me.

Why did I have to get those scales so late? What was I thinking carrying that amount of hash on me? What the fuck am I gonna do now all my money's gone?

I had no idea what I was going to do next. I got bailed and went straight home. I could think clearly there.

Maybe they didn't find all my hash. At least there might be something left for me to get high.

Mum was standing at the top of the stairs. She was wearing her face. The disapproving one. All scrunched up as if she should be shaking her head and wagging her finger. I wasn't having any of it.

This is all her fault.

'Why the fuck did you let them in, Mum?' I asked.

'What do you mean, let them in? They're the police! What do you expect me to do when the police come round here in the middle of the night and—'

I cut her off. 'But you didn't have to let them in, did you? Did they have a warrant?'

'Don't talk to me like that, Mark.'

'Mum, I asked you, did they have a fucking warrant? A warrant – did you see the warrant?' If they hadn't had a warrant I was a free man. I'd heard enough stories from friends and seen enough TV shows to know that.

'I don't know what you're talking about. What did you expect me to do, not let the police in? This is your fault, Mark…'

I barged past her to my room while she carried on wailing in the background. At some point she trailed off. I don't know what she said after that because I had found enough hash to get me high. I sat there puffing and huffing about Mum letting them in and the police taking all my money.

What the fuck am I supposed to do now?

I had to think.

I can't do this any more. Work all day and then sell hash at night. It's too much.

Things had to change. I wanted what the hippies had. The hippies had a freedom I had always longed for. It was what I had seen in the rough kids on my first day in big school – not caring about what anybody thought. The problem with the rough kids was that it took a lot of work to not care about what anybody thought. Being a hippy looked like work too. Drug dealing seemed like a better bet. I had watched Ronnie deal and seen the respect he got. Everybody knew who he was. Nobody messed with him. I saw the girls he got to be with. They were all attractive and sexy girls. I saw the other dealers and their flashy cars, their money. I knew it was hard work, but the respect they got looked like it was worth all that graft.

If I can just make it to the big time, if I can deal my way to respect and fortunes, then I won't need to care about what anybody thinks.

The problem was reality. I had a vision of where I wanted to be – a big time dealer with the money and respect that goes with that. The reality was that I had broken scales, no drugs, no money, and a dopey mum who lets the police in. Things had to change.

If I get away with this, things are going to be different. I'm going to shape up and get professional. Get clever.

I did get away with the drug charges. At least I didn't go to prison, which was good enough for me. Old Man Trammy, who had helped Dad get off a drink-related crime, got me off a drug-related one. Manslaughter was as serious as drug dealing, but Trammy told the judge I had got into a bad crowd and was now a reformed character - that I would have to live my life with this mistake and that prison wouldn't help anybody. I was sat in the dock, wondering if the judge was buying this crap. I didn't notice Mum watching and crying, and Dad shaking his head. The judge asked if I had anything to say. I didn't, but I said what I was supposed to anyway. Just like confession, getting my sins out to the priest as quickly as possible: 'Yes, Judge, I've learnt. I just got in the wrong crowd. I'll never do this again.'

I'll never get caught again.

It didn't matter that I didn't mean what I said. Old Man Trammy did a good job of convincing the judge of what he said.

'You got off lightly, son,' Mum said.

'I know. I'm sorry, Mum.' I didn't think I had got off lightly. A five hundred pound fine and a two year suspended sentence. All I could think about was the fact that I wouldn't be able to deal for two years. If I got caught dealing in Glasgow again I would go straight to prison.

Dad said, 'You have disgraced this family, son.'

Who the fuck are you to be telling me I've disgraced the family?

'I know. I'm sorry, Dad,' I said.

Clare was the only one not to give me a hard time about the sentence. She wasn't happy, I knew that. Luckily for me, though, her parents were even less happy than her. They thought that she shouldn't be dating boys like me. Boys from the rough, mean streets of Glasgow who get caught for dealing hash. I think Clare was happy with her bit of rough, though. Going against her parents' wishes simply made me more desirable.

The bosses at the nuclear base weren't too happy either. But they had spent two years training me and that had cost them a lot of time and money. I just needed a bit of character building, they said. I got given a verbal warning and sent to a character building course in the middle of Dartmoor. Building character meant potholing, kayaking, rock climbing, and walks. One minute I was facing a long prison sentence with the likelihood of slashings, beatings, and rape. The next I was in the middle of the moors exploring mad holes down the rivers. There must have been lots of shady characters in the

Ministry of Defence because the camp was full of us from all over the country. It was mushroom season on the moors. We spent a lot of our free time picking, eating, and tripping on magic mushrooms. We couldn't have been happier if we had been sent to Barbados with a bunch of braless hippies.

At the end of my character building course I had learnt two things. The first was how to find magic mushrooms on the moors. The second was that I needed to get out of Glasgow if I was going to be a dealer. I had seen the other fuck-ups on the character building course and I knew that I was different from them. They were staying where they were for good. Either they would learn their lesson and reform – get serious about their life and career at the base - or they would drop out and live off the welfare. I didn't want either of those options. Staying at the base and making a career wasn't working. My bosses could see I wasn't serious. I turned up for work in hippy clothes, stinking and steaming of weed. I even got stopped by the Military Police once because they thought I was an infiltrator from the peace camp. I didn't want a life on welfare either – or running from the police all the time.

I decided to leave Glasgow. The nuclear base let me leave shortly after I made that decision. I was happy about that as it gave me my pension, which was a couple of thousand pounds - enough to get me started. I didn't know where though. I wanted to travel to India and the places I had visited in *The Great Book of Hashish*. I wanted to get dealing and start my career in the big time.

Chapter 7

Walshy and Ronnie had been spending time with the New Age travellers. Those travellers were *real* hippies. We all thought ourselves hippies because we *looked* like them, we *talked* like them, and we smoked hash and tripped on LSD. But the New Age travellers were hippies because they *lived* like hippies. The real hippies dropped out of society and took to life on the open road – travelling from camp to camp. They disowned society as we knew it. They damned the weapons and the wars. They discarded the rules and the laws.

The real hippies created their own communities that relied on everybody taking part. Campsites had to be set up; the vehicles they travelled in had to be maintained. But the idea was that people were free to do as they chose – they could wear what they liked and do what they wanted. Ironically, it turned out that almost all the hippies I met travelling wore the same thing and behaved in the same ways.

Although the hippies were free of permanent locations, a lot of the things that existed in the community I grew up in to keep people together and socialising existed with them, too. That's how the free festivals of the seventies and eighties started. They were a way for the travellers to come together, drink, sing, and dance – just like we had with the pubs. The hippies travelled in a battered entourage of vehicles known as the convoy. The peace convoy led the way from festival to festival. It was made up of families, couples, groups of friends and solo travellers. Along the way to a new festival, other travellers would join at the lay-bys, and everybody would exchange advice and food.

The mantra was: *You bring what you expect to get.* So, most of the travellers welcomed newcomers and gave them what they needed. More young people, disaffected from the unemployment and poverty of the seventies and eighties in Britain, joined the travellers at the festivals. Newcomers needed the advice and help of the experienced hippy travellers. In return, they bought the goods that the travellers sold, which funded the petrol and food they needed to sustain themselves.

Every community has its 'undesirables' - the people that ignore the spoken or unspoken rules. They act like they have no interest in being part of the community, yet refuse to leave it alone. The undesirables of the hippy traveller community were called the Brew Crew. They were the last ones to arrive at a free festival and the last ones to leave. They didn't bring anything, yet expected everything. They were made up of drunks and some bikers and they stole other travellers' food and money, slept with other travellers' girlfriends, and pissed all over other travellers' tents.

The Brew Crew were disliked by almost all the real travellers. The real travellers had spent years on a spiritual journey, learning from their travels in India, and the Brew Crew were showing up and drinking away their personal freedom. I wouldn't have known about the mid solstice festival at Stonehenge had it not been for them. They were responsible for all the negative news reports and outrage from politicians. Those who didn't know anything about travellers only saw or heard of the destruction caused by a small minority of them. I watched the festivals on the news and I wasn't scared by the travellers. I didn't see chaos. I saw hippies – like the ones at the peace camp – singing, dancing, and having fun.

Clare, like every middle-class young hippy at the time, wanted to spend her summer travelling the festivals. We both wanted to go to Stonehenge. There were plans to shut it down, so in 1984 we knew that it might be the last year we could go. Clare wanted to experience the atmosphere, the adventure, and the freedom as much as I did. When we arrived, we could see the camp below a fog of smoke from the campfires. It was like a refugee camp with thousands of tents, old buses, caravans, tepees, and carts. We were told that there were about a hundred thousand people. Everybody was scattered about, so it didn't look like anywhere near that number. There were people of all ages surrounding their tents with kettles boiling on wood fires.

I knew there would be lots of drugs at the festival. I knew hippies smoked hash and took LSD. I didn't expect drugs to be so openly available, though. Every other tepee or bus was adorned with billboard menus of hash, LSD, and coke. Better still, because of the supply, every other tent had something on offer, and they were price-cutting. They were the cheapest drugs I had ever bought.

I could easily get into this life and set up my own drug tent.

I didn't tell Clare what I thought about this life of freedom, adventure, and cheap drugs. For her this was a romantic trip. She wanted to listen to the music and dance with me. I wanted to trip out and watch the summer solstice. It was all about compromise with Clare – so we did both. Besides, a life dealing drugs at festivals wasn't really an option. This anti-capitalist movement didn't have free trade. The drugs were all supplied by one or two key players who had a string of dealers and heavies at campsites and festivals across the country. One group of dealers from Wales offered to sponsor the stage the following year. They were dealing heroin. The travelling community were anti-smack. It was the only drug that they frowned upon and actively discouraged. The festivals were self-policed, mainly by the Hell's Angels. They would burn the vans and cars of smack dealers and beat them into hospital.

The Brew Crew were busy drinking and stealing food and

94

valuables from campers' tents, the Hell's Angels were busy burning vehicles that belonged to the heroin dealers, and the rest of us were tripping on LSD and swaying along to Roy Harper and Hawkwind. I considered adopting this style of life – getting a van and joining the convoy. Claire would have definitely left me if I had done that. She liked smoking a bit of hash every now and again, but it was just a holiday for her. It was a gap year from her middle-class life. She still had middle-class plans for the future. She wanted to finish university, get a job, get married, buy a house, and have a baby. If I'd had to choose between that life and the life of a traveller – I would have chosen the traveller's life.

I didn't need to choose, though. I could see there was no business to be done at the festivals. Clare was right about me having potential, being able to achieve things with my life. My potential as a drug dealer went beyond selling a bit of hash and LSD out of the back of a van. There was no future for the festivals, either. The drugs, the drinking, the Brew Crew, and the bikers were the only things that the public saw. They didn't like their landmarks hijacked and fields trashed. Thatcher had crushed the miners and now she could crush the travellers. She ordered the Stonehenge festival to be shut down and the next year thousands of police, armed with water cannons and batons, beat back the hard-core group that ignored the ban. They didn't just shut down the festival; they destroyed hundreds of travellers' vehicles. They hoped that this would destroy the spirit of the movement.

In some ways it did. The public were happy to see such a free group of people taking a beating. That made it easy to bring in laws that banned groups of three or more vehicles setting up camp together without a licence. Some of the travellers emigrated to Spain and other hot countries, forming their own permanent camps. Others started all-night festivals - raves. A rave could get around the law for a while as nobody was sleeping at raves. The music changed to beats and the hash to speed and Es.

Although I could see there was no future in joining the travellers, I didn't plan to go the way of life Clare wanted me to, either. I wanted to get set up as a dealer as soon as possible. I couldn't deal in Glasgow. With the suspended sentence the drug squad would be keeping their eye on me for a while. Ronnie, Walshy, and Davey were getting set up in London. That was where a lot of the travellers and hippies set up squats for the winter months. They took over unoccupied flats and houses and signed on for benefits.

Walshy didn't think much about my plans to deal in London. He pissed me off sometimes with all his worrying.

'What if you get caught again, Mark? You still have a suspended sentence in London!'

'Yeah, but they won't be watching me in London, will they?'

'Why don't you come travelling with us? Ronnie and I are thinking about getting a bus and joining the convoy. You can still deal a bit to the travellers.'

'No, Walshy. I can do better than that. I have a plan.'

Walshy couldn't understand why I wanted to be a dealer, when I could be free like him and the other travellers. He couldn't see that if I had the money and the respect that comes from being a big time dealer then I would still be free. Then he would come begging me to be part of it. He liked the idea of travelling and thought he was more of a hippy than the rest of us. But he liked taking drugs and gambling more. That required money. It wouldn't be long before he needed some.

I needed money to get me set up in London. We were all scamming the state. We wanted to drop out of society, but still expected society to support us in doing it. I got signed up to a college course in Glasgow. I wasn't going to attend the college - I was just taking the grant and leaving town. When we got to London we all signed on for unemployment benefits, using several different names. We got housing benefit for B & Bs, but pocketed the money and stayed in squats instead. It was more than enough money to live on.

96

Ronnie was already set up in London. He had made connections and let me stay with him for a while, until I found my own squat. He had found a dealer and took me to see him. We entered a room with Hawkwind music playing. A slim man, slightly older than I was, with long hippy hair, was sitting in the middle of the room. He was rocking his body to the music and reading a book on philosophy. He was surrounded by piles of hash and hundreds of LSD trips.

He looked up at us. 'Oh hey, Ronnie,' he said, 'who's your friend?' Ronnie introduced me.

'All right, Mark,' he said. 'I'm Nick. Make yourself at home. Smoke a joint?'

I didn't need to smoke a joint. I thought I was already high. There was a girl coming down the stairs. She was wearing sexy black leather trousers and her bum was sucked into them. Her body left me drooling at the mouth. That was until I saw the ten foot reticulated python draped around her neck.

What is going on here?

'Don't worry about the snake. It's harmless,' Nick said, as if he could read the worry on my face. He introduced me to the sexy girl with the python wrapped around her neck. 'Hey, Kerrin. This is Mark.'

Maybe I do need to smoke a joint.

I sat with Nick and smoked a joint and spent most of the week smoking with him. I watched him pop trip after trip – he took five trips at a time - yet still functioning. An endless stream of people kept coming and going and Nick sat dispensing trips and hash like a doctor.

How can he even move his head with that much LSD inside him, let alone read and listen to music and dispense drugs, knowing exactly how much he is owed.

I got high, but I didn't need to with the madness going on around us. The squat was as manic as Piccadilly Circus on a Friday night. They wore different clothes, came from different walks of life, but had one destination: drug-induced nirvana. Kerrin was bouncing down the stairs, her body more ravaging, eyes more lustful the more I

97

smoked and got high. It felt like the snake was hissing at me, *'Thisssss issss heaven, my friend.'* She was cutting up Sellotape and putting LSD microdots on the strips of tape. One night, through the partition doors to the kitchen, a band appeared. The band had every kind of instrument they should have – drums, guitar, keyboard, and a singer. It just looked out of place and added a surreal spin to see it appear in the middle of a three-storey squat in Vauxhall. All through this chaos, Nick would be sitting in the same position, swaying his head to the music, popping and dispensing pills.

I've got to live here.

Gordon was the odd one out in Nick's squat because he was actually quite normal. He tried to be as cool as Nick, but he couldn't pull it off. He bought hash from Nick and baked hash cakes to sell. Amongst the chaos of the squat, Gordon would be standing at the cooker in his apron, with stacks of cakes nobody was going to eat.

'Have some hash cakes, Mark,' he would say.

'No, Gordon, I'm okay, thanks.'

'No, Mark, you must have a cake. Come upstairs and I'll make you a tea. We can have a chat.'

Gordon always wanted to make me a tea and have a chat. He didn't have a reputation for being rough and hard. I did – it came with being Scottish in London. People just assumed I was rough and hard because of my accent. Gordon thought that being friends with me would rub off on his reputation - that he would be seen as rough and hard by having a rough and hard friend.

'Okay, Gordon. Just a cup of tea.'

I didn't want to have tea with Gordon, but I felt sorry for him. Besides, he was almost pushing me up the stairs. His room was covered with papier-mâché lampshades. I was sitting in his room, sipping on my herbal tea, looking around at them. There were more lampshades than anybody would need, more lampshades than a street of families would need. Gordon was standing there with a big grin and a plate full of hash cakes held out for me.

Gordon, man, I'm sure you're destined for better things than this.

His skills weren't completely useless, though. Luckily for me, his entrepreneurial skills extended beyond hash cakes and papier-mâché lampshades. He had developed a co-op of squats with the place next door and offered to rent me the basement.

With Gordon's help I had found my London home. I blended into the chaos and craziness of the squat like it had always been my life. I spent most of my time at Nick's, smoking, drinking, and tripping. I never tripped much, other than a few mushrooms or LSD. Hash and alcohol were my staple. I was always worried that I would get a bad trip, like the time I had been frozen in the pub. Taking LSD was like going on holiday to some far-flung place with a girlfriend, realising halfway through that you couldn't stand being with her, but having no way out. You just had to get through it without killing her. That was exactly the experience I got when I tripped with Nick in the squat.

'Just try a few of these trips, Mark,' he said. 'They're really fresh,' he promised.

Why not? If Nick can still read and deal while tripping, then I can handle a few trips.

I swallowed the trips and sat there. I watched Nick. He was silently watching me. Everything was okay, until I started to sweat and panic. I knew it was going to be a bad trip soon after I took the pills. Taking a bath during a bad trip sometimes had a calming effect. I tried that. After my bath, which did little too soothe me, I went back downstairs to join Nick. He had two customers with him – a man and a woman. The woman had a beautiful dress on. She was smoking hash and was letting the burning hash fall on to her dress.

Use a fucking ashtray.

It bothered me that she wasn't using an ashtray. It bothered me that she was letting it damage her dress. I was angry that she could afford to let her beautiful dress burn.

Posh bastards – too much money.

Then Kerrin came in the room. Usually I was pleased to see Kerrin because she was so sexy. This time she scared me. Her face was different from how it usually looked. It was like she had two faces. The second face was ugly. I could tell that the second face was evil.

That face will get me. That face will eat me.

The face and the woman burning her dress were too much for me to handle during the bad trip, so I fled to safety. I headed for my room in the basement next door and hid under the covers. I tried to sleep, but I couldn't. My mind was active and all I could see when I closed my eyes was Kerrin's second face. I started pacing the room. I saw the picture of the spiritual guru Krishnimati on the wall. He was sitting in the lotus position.

Why have I got that picture in this room? He looks fucking depressed.

It was the first time I had noticed he looked depressed. He didn't look at peace. Before I could tear down the picture from the wall, Davey turned up. He had been tripping too.

'Nick's a fucking nutter, isn't he,' he said.

I looked at him. He looked at me. Then we laughed hysterically. We had no reason to laugh, but he had taken me away from bad thoughts, and that was a good thing.

'Hey – let's build a fucking fire. I love fires,' I said. Then I got the axe from beside the fireplace and went out to the garden to chop wood. I raised the axe and started chopping lumps of trees. I looked back at the window and saw Nick looking out at me. He was looking out at a crazy Scottish guy chopping up wood with an axe, for a coal fire.

I never once thought: *This isn't normal.*

I was spending so much time around these people that what started as abnormal had become normal – I thought everyone lived like this because I didn't know anyone else in London. Clare was the only person in my life who was different from the madness around me. She came to visit me and stayed in the mad squat a few times. She was always in between being impressed and happy to be associated with the hippy lifestyle and disapproving of the new characters I was hanging around with. She didn't think I should be hanging around with guys who tripped and baked hash cakes all day. Clare was starting to worry more than Walshy did. She was worried that I would get lost in the chaos and forget about our future together. I hadn't forgotten the plans we had made to travel to India together. I had even got a job as a security guard at Earls Court to help pay for the trip. It was shit pay for boring work. As much as I wanted to go to India with Clare, I wouldn't have stayed in the job for long had I not discovered the other perks.

It happened by chance while I was just doing my patrol around the office.

Nothing wrong in that.

I was just checking out the desks to make sure all the drawers were closed.

Nothing wrong in that.

One of them was open and I was just checking if anything was missing.

Nothing wrong in that.

There was a big pile of blank giro cheques, and I didn't think there was anything wrong in taking a few. Only a handful. Nobody would have noticed a handful missing.

I'm only taking what they should be paying me anyway, right? Honestly, who can live or do anything on what they pay?

One of the guys from the squat band was out of work and agreed to cash the giros for me. I gave him clear instructions: go to the Births, Marriages and Deaths at St Katherine's House. Get a death certificate, someone about your age. Then, the next day, get the birth certificate. Find a post office, somewhere far out of Tottenham, and use that birth certificate as ID to cash the blank giro cheque, with the new name. It couldn't be any clearer or easier. With the promise of thirty per cent commission, he didn't need a sales pitch.

Three weeks later, the giro cashing had become a conveyer belt of more and more. Whatever we cashed was never enough. The more I had, the more I got away with, the more I did it.

Maybe security isn't such a bad job after all.

I knew somebody would notice the scam at some point. I just planned to be in India by the time they did notice. I didn't expect it to happen so soon. I was in the middle of one of my patrols around the exhibition centre. There was an antique fair using the exhibition space. On one of the stalls I saw a vase.

That's gotta be worth a few grand; I could just put that in my jacket and nobody would miss it amongst all these other vases and old shit. Nobody would know.

Before I could slip it under my jacket, my radio went. I was wanted in the office. My mind immediately shifted to overtime.

Finally they're going to give my double pay for the extra hours I've been doing. Finally somebody has noticed what a great employee I am.

I saw the shit-coloured suits and wrinkled faces the minute I entered the room. I could see my name appearing in them, just like back in Glasgow. It was a different face, different accent, but the same shit-coloured suit and the same wrinkles.

'Fraud Squad, Mr Dempster,' the suit said. My stomach shot through my arse. 'We've spoken to your friend Mark – he's told us everything, told us about the giros, told us where he got them from. It seems you're in a bit of trouble.'

What has that little shit done? Has he grassed me up?

'I don't know who you are talking about,' I said.

'Ah. That's funny, because we thought you lived with him?' He smiled like he had got me.

'No, I think you made a mistake. I don't know what you are talking about.' The suit kept smiling then looked over to the other suit who shook his head.

'But we spoke to another guy who says you live there.'

'No comment,' I said, but that didn't matter because I was in the cells, pounding my fist on the wall.

How did I end up back here?

102

The guy who had been cashing the giros for me hadn't bothered to buy a death certificate or a birth certificate. He had been cashing the giros in his own name, from his local post office down the road. It hadn't taken them long to find the post office, find him, and find me. I was going to prison and no Old Man Trammy was going to get me off this one.

After getting bail, I rushed to seek advice from the wisest person I knew. Nick sat there, listening intently to what had happened. All the while he had his eyes closed like an oracle, moving only to nod and smile.

'It's fucking serious, Nick,' I said. 'I don't want to go to jail. They're going to sentence me this time.'

Nicked remained silent for a while longer. Then he opened his eyes.

'I know this guy. His name is Brian. He's Irish and has had lots of trouble with the police. He's a friend and he can get you out of this fix.'

I couldn't believe him. I didn't believe him. But it was my only hope.

'What was he in trouble for?' I asked.

Nick closed his eyes again and said: 'Terrorism.'

Fuck, fuck, fuck.

* * *

We stood outside the door of Terrorist Brian's flat. It was on the ground floor of a large Victorian terraced house in Brixton. Nick knocked on the window and, a few minutes later, the front door swung open.

Am I tripping?

Nobody was behind the door. I felt like this was another bad trip, that maybe my drink before we had left Nick's had been spiked. As we entered through the door that had opened by itself, we walked through another flat door and then to the lounge. The flat was decorated as if it was a luxury mansion in the countryside. The room was adorned with miniature African tribal art. The large French marble fireplace looked at odds with the man that sat beside it. He was shortish, had long black messy hair, and a scar from his eye to his lip. He was staring at us as we came to the entrance of the lounge.

'Who's the fuck is this, Nick?' he said, nodding to me as if flicking away a fly. The air was shrill and cold. I had a feeling that armed cops were going to ram the door screaming 'Everybody down on the ground' any minute. The man on the sofa looked at us like we had just done that.

'No, Brian, everything's cool, man. This guy's a friend.'

So this is Brian. He looks like a nutter. How is this guy going to help keep me out of prison?

Brian's eyes were wide and manic. He looked at Nick like he was going to break his neck. He could have broken it easily. He wasn't well built, but his arms looked strong. He looked rough.

Nick stuttered out more words. It was the first time I had seen Nick in a stressed state. He was shitting himself and so was I.

'A good friend, a really good friend. Mark could actually be useful to you – but he's in a bit of trouble with the police.'

Brian's psycho eyes continued boring into us.

'Nick, you're fucking cheeky bringing a stranger into my house. You know the Terrorist Squad are watching me night and day. I told you to be fucking careful coming round here, didn't I?'

'Yeah, yeah, man, but nobody saw us. It's okay, Mark's cool.'

Brian went psycho.

'THEY SAW YOU! Didn't you hear what I said? Always watching. Can't take a piss without those fucking snoops knowing.' He turned to me. 'So who are you, then?'

'Mark. I'm Mark,' I said. That seemed to be enough to pass whatever test I had to pass because his eyes relaxed. They relaxed as much as they ever would with the amount of coke he had stuffed up his nose. He had a pile of white powder on the mahogany coffee table in front of him. I had never seen so much cocaine.

'You're Scottish, right? Hate the British. Fucking wankers the lot of them. You don't like the British government, do you, Mark? You know what I'm talking about. They screwed the Scottish as much as they screwed us.'

We sat down and my heart started to calm. I was safe, safe as I was ever going to be in this house.

Brian had accepted me because I was a Scottish Catholic and he was an Irish Catholic. Brian hated the British because of history. It was a history I could understand only because I had been brought up in Scotland, knowing the English screwed us. It didn't matter that it had happened hundreds of years ago. I'd never really cared about any of the history affecting everybody else's judgement of the British back where I grew up. Brian cared, though. Nick had already told me that Brian used to be in the IRA and had bombed a military house back in Ireland. That's why he had moved to London. There was money in drugs and only fight in terrorism.

Nick was a drug dealer, but he bought his supply of drugs from Brian. Brian was a real drug king – he supplied Nick and a lot of other dealers in London. It looked like a small, two-bedroom flat; however, the floorboards were stashed with tens of thousands of pounds' worth of hash, LSD, speed and coke, hoarded like stocks of ammunition. He had guns, too, and I was sure by this point that he could have shot us both in the head without a second thought if he'd chosen to.

I sat next to Nick, facing Brian. I was scared to move. I didn't know what to say, how to say it, and was thinking that, if this was the guy that was going to help me, I was fucked. If he did help me - if he kept me out of prison – what would I have to do for him? Blow up Buckingham Palace?

I took a deep breath and explained my problem. Brian listened. His psycho eyes flitted from me to Nick, Nick to me. Every few

105

minutes his head shot down to snort another line of coke. He kept his hands rested on his knees, yet his fingers stretched out tightly. When I'd finished talking, he started talking. He talked rapidly and sounded angry with every word.

'You don't have a problem. What's giro fraud? Fucking nothing. I'd be embarrassed about a bit of giro fraud, Mark. Just plead it out and get a slap on the wrist. You're not gonna have to go to prison for that. You should get a fucking slap in the face for being so stupid, though.' He was right.

That lazy, stupid tosser. If he had just got a fake birth certificate like I told him, then I wouldn't be in this mess.

After Brian had finished giving me his advice, he told me I might be of use – that I could repay the favour one day. Brian was a drug dealer of a different kind. He was at the top of the chain and being at the top carried more risk. Anybody who came close to Brian, who did favours for him, had to know the rules.

'Nick's okay for a British guy, but he's a cunt coming here with you like this,' Brian said. 'You have to understand I'm being watched all the time. Those fucking Terrorist Squad wankers. When you come here, I don't answer the door. If I do they get me on their cameras. You knock on the window, I'll come and open the door, but you won't see me. I'll open it and move out the way before you come in.'

I wasn't tripping.

'If you ever get caught, if anybody ever asks you what you're doing here, you say fucking nothing.' His eyes finished the thought: *'If you say anything I'll fucking kill you.'* After a pause, to emphasise the point, he continued: 'If you get caught, you say you were here to see Michael. He lives on the second floor and is an artist. You're seeing Michael for a portrait. He's doing a portrait for you and you were coming for a sitting.'

When he'd finished speaking, he started cutting up a line of coke and raised his head to motion Nick to the door. I was relieved to be out of that pressure cooker. As I left, my eyes searched the area for the Terrorist Squad - guys with cameras or guns. I couldn't see anything but I felt watched. I felt a chill. I had been scared from the moment I had entered the flat, but it was a buzz. I got a buzz from being around Brian – a terrorist, a drug dealer. Brian was big stuff and somebody that could help me make my plans a reality. The buzz I felt was bigger than the fights I had got into as a child in school or jumping the bins back in Partick. This was the buzz of danger. I was part of that danger now. I was heading towards the big time.

Chapter 8

I had followed Brian's advice and he had been right. I pleaded guilty in exchange for another suspended sentence and a fine. Clare wasn't happy that I had got myself into trouble with the police again.

'You need to sort yourself out, Mark. You need some direction in your life,' she moaned.

'I know,' I lied. *Anything to shut her up.* 'Look, let's go to India. We need this trip. I'll have a fresh start with things when we get back.'

Clare wanted to go to India for the spiritual journey. She wanted to experience what the Beatles had experienced on their trip to see the Maharishi in an ashram in Rishikesh, 1968. She wanted to meditate and discover her inner self.

'It will be a really spiritual experience, Clare. We can meditate in Rishikesh.'

I didn't tell her Davey was coming with his girlfriend, Alison. I didn't tell her Alison was pregnant.

'Okay, Mark, but things have got to be different when we get back. You have to change.'

When I came back from India I was going to start dealing in London. That had been my plan from the moment I moved down from Glasgow. The spiritual reasons for visiting India were not at the top of my list. I wanted to go to experience the best hash in the world – as was written about in *The Great Book of Hashish*. I wanted to smoke the best hash in the world and then smuggle it back to London to sell. I could have done that without Clare, but I still loved her. She was my first girlfriend and my first love.

This trip to India could repair our relationship.

'Yes, Clare. I promise. When we get back things are going to be different,' I said.

Maybe she'll help me smuggle back some hash.

* * *

Arriving at Delhi airport in 1985 was a culture shock. We had left Heathrow airport cursing the queues and delays. We arrived in Delhi experiencing Armageddon in comparison. The queues were longer and we had to complete more paperwork to enter India than if we had bought one of the planes we'd flown in. Every customs officer, passport controller, guard, or other worker we met nodded their head, chanting 'Acha, acha' at us. The chant meant, 'Okay, everything's cool.' Everything was not cool. There were giant fans everywhere trying to keep us cool as we queued for hours. But we were still dripping with sweat.

By the time we left the airport I wasn't feeling spiritual. I wanted to smoke some hash or drink some whiskey, whatever came first. We passed through the airport exit, avoiding the cows trying to get into the airport. The guards were trying to shoo the cows away from the doors with their voices. The cow is a holy creature in India, so they wouldn't just kill them. It was frustrating being on the bus to Rishikesh, having to stop every ten minutes to allow a cow or two to pass by. I was starting to wonder if the stories about finding spirituality in India had been exaggerated. It was more dangerous than spiritual. The bus was crammed with people. Those who couldn't fit inside sat on the roof and hung off the sides.

We had to find somewhere to stay. I wanted to score some hash as soon as we could, though. To score hash in India, I had read that I needed to look no farther than a wandering monk. The monks of Hinduism in India were called sadhus. There were many sadhus in Rishikesh, and it didn't take long for a sadhu to find us.

'Where are you from?' one of the sadhus asked. He looked like he was in his forties with his hair in dreads and skin wrinkled by the sun and dust.

'Scotland,' I said.

'Oh. Scotch whiskey.' He laughed. I didn't. It's what everybody said to me in India when they learnt that I was from Scotland.

'Do you know where we can get hash?' I asked.

'Oh, yes, yes. You need a place to stay?' he asked. There was always somebody who would find you a place to stay and sort out some hash. The sadhus lived without worldly possessions – material wealth was not important to them. They relied on donations for everything they needed, which mainly came from tourists in return for advice on where to stay and where to get hash from. The sadhu said his name was Bangee and he became our holiday rep for the duration of our stay.

I had imagined smoking chillums in the mountains of the Himalayas ever since reading *The Great Book of Hashish*. My first experience of smoking hash in India was actually in a rusty, dusty, noisy marketplace, sitting on the ground, alongside a group of sadhus chanting the names of where hash grows.

Most of the names I knew from *The Great Book*. Watching them, I wondered why they sat around the Shiva statue smoking the chillums and chanting names of places. Bangee explained it was because Shiva smoked hash - that it was a holy thing to do. I thought that was just as much bullocks as the Virgin Mary, but was happy to adopt a religion that insisted I smoked hash.

The sadhus were passing around a feast of samosas, sabji, and pakera. I was stoned and trying to remember not to pass or accept anything with my left hand, the hand the sadhus wiped their arses with. Bangee had found a place for us to stay that was no bigger than the concrete block I'd first had sex in. The hut was made out of tin with a corrugated iron cover. The hash was strong enough to make it habitable, strong enough for us not to care that we had to piss and shit into a hole outside. Strong enough for this to seem like the life we had been missing all this time.

The problem with the new life, the life we had been missing all this time, was that it was the same every day – sitting around smoking chillums. That wasn't a problem for me, but there were tensions in our group. Clare was getting agitated with me smoking chillums all the time.

'It's only while we are here, Clare. It's what people do when they are in India. Shiva did it!' I would argue.

'Mark, I don't care if Shiva did it. You are not bloody Shiva. I want at least one day where you don't pick up a chillum.'

Clare smoked sometimes, but not much. Not enough for me to defend myself by accusing her of being a hypocrite. She and I had different expectations of what the trip to India was going to be. She wanted to meditate and explore the sights. I wanted to smoke hash and have fun.

Alison was getting agitated with everybody. Alison was pregnant, so she couldn't smoke or drink. Davey and Alison had come to India to have the baby at Dharamsala, the spiritual home of the exiled Dalai Lama. Alison considered herself an expert in spiritual matters, but Clare had done the hard work – she had studied meditation and practised it to near perfection. I could see Alison and Clare were clashing. They were niggling and snapping over the smallest things. Davey didn't know what to do about it, so he smoked chillums with me.

The other problem with this life was the attention that Clare was getting from all the men. Everywhere we went the men were staring at Clare and trying to talk to her. I was going nuts with jealousy. Only a few weeks into the trip, I was starting to wonder how I was going to cope for another five months living with all this tension and

111

pressure. It was about the time I was ready to crack and lose my temper at the Indians that I heard this loud, Scottish voice over the beeping cars and mooing cows.

'Oh, BIG MAN.' The voice belonged to James. He was somebody that I used to smoke with back in Glasgow. He had been in on the college scam too.

'You fucking DANCING BEAR!' I shouted back and we slapped each other's back and had a pretend box. 'What are you doing here, James? This is mad!'

'Yeah, well I had to get out of Glasgow. I got nicked for a kilo of hash, right, so I thought, you know what? FUCK IT. I'll just come here and hide out.'

I nodded. It made sense: prison or India.

'I've got two kilos of Kashmir in my bag and a kilo of opium,' he said.

What a fucking god.

I looked around to the others to share my joy, but discovered that they didn't. They were glaring back at me, clearly unhappy with the new arrival. Clare was scowling at me.

'Oh… James, let me introduce you to my friends Davey and Alison. And this is Clare, my girlfriend.'

James will charm them into joy.

'Hey, Clare, how you coping with this wee scally, then? This place is mad, isn't it? I don't know how you pretty girls cope with all these skinny guys leching after you.'

Alison perked up at being included as 'a pretty girl'. Clare even looked like she was warming to him. Then he pulled out a Smith and Wesson knife.

'Don't worry, Clare, any of these cunts try it on with you I'll fucking slice their skinny balls off.' In the space of a minute James had won Clare over and then lost her again. She looked at me with her eyebrows raised and no smile. I knew that look. It said, *'You better not even think about inviting your friend to join us.'*

112

I looked at Clare's commanding face, Clare's beautiful face.

I love Clare.

I looked at James's grin, a grin full of adventure and madness.

I like James.

My love for Clare was more important than my like for James. I knew I had to say goodbye to him.

Then I looked back at his rucksack. He had said he had two kilos of hash and a kilo of opium in it.

I've never tried opium. Fuck it.

'Come on, you dancing bear, come with us,' I said.

That night we ate and talked and the hash cleared the tension. I didn't notice Alison's scowls or Davey, who was torn between Alison and the hash. James got out the opium.

'What's the opium like, James?' I asked.

'Fucking big, like you're dreaming that you're racing cars and crazy shit.'

Racing cars is exactly what I wanted to be doing. He broke off a big chunk and gave it to me. It was about three grams.

'Don't even think about it,' Clare said. 'It's bad enough you're smoking bloody chillums every minute of the day. I'm not putting up with you high on opium.'

Clare was really getting to me with all her moaning. I felt henpecked from morning to night.

'Come on, Clare, it's just a bit of fun. I've never had it before – I'm just going to try it. You could try it too?'

James helped me out. 'Yeah, Clare. It's safe as houses. I do it all the time. Let the big man have some fun.'

Clare still huffed and puffed about it.

'Okay, Clare, I'll just take a little bit of it,' I compromised. Three grams was a lot. I broke it in half and swallowed it. Within thirty minutes I was throwing up and sweating. James was already packing more opium into the chillums with the hash. We started smoking it just as my body was going numb. It was another few minutes and

113

then my whole body felt paralysed. Clare was patting me on the back, soothing my head as I was sick. But then I couldn't feel her hand any more.

'I can't fucking move,' I was saying to Clare.

'I told you that was too much,' Clare said.

James passed the chillum to me. It was packed with more opium and hash. 'Chillum, Mark?' he said.

I picked it up and smoked it. I managed to get it into my mouth, despite feeling like I couldn't move.

'Mark, you can't move, but you can smoke more chillum?' Clare asked.

Your point is?

At some point Clare went to bed and sulked herself to sleep. Davey had headed off to bed with Alison a while before. That left James and me to continue smoking opium and hash. I was starting to get very paranoid. I tried to lie still and calm myself. But, as I lay there unable to move, Bangee kept entering my thoughts.

Bangee looks dodgy. I bet that dodgy wanker's gonna steal my traveller's cheques and passport.

Next I was on a race track. I was zooming around, but there were no race cars. I was the race car. I was going at ultimate speed, faster than my legs could ever carry me. I was zooming round and round and round and seeing lights. They were magnificent, multi-coloured lights streaming down on the track, lighting my way, faster and faster. Then I was back to Bangee.

He better not steal my traveller's cheques, better not take my passport.

Then I was drifting out. As I was drifting into unconsciousness, I wasn't thinking about death. I wasn't wondering if this was it for me. I wasn't racing. I was just drifting into nothingness with one thought left dangling:

I've got to do this all the time. This is freedom.

* * *

114

James came back every day, which I thought was great, but I was the only one. As the sun rose, I was outside the back practising with my nunchakus, swinging them around when James arrived.

'All right, BIG MAN. You can wrap that around some wee Indian's fucking head,' he shouted.

Davey was sitting, watching me with my nunchakus. As soon as James arrived, his face turned into *Oh fuck*. James being around was getting him into trouble with Alison. I knew what that was like, because Clare had been on at me every day for several weeks. She didn't want me to smoke any more opium with James.

'In fact,' she stated, 'I don't want James hanging around with us any more. He's rough.'

It was getting to the point where I would have to choose between James and Clare. James was becoming more of an attractive choice. We spent hours every day talking about our respective plans to smuggle hash back to London and deal. I was starting to think James could be a good business partner. Like me, he had big plans for the future. We talked into the early hours, smoking hash, eating opium, and exploring the extent of our ambitions. It was like I was having an affair with somebody else. I had to make sure that our plans for the future were hushed so that Clare couldn't hear. It didn't matter, though – Clare was getting more agitated with me the more time I spent with James. She was on the verge of making me choose. Luckily for me – and for Clare - James decided to leave for his reasons before I had to.

'I'm heading back to the mountains, Mark. Going to get some more hash and smuggle it down to Goa. Fancy coming?'

I could leave Clare here with Alison and Davey for a few days.

As much as I wanted to, I couldn't leave Clare on her own. Alison and Davey were leaving too. Alison and Clare were not even on speaking terms now. They couldn't even unite in their disgust at James. So they left for Dharamsala for their spiritual birthing at the home of the Dalai Lama and James left for the mountains to

115

smuggle the best hash in the world. He left us with his rucksack so that we could take care of it until he got back from Goa. It only had a bit of hash, an air ticket in it, and a Smith and Wesson knife. I took the knife and gave the rest of it to Bangee to take care of.

With all the tension that Alison brought with her, Davey wasn't much fun to spend time with. I was glad that they had left. Having James around had become a problem too – but only because Clare didn't like him. With James gone, I didn't have anybody I could have fun with. Spending time with Clare was rarely fun any more. It had become a chore. Mainly because she always had an idea of what she wanted to do that completely interrupted the plans I had for what I wanted to do. I had to work hard on my persuasiveness to convince her we should head to Goa.

I told her I wanted to go to Kerala to see what the beaches were like. In truth, I wanted to go to Goa so I could take a trip to Sri Lanka to buy a video recorder. Bangee had told me that if I bought a video recorder from Sri Lanka for a hundred dollars, I could sell it in Goa for seven times that. I didn't tell Clare that was what I planned to do until we got to Kerala. She thought it was nuts to travel to Sri Lanka for a video recorder. I thought she was just annoyed that she couldn't come with me. To save money, I'd only bought one ticket. I would only be gone for a day.

I got a plane to Colombo very cheaply. I bought the video recorder and waited for the return flight. The flight was cancelled. I had to wait another two days for the next one. There was no way of telling Clare. She wasn't staying in a hotel in Goa, with access to a phone. I was stuck. I was in a beautiful country, yet confined to a dingy, cheap hotel – my only possession a video recorder.

Why the fuck did I do this? If I had some hash on me, this would be bearable.

Just as I was trying to think of a way to get my hands on some hash, there was a knock at the door. I opened it to find this man, a little older than I, standing at the door with a big grin on his face. He looked like a tourist, dressed in shorts and a baggy T-shirt.

116

'Hey, man, I'm Pedro. The hotel said you're waiting for your flight?'
What's it got to do with you?
'Yeah. I'm stuck here for another day. Are you going back to India too?' I asked.
Now fuck off and leave me alone.
'Yes. I'm waiting here with nothing to do. I have some hash, though. I was trying to find someone to smoke with.'
I love you.
'Come in,' I said.

I liked Pedro immediately. Maybe it was the effect of the hash, but everything he said was funny. He was from Peru and had had many more experiences of travelling than I had. We spent the night smoking and discussing the finer points of shamanism.

'I'm right into shamanism, man,' I was saying.

'Listen, believe, brother,' he was saying.

Only a few hours earlier I had been sat in a grotty hotel, missing Clare, and wondering what I was doing here. Now, my new best friend and I were sitting in the most spiritual place on Earth, feeling like the most spiritual people on Earth, and thinking we could see what Buddha saw.

We flew back to Kerala the next day. Clare wasn't happy that she had been left without any knowledge of my plans for several days. But I had Pedro with me, so she couldn't be too annoyed. She was polite that way. I was happy not to get a lecture and to have a new friend. It was boring with just Clare and me. Clare seemed to be happy with Pedro, too. After a few drinks, she was talking to him. She seemed happier than when I had introduced James. Much happier than when Alison was around.

This is great. Sitting, smoking chillums, and chilling with my new best friend Pedro and the love of my life, Clare.

They were laughing. They were chatting. I was laughing at them laughing. Clare was looking at Pedro. Pedro was looking at Clare. I was looking at Pedro, looking at Clare.

117

Wait a fucking minute, what's going on here?

As soon as Clare went to the toilet, I fronted up to Pedro.

'Hey, big man, what do you think you're doing looking at my girlfriend?' I said.

'What are you talking about, Mark? We're just chatting; we're all just chatting.'

'No, no, don't deny it, you've been thinking you got a chance with my girl, haven't you?'

'No, man. I'm just feeling the connection. We're all spiritual brothers and sisters.'

I looked at him, and noticed, for the first time, that he was better looking than I.

'Fuck that, you stay away from my girlfriend.'

With that, I sent my new best friend off on his spiritual journey with a cut lip. As much as I wanted Pedro along for the ride, as much as I didn't like Clare's moaning all the time, there was no way I was letting her get it on with somebody else. Clare was surprised to see him gone when she got back from the toilet. I told her that he had to leave for something he had forgotten about. I didn't tell her about the cut lip I had left him with.

We spent several months in Goa. There were lots of drug tourists around at that time. They came from the West, mostly Britain, to experience the spirituality of the East. They came in search of peace and found that inner peace in vast quantities of cheap, high quality drugs. It was always easy to make friends with people like me while travelling. I could spot the ones that were high and they could spot me. It wasn't even the eyes or the behaviour – it was as if we could just smell each other.

That was how I met Mickey. I had rented a motorbike for a month to get around a bit easier and see Goa. I was filling up on petrol and had the video recorder in a bag. Mickey asked if I wanted to sell the video recorder. I think he just wanted a lift back to the villa that he and his friends had rented. I didn't care. If he could afford to buy

118

a video recorder from me, I wasn't going to say no.

As we drove up to the house, we passed a line of palm trees that had been painted in different colours. It was a big house, the size of a small mansion. A lot of the big houses were rented out to wealthy tourists. The rental prices were still peanuts compared to what you would have to pay for a hotel of the same luxury. The house was being used as a party house. There was a group of people, slightly older than I was, sitting on the porch playing cards. They were surrounded by empty bottles of beer and spirits.

'Fancy a line, Mark?' Mickey offered. I hadn't had any coke since being in India. It was one of the only drugs difficult to get. These guys had lots of it. Mickey was an impressive character. He was a proper cockney, born and bred in the East End of London – yet he was mixed race, had long dreadlocks, and lived in Amsterdam.

'So, how much do you want for the video recorder?' he asked.

'Eight hundred? I thought I could get a thousand on the street.'

'Let's say seven fifty.' I could tell by the way he said it that it wasn't a negotiation. That was all I was getting. It was still a big profit, although he paid me in rupees.

I spent a while chatting to Mickey about what he did in Amsterdam. He dealt hash and LSD, but mainly LSD. He said he would link me up with some supply if I needed it when I was back in London. As I drank with Mickey and looked around at the other guys playing cards and doing coke, I could see what I wanted in the future much more clearly. I wanted the success that these guys had. They had a big house, with lots of friends and as many drugs as they wanted. They didn't have a moaning girlfriend and they didn't have to travel to another country to buy a video recorder to sell on the black market to replenish their funds. I took Mickey's number and told him I would call him when I got back to London.

India was two worlds in one. There was the world with Clare – which she would have liked to be a world of hugs, romantic walks along the beach, and talks about our future as the sun set over the sea. In reality we mostly argued about Clare wanting to 'spend time together' and me wanting us to have fun. Then there was the other world – where I met random strangers who took me on new adventures, gave me lines of coke, and smoked hash and opium with me.

Of course, with the world that Clare offered, I knew that everything was going to be pretty much okay. There wasn't going to be any chance of danger or things going wrong. We would have a lovely trip in India and return home. I would get a job; she would finish university. Then we would get married and have children.

The other world had nothing to offer but uncertainty. Yet the other world was the one I was being pulled to all the time. Even when we did what Clare wanted to do, the other world would present something to tease me back.

Clare wanted to go to see where the Dalai Lama lived and I thought it would be a cool experience to have an audience with him. When we got up to the Dharamsala, I asked around the locals to see if they had seen a pregnant British girl staying nearby. It made sense to stay with Alison and Davey while we were there. I thought that enough time had passed for any tension to have disappeared. I was wrong. As soon as they spotted us coming towards them I could see their faces drop. But there was a new face with them – a face that I didn't expect to see and a face that didn't drop at the sight of me and Clare.

'Nick!' I shouted.

'Mark!' Nick shouted. We ran towards each other and gave each other a bear hug.

'What the fuck are you doing here?' I asked.

'The squat got busted. I got arrested for intent to supply. So I skipped bail and thought I'd get out of London. India seemed the best place to come. I could see my sister and thought I might catch up with you.'

Alison was Nick's sister. That always surprised me. Nick was so chilled out. Alison could be miserable, and remained that way for the few days that we spent with them. She made no effort to be friendly with Clare, which left Clare in a grump with me the whole time. The only refuge I got from all the hassle was tripping with Nick on black microdots in the Himalayas.

At some point I must have zoned out with the intensity of the trip. I came to with a local woman standing over me. She had her hands out, begging for something. Her body was thin, so thin I could see every one of her bones poking through the skin – the skin only just holding them together. She was ravaged by famine. I could see right into her eyes. They were big, bigger than the rest of her face. I could see her soul through those eyes. I could see her spirit.

It's not black. There's no black in her soul, it's just ravaged by hunger.

The old beggar woman kept her hands out, pushing them towards me. She was seeking something from me, but I had nothing to give her. She kept trying to speak, but I couldn't hear what she was saying. I just felt sad. I didn't feel sad for her. I felt sad for me.

I'm not ravaged by hunger, but my soul is as black as it could be and no Hail Marys are going to stop me going to Hell this time.

I started to freak out. I couldn't see what I was doing here any more. Even though I was tripping with Nick in the Himalayas, one of the most beautiful and spiritual places on Earth, I felt that not all was well. I could see that this beggar woman, ravaged by hunger, had more of a soul, more of a life than I did.

Maybe Clare's right. Maybe I do need to think about sorting out my life. Settling down might be the right thing to do.

I turned away from the beggar woman and looked at Nick lying next to me. He got up and passed me a few more trips. I looked back at the beggar woman – but she wasn't there any more.

Where did she go?

I popped the pills in my mouth and swallowed them. Then I lay back and sank into the mountains.

I don't need a soul. I don't need God. I don't need heaven. Not when I'm sinking into the Himalayas.

121

* * *

Our trip to India was coming to an end. I knew that I had a choice to make when I returned to London. Clare was going to make me choose between the life she wanted for us and the life I wanted for myself. I don't think she knew what life I wanted for myself – she just felt that I didn't want her.

'You don't act like you love me, Mark. All you do is smoke bloody chillums. What's the first thing you do when you wake up in the morning? Smoke a chillum. Even before you kiss me, Mark, before you kiss me in the morning, you reach over to the side of the bed and smoke a chillum.'

I told her it was because we were on holiday. I told her it was because the hash was really great in India, that I wanted to make the most of it. I told her it was because I was just chilling out. I told her it had nothing to do with her, that I could do what I wanted.

The problem was, she wouldn't be told any more.

'Mark, I'm telling you now, you have to stop smoking chillums and taking drugs or we are over.'

I had to think about what to do. I thought about staying in India for longer. The life in India was good and the longer I stayed there, the longer I didn't have to start life, whatever that was going to be, back in London. As I was contemplating what to do about Clare's ultimatum, I heard a voice from across the street.

'Oh, BIG MAN.' It was James. He was running across the road towards me and this time he didn't slap me on the back and we didn't pretend to box.

'Where's my fucking rucksack?' he asked.

Shit, I left the rucksack back in Rishikesh with Bangee.

'No, no, Mark, don't fucking lie to me. I just been there and Bangee said you took it.'

He's going to hit me.

'Listen, James, I promise you I left it with Bangee. The only thing

122

I took from your rucksack was your Smith and Wesson knife and I left the rest for safe keeping.'

He doesn't believe me.

'I promise you, mate, I left it with Bangee.'

James paused for a moment to think.

'That fucking Indian cunt. Right, I want you to come with me and we're gonna go see that thief and send him down the Ganges in concrete boots.'

There was no way I was going to go with James to put Bangee in concrete boots. James would stab the guy, jump on a bus, and leave me to take the rap. But there was still a voice inside my head egging me to go with him.

It would be a rush to put the little bastard in concrete boots.

Clare wasn't happy to see James again. I shrugged my shoulders as if to say, *'Nothing I can do about it.'* I was pleased James had appeared out of nowhere. It gave me more time to not think about Clare's ultimatum. The minute we sat down James started staring at an Indian man who was sitting opposite us, staring at Clare. James suddenly thumped the table.

'I'm gonna fucking teach these Indians a lesson.' He got up, took his knife, and sat next to the man.

'Listen, you little cunt,' he said to him. 'I'll stick this fucking knife in you.' He pushed it to his ribs. 'That girl over there don't belong to you. You look at her again, I'll fucking slice you open.'

Claire glared at me. I shrugged my shoulders as if to say, *'What can I do? Nothing to do with me,'* but she continued to glare at me.

Why are you glaring at me? What have I done now?

'You are not going with that man anywhere,' she said.

I wanted to leave with James to punish Bangee. It would have been a rush to be part of the adventure of it, the chase of it. But, as Clare continued to glare at me, I could see tears forming in her eyes. I thought – I had hoped – that her ultimatum had just been one of those things she said in anger. Like the times she told me she hated me when I did something she didn't like. She always said, *'I love you,*

Mark,' and I always said, *'I love you, Clare,'* and we would make up with a kiss and sex. This time, I could see that she wasn't going to say, 'I love you, Mark,' and we weren't going to be making up at all if I went with James.

'Okay, Clare. I won't go with James,' I said.

'And you will stop using drugs for a while?' she said.

Maybe I will try it for a bit.

'Yes, Clare. I'll stop using drugs.'

'I love you, Mark,' she said.

'I love you, Clare,' I said.

She reached across the table and hugged me. She hugged me tight and I could feel a tear drop from her face to the back of my neck. This trip to India had been hard for her.

'Things are going to be different, Clare. I promise,' I said.

I think she believed me.

Chapter 9

Clare was the love of my life, but she had no common sense. All I wanted to do was smuggle some hash back to sell.

Maybe one kilo.

Nobody would have noticed one kilo.

'What if you get caught? What if you got strip-searched? What then?' she whinged.

'For fuck sake,' I told her. 'Nobody's going to bother searching me. If you're that bothered we'll walk through customs separately. It's only two kilos. Who's going to notice two kilos?'

'Two kilos! It's growing by the minute, Mark, and I'm not doing it. I'm not letting you get locked up for a bit of hash.'

She was nuts! I could have sold three kilos in London and made a ten grand profit.

We could go wherever we wanted with that money. Besides, who is going to notice three kilos?

But no, she wouldn't have it. She couldn't see sense and she whinged until I just let it go. I was pissed off because I had done what she had asked me and laid off smoking the hash. The least she could have done was let me smuggle some hash back to make some money. It was only four kilos. Now I was just fat, poor and pissed off. To top it off, nobody noticed us as we went through customs.

'I fucking told you, Clare. They didn't check, did they? I would have got away with it. Now I've lost ten grand.' She didn't care. She could be selfish sometimes.

I was telling Rossie all this, sitting in his lounge, while smoking a joint. I had started smoking hash again the minute we returned to London and Clare had gone back to her granny's house.

'Yeah, man, it's an easy deal. You get a kilo for seventy-five pounds. Look…' I scribbled it to life for him: 'Seventy-five pounds to buy the hash, there's thirty-six ounces to a kilo, and we can sell it for a hundred and twenty pounds an ounce back here. That's nearly four grand when you take off the flight and cost of the hash.'

Rossie's eyes lit up.

'Okay…' He was thinking. 'Okay…but how do you get it back?'

'Oh, Ross, it's easy man. You can either swallow it, or put it in the luggage, and spray neutraliser to get rid of the smell. They don't bother checking the bags. Look, Clare and I came through and they didn't even look at us. Yeah, but it's fucking shit,' I said. 'If only Clare hadn't fucked it all up.'

'Yeah, yeah.'

'But I don't know how we would do it again. I don't have the money and you really have to go in twos.'

Without another thought he said he'd do it.

'Oh no, Rossie, you don't want to do that. Do you?'

Result!

'Yeah, man, yeah. Sounds simple and you're right – we can make a packet. I'll come with you and we'll bring the stuff back.'

I don't know how much it was me convincing or him deciding through his own initiative. I only knew that I could make someone do what I wanted through fear of a beating. I had experience of that from bullying my friends as a kid. That was the first time I had ever made someone do what I wanted them to do by selling the positive. It was alien to me, but effective.

Once I had convinced Rossie he should join me on the smuggling trip, the rest of my plan was simple. I knew where to go for the hash from *The Great Book of Hashish* and the research I had done whilst in India with Clare. Malana was a tiny village nestled in between the mountains. It would take a good eight hours up from either the Kulu or Paruati Valley to get to the village. There would be no roads - just tracks carved out from the feet of those that had gone before us.

It was a simple plan, but the trip was still dangerous. I knew a few people that had been caught for smuggling and were in prison. That wouldn't happen to us. I had already escaped prison sentences. Getting caught wasn't what I was worried about. I was more concerned about getting lost up the mountains. To avoid this happening, we enlisted a Nepalese guide. They were locals who knew how to trek through the mountains. They knew the routes and they knew how to keep safe on the trek. If we went alone we could end up getting lost. I still resented the thirty dollars we had to pay him.

That's already thirty dollars less hash.

We would definitely need him on the way back. Even if we had made the trek safely by ourselves, there were police checks coming back off the mountains. The whole area was full of hash crop. The police knew that tourists were not hiking for the scenery. They wanted to get a bribe or take the hash and sell it themselves. The Nepalese guide was our Trojan Horse.

Trekking across the Himalayas was hard. At the start of the trek it was the beauty that kept my thoughts occupied. Then, after a few hours, the magnificent beauty of the Himalayas descended into freezing conditions. The top, before the descent to the village, was covered with snow and we were struggling to see. I was slipping and sliding all over the place. We made the mistake of smoking a chillum on the hike up the mountain with some German tourists on their way down. I regretted it immediately because it wasn't fun being stoned and trekking up a freezing cold, snow-covered mountain. If it wasn't for our guide we would have got lost or just stuck there as both of us would have given up. We would have fallen asleep in the snow and frozen to death.

127

Our Nepalese guide kept pushing us on and was starting to panic. 'We have to get to the village before the sun sets,' he kept saying.

I was focused on not falling over. If we fell forward with our rucksacks, we would roll down the mountain. Rossie was moaning out loud, I was moaning inside, and the guide was kicking our butts. We went down the mountain slowly, but we arrived alive and before the sun set.

Malana was very different from Delhi or Goa. It was an ancient village with wild and rough huts scattered over the hills. There was a Shiva statue and a trident. It all reminded me of *Raiders of the Lost Ark*. The locals were milling about. I remembered that these Indians were Brahman, which was the highest caste, the highest level of spirituality. They were dressed in traditional mountain clothing, which looked cool to me. The women wore saris and the men had matted hair and teeth missing. We were getting harangued over and over by the locals: 'Charis, charis, do you want to buy charis?'

Rossie, our guide, and I sat in the village square smoking chillums. I was desperately trying not to touch anybody. Our guide had warned us that it was a spiritual tradition that you can't touch the houses or anything else in the village. Anything from outside the village might be infectious. Everything in the village already looked infectious compared to where I came from. It was hard to remember the things I shouldn't be doing when I was high. There was a hut where you could buy food and drink, so obviously the money from outside wasn't infectious. I was trying to remember not to touch any buildings as the chillum was being passed for smoking from one guy to the next.

I thought I had got used to the not touching anything rule. But then, as we were heading to the dealer Siteram's house, I began to sense some tension in the air. Things were not feeling good. They were not sounding good. They were not looking good. This feeling went beyond the usual paranoia I felt when smoking hash. The local villagers were gathering around us, circling us in. I couldn't hear what they were saying. I was so stoned by this point that all I could hear were sounds.

RAHH, RAHH, RAHHH.

I was getting agitated.

'Oh, this is a problem, a very big problem,' our guide said.

'What's the trouble?' I asked.

'It is a problem. Your bag touched their house. Your bag cannot touch the house,' he said.

'That's fucking rubbish. The house isn't even a house, it looks like rubbish.'

'It is still a problem. They say they want you to buy goat.'

'Why do I have to buy a fucking goat? I don't want a goat.'

'Because your bag touched the house. You must buy goat so they can kill goat, drain it of blood, and purify the wall your bag touched with the goat's blood.'

This is crazy. I don't want to buy a goat. I'm not even going to eat the goat.

There were more people surrounding us and the crowd began to contract like a snake, squeezing us in.

They're going to kill us.

It dawned on me that this might be it. After surviving the mountains, we were going to be killed by the village people and nobody would know about it.

Nobody knows I'm here.

I hadn't told anybody I was coming to India. It was a quick trip to get some hash and smuggle it back to London to start my dealing business. There were no roads to the village. There were no police that I could see. These people could have just murdered us and buried us and nobody would ever have known where we disappeared.

I'm not going to die in the middle of nowhere for the price of a goat.

'Okay, how much is a goat?' I asked.

'About thirty dollars,' the guide said.

Thirty dollars.

It was thirty dollars for us to be able to escape a brutal death.
Thirty fucking dollars.

It was also thirty dollars less hash. Thirty dollars' worth of hash would net thirty times that when sold on the street back in London.

Fuck the goat.

'Tell them to fuck off. There's no way I'm buying a goat,' I said. If it had been a fiver or something, maybe, but thirty was taking the piss.

We gently broke through the snake ring and, as they realised we were not going to be buying a goat, they let us pass without harm. I like to think that they were scared off by my bravado - they knew they would have a fight on their hands with me - but it probably had more to do with us heading to Siteram's. He wouldn't have been happy with the loss of a customer - at least not for the sake of a goat. Spiritual traditions were one thing, business was another.

Siteram was ready for business when we arrived at his house. He was already loading up a chillum with a big lump of charis to welcome us.

'You want to buy much charis,' he said.

'A couple of kilos,' I said.

He took us into a separate room. There were four other people already sitting in the room, each smoking their own chillum. It was like the European Union had sent a trade delegation. There was a French guy, an Italian, and two Germans. They looked like hippies. We all looked like hippies. We were sitting in a hut, in the middle of the mountains, getting mashed on charis – thinking we were amongst the most spiritual beings on Earth. Siteram was a good host. He brought us sahgi, rice, and dhal. We ate and smoked our way into a nightmare-filled sleep of toppling down mountains and being buried alive in the hills by the locals.

The next day Siteram took me through to the room that housed the greatest charis in the world. He opened the door and my mouth dropped. In front of me sat bags of charis, neatly stacked, like bars of gold in a bank vault. Hundreds of kilos of hash that had been hand rubbed into shiny black sticks, just as I had read about in *The Great Book*. There's a big difference reading about such treasure, seeing the pictures, and being able to see it, touch it, smell it - and *buy* it.

'You like?' Siteram asked.

Yes I like, Siteram, you god. Yes, I like it very much.

I asked for a kilo of Cream and a kilo of Bagetcha. I tried to haggle the price with Siteram, but with hash of this quality he didn't need to discount it. He had one price and wouldn't budge: three thousand five hundred rupees a kilo, which was about seventy-five pounds.

I still make four thousand pounds or so a kilo. Even with expenses I'm at least seven grand up. Not bad for two weeks' work.

Siteram weighed the hash on large scales, like the scales of justice - weights on one side, a pan on the other.

'Hey, don't fucking cheat me. You weighed that twice. Get it back on the scales. Start again.' I was watching him like a hawk. I had been warned about the dealers in the mountains. They would cheat me if they could get away with it. Siteram held his hands up and started again. 'I'm fucking watching you,' I warned.

As we left Siteram's palace of hash, I was pleased that we had our guide. He was going to be doing the heavy lifting on the return trip. Two kilos starts to feel like a lot more than that after a few hours of trekking. That didn't stop the little fella. The guide loaded the hash on to his small back and started zooming ahead.

That little fucker's going to make a run for it with our hash.

'Hey, don't fucking run off.' I pulled out my knife and waved it. 'I'll have you if you run off. Stab you, kill you – you understand?'

'No, no, I'm not running. We must go separate; cannot be seen together.' What he said made sense, but I still kept watch, ready to pounce and beat him if he ran.

We made it to Delhi with no tumbles and no stabbings. When we got to the city there were police everywhere in the bus station. I was sweating fear.

131

We're going to get busted.

We escaped to a rickshaw and got to the hotel safely. The guide had done well by us - so well, I gave him his thirty dollars and a Sony Walkman. He could still grass us to the police when he left, and they could come and take the hash from us. The Walkman was to keep him happy and quiet.

We were so cocksure after such an easy ride that we didn't use neutraliser on Rossie's bags. We just packed it in under the clothes. Rossie was wearing a suit and looked smart. Our thinking was that people wearing suits don't get stopped by customs officers. I looked like a hippy with torn jeans and beads, which made me the decoy and Ross the Trojan Horse. We were flying via Damascus, but the Libyans messed that up. Britain and America were bombing Libya and the pilot announced mid-flight that we had to debark at Damascus and fly to France or Germany and continue to Britain from there.

We spent a frustratingly long few days stuck in a hotel in Damascus. Our luggage was still in the transit lounge of the airport and they could have checked the bags at any time. Some of the other passengers I talked to had hash and had to go through a cycle of shitting it out and then swallowing it when the next flight was announced. I used the time to make contacts for new customers that I could sell to when we returned to London. Rossie wanted to fly to France and then back to England, but that was too many borders and we had pushed our luck too much already. If we got through France the next day without exposure, I wasn't going to risk another border check. We settled on flying to France and offloading the hash with arty types there.

There was no green zone as we went through the French customs at Orly airport - just a red zone where they could check everybody if they wanted to. I was close to the exit. Rossie went behind me so that he could shoot through after I distracted them with my hippiness.

'Do you want to look through?' I asked the customs officers as I passed through and coaxed them with a set of weighing scales and

132

some chillums. They weren't illegal to take through customs, but would capture their attention long enough for Rossie to get by unchecked.

I was in the Portakabin and the customs officer's eyebrows were going up and down as he got the scales and chillums. I had one eye on Rossie walking through the gate until I saw him at the exit door.

Fucking brilliant, we've done it – seven grand in the pocket.

'What do you mean?' I heard from the cabin next door.

That's Rossie's voice. Fuck.

'I said how much is in here?' another voice said. Then I heard the unzipping of a bag.

'How much is this? Two kilos? Three kilos?' the voice said. I walked through the exit, my body violated from the strip search. Rossie was heading for more violations in the months to come. They had taken him away and I didn't know where to. I didn't know for how long. All I knew was that I was heading back to London with less than I left with.

Fuck, fuck, fuck.

Chapter 10

I was back in London with two paths in front of me. The path I wanted to take – to become a drug dealer – had already claimed a victim. It had been a bad deal for Rossie. I was sad for him that he had got caught. But he had known what he was getting into. He'd practically begged me to let him in on it. Anyway, he got off lightly with a two year sentence and a fine. The only thing I could do was tell his mum what had happened. I owed him that. As for a sign against going down that path – I was better at this than Rossie. I wasn't going to get caught.

The other path in front of me included Clare. She couldn't understand that I had plans. She wasn't from my world and she was trying to get me to join hers: get a job, have some kids, and live a happy life together. That was the path she was taking me down, and it sounded like the worst kind of world to end up in. Besides, I still couldn't get over how she hadn't let me smuggle some hash back. Rossie wouldn't be in prison if it wasn't for her.

Breaking up with Clare wasn't difficult. We had been together for four years and I had loved her. Yet she had become a barrier against everything I wanted in my life. I needed freedom from her nagging and expectations. I told her we were over. She didn't want it to be over, but I walked away. Clare wasn't going to get in my way any more.

In fact, nothing was in the way of my ambitions. All I needed to do was get somebody to front me some hash. Terrorist Brian was willing to do me another favour and give me some hash. I would pay him when I sold it. He wouldn't have done it for me had Nick not been my partner in the drug business. Nick had returned from India and, as long as he kept a low profile, I let him come into business with me too. I could use Nick's experience, I thought.

With my hard work, Brian's drugs, and Nick's knowledge of dealing our new business grew pretty fast. It was definitely a business. Our product was hash, speed, and LSD. We bought the product from Brian and sold it on with a twenty-five per cent mark-up for us. Our customers were mostly the connections Nick had from his dealing days before he got busted. Over time, I added to that with travellers that were squatting in the area.

We started selling more speed and LSD than hash. Raves and all-night parties were taking off. Speed kept people dancing until the next day. Brian set up a speed factory out in the countryside. Nick acted as his 'chef'. Brian became one of the top distributors of speed in the country.

Nick was the weakest link in our business. He was supposed to know what he was doing, but he forgot the cardinal rule of drug dealing: never get high on your own supply. Nick was tripping more than ever before, now that he was making it. One night he took too much speed, forgot he had a warrant out for his arrest, and was nicked speeding in Hyde Park. I wasn't concerned about the loss of Nick. At one time we had been friends. My friends weren't so much friends any more – more like rungs in a ladder I needed to climb. Nick was a broken rung. He had to go.

Brian was the top rung on the ladder. At least, he was as far as I could see up the ladder at that point. He had a sophisticated operation. The more time I spent with Brian, the more of that operation was revealed to me. At first, it was just on the visits to his flat that I would notice small things. There were Sainsbury's bags full of twenty-pound notes lying at the side of the sofa. I had never seen that amount of money, not even with the drugs I was selling – and by that point I was selling several thousand pounds' worth a week. I got a thrill seeing that money. It gave me a something to aim for. Brian became my mentor.

We sat and drank together in the Windmill pub, Brian dispensing his wisdom and me listening. One day an elderly man came by and whispered in Brian's ear. I thought that was strange. The man looked like he was in his sixties. He was big, bald, and had stubble across his chin forming an early, unplanned beard. When he'd finished whispering, Brian pulled a wad of cash out of his pocket and gave it to the old man. Then he turned to me:

'Mark, this is Jerry. Jerry works for me. Does odd jobs – answers the phone, sorts the deliveries. You might be dealing with him sometime, so get the guy a drink.'

Jerry drank strong beer and lots of it. There was another guy that worked with Jerry. His name was Marty and he was just as old, just as bald, and just as unshaven as Jerry. They were both gophers for Brian. They did anything he needed doing. I wondered whether that included killing people.

I wasn't scared of Brian when I was drunk – quite the reverse. I had lots of confidence around Brian when I was drunk. I would tell him about my adventures in India, making them much crazier than they actually were, much more profitable than was possible. It was all about image. I had to keep up an image that said I was a hard, rough guy. I knew I was okay with Brian when he was telling me about his adventures. There was a difference in our stories, however. Mine were about smuggling drugs in India; his had a darker tone to them. People got hurt in his stories. I sometimes thought he was making up the stories he told me – that it was just part of the image he needed to create for me, just as I had to create mine for him. Then others would tell me the same stories when Brian wasn't around. When I started to see that what Brian told me wasn't an

136

image, wasn't just bravado, I worried that one day he might turn on me that way – that I might end up dead because of something I did or something I said that Brian wouldn't like.

It had happened to other people. Brian had been dating a girl called Carly. She had got away from her ex-boyfriend to be with Brian. The ex had been beating her up during the relationship. When he bumped into Carly one day and found out she had a new boyfriend, he slapped her round the face. Brian and his gophers caught the ex-boyfriend, tied electrical cables around him, and tortured the guy with kicks and punches to the face. After that, they lowered him off the balcony and dangled him from the third floor of a building. Brian and his gophers joked about it while we drank in the pub together. I laughed. I had to. There was still that lingering thought, though:

What the fuck have I got myself into?

All of the people around Brian – his friends, the people who worked for him, the other dealers – were all bigger than I was, and I was just as much scared by them. I made the mistake of thinking that they were my friends a few times. Just because I laughed with them and drank with them didn't make me one of them.

I got a reminder of my place when I was drinking with Brian and another of his Irish friends. We were all having a good time. He was mocking his friend, calling him a country boy, which he could get away with. Brian could get away with anything. Country boy meant soft, it meant weak. This guy was anything but weak. As soon as I joined Brian in mocking his friend, the guy got up and went for the axe by the fireplace. I don't know what happened next because I didn't wake up until the next day. I was lying in the same place, surrounded by bits of wood. I thought I might be dead, that he had sunk the axe into my head.

I was lucky that there had been a bass flute nearby, which was now lodged into my head. That, and there was a bit of my ear missing. When I saw Brian he acted like he was concerned, but I

137

knew it was just that: an act.

'Oh, Mark, that fucking nutter. I flew into a rage after he done that to you. I chased him down the street and gave him a good beating,' Brian said. Most likely, they carried on drinking, laughing about what had happened, with me out cold next to them. I didn't care. It was dangerous being Brian's friend. But drinking with Brian made me more of a villain than I was. He made me look harder than I was. I felt more loved and needed than I had ever felt, even with a bit of my ear missing. I was part of a gang.

Although we were friends, a lot of our relationship was business. Brian had a lot of crime enterprises. It was hard to keep up with them all. Just when I thought I had a handle on what he was involved with, something else would pop up. As well as my own drug dealing business, Brian had me doing other things for him. I stole furniture from probate houses and took it to the antique shop that he owned. It was a front – a place to funnel the drug money – yet he still made some money selling furniture from the shop. The other crime enterprise was selling on stolen paintings. He asked me to keep my eye out for stolen paintings that he would buy and then sell on for a profit. Everything was a scam with Brian.

I never could tell whether he was a real terrorist or whether it was just a charade – something to instil fear and uncertainty in the people around him. He talked a lot about sectarianism, how he hated the British, and about politics in Ireland. I knew from Nick that Brian had fled Ireland because he was involved in blowing up a house. But that could have been a rumour or just something Brian made up to look big. I made things up to look big too. I made something up just on the way from the shops. I'd walk in and tell everybody I had just seen a massive car crash. It wasn't true, but I thought it made me sound more interesting. I began to think the whole terrorism thing was just another one of those made-up things to sound interesting.

I didn't see anybody watching his house either. I checked every time I left the house, but after a while I stopped bothering. It wasn't until I was leaving the house one day with two other dealers - Pearl and Jake – that I got the rude awakening. As we got into the car Pearl shouted: 'Old Bill coming!'

Behind us were a dozen or so plain-clothes police running to the car. Jake threw his hash back at us but before I could throw it back we were dragged out of the car, put against the wall, and searched. They found a couple of grand on me and Jake and seven grand on Pearl. They also found the hash. We didn't have much of it, though. We hadn't gone to Brian's to get drugs that day. If we had, we could have been in serious trouble. We were taken in for questioning, regardless of the fact that we had very little hash on us. This type of police were not interested in drugs.

It was dark and shady in the station. The officers questioning us were not like the Scottish Drug Squad or the Fraud Squad. These guys carried guns and they didn't play nice.

'Why the fuck was you there?' they shouted.

'For a painting,' we answered.

They laughed.

'Why do you have seven grand,' they asked Pearl.

'To buy a horse,' he said. He was a traveller so this wasn't so strange, although he was unlikely to find a horse to buy in the back end of Brixton.

'A fucking horse,' one of the officers said. 'We know what horse you were buying and it doesn't have four legs.' They all laughed at that except the officer who said it. He just stared at Pearl. 'You smell. You fucking stink,' he said. Then he turned to his colleagues again. 'Fucking travellers. They all smell.'

I thought that was rude. Pearly didn't smell. They were just trying to get us to lose it so they could have us on something. They could use the fact that we lost it at them as leverage for information on Brian. That's what this was all about.

They questioned us all individually as well. They continued with the questions about why we were there and they kept mentioning

Brian's name. Brian had warned me about that tactic and I held my nerve. They had nothing. It wasn't illegal to carry money, even in those amounts, and the hash was too small for these guys to care about.

They let us go and there was no charge. From that day I knew there was nothing phoney about Brian's image. He was a terrorist who would think nothing of popping a bullet in my head. Everything that happened around Brian made more sense after I accepted that truth. Brian would disappear often. He would be gone for several weeks at a time and not tell us where he was. Sometimes I knew he was in Kenya – that was where he got some of his drug supply. I drank with Brian's brothers and they told me that he would have big suitcases of grass smuggled in from Kenya.

After we were busted by the Terrorist Squad, I started to question what I was doing in this world of crime. I also knew there was no going back. For a start, my business was booming and Brian was my main supplier. Secondly, Brian just might hurt me if I left. I was close to him by then. We drank together, we did coke together, and he trusted me. He trusted me enough to ask me to look after the ammunition for his guns. I didn't particularly want to – but what could I say? What could I do about the situation I was in other than embrace it and get on with it? What else could I do but continue to sup with the Devil? Besides, the Devil was my friend.

I had a pocket full of bullets and a house rammed to the rafters with speed and hash. I had built up hundreds of customers. But the pressure was high. I could cope with the twenty-four hour work, always on call like a doctor. I could handle the constant fear of being busted by the police. I could push to the side the idea that I might get really hurt by Brian or one of his henchmen. But I couldn't handle the feeling that I was faking this.

I don't really know what I'm doing.

I'm not a big time drug dealer. I can't match up to the reputation of Brian or that crowd.

I even struggled with my customers – people who needed me and my product. I felt beneath them, especially the big time customers. There were a lot of heavy characters that bought drugs from me. They were harder than I was, had more money than I did, and talked like they had a handle on the world and everybody around them. It was a talk of macho confidence. My self-esteem was zero most of the time. So I drank.

I drank as much as I could, which allowed me to play the game. Drink allowed me to make out like I was a drug king, a god amongst gods, a leader of men. Pumped with beer and liquor, I didn't worry. I didn't think about how good I was or how bad I was. I was drinking nine per cent proof Crucial Brew, dosing with hash, and picking myself up with cocaine and ecstasy. It was a daily concoction of self-prescribed meds. The drink gave me confidence and bravado; the drugs gave me the ability to keep going and do the job.

Something felt amiss, but I couldn't see any other way of life. I could still do my job and the people I worked with - the people I spent my time around - all drank and used drugs like I did. Brian was a drinker and a cokehead. He had so much of the white powder that when it was spilt I would be on the floor trying to hoover it up with my nose from the carpet. 'What the fuck are you doing, Mark?' Brian would say. 'I have bags of the stuff here.' I thought he was nuts, letting any of that beautiful white powder go to waste.

Jim was a character who spent a lot of time at Brian's. He was Irish too. Even though he was small, he had a shaven head and still looked like he could kill me without much effort. He would shout 'Shut the fucking door' as soon as I walked in. As he always carried around a claw hammer, I was always quick to do what he said. Whenever we went out, Jim would start a fight with someone because they were black or English. It was a pain having to jump in all the time, but I couldn't stand and watch. I was expected to hate the English as much as they did. I didn't really care about whether somebody was English or black or Scottish or Irish. I don't think they cared either. It was just all part of the image we had to be - rough and hard and mean criminals.

The business itself was becoming dangerous, which wasn't the rush I was looking for. With Nick gone I had more customers than I could handle alone. On top of that, some of the customers were starting to get demanding. Some of them started to get aggressive when they didn't get exactly what they wanted, when they wanted it. I had to enlist the help of some people that I could trust.

Ronnie and Walshy had bought a bus and were travelling on the road. They were camped in Wales. I went to try to convince them to join me in the business. I ended up spending a week with them on the bus, drinking and tripping. We broke in to a rock star's cottage and spent the night drinking his tequila and feeding his furniture to the fire. I should have felt guilt, but all I felt was the return of the feeling of freedom and adventure we had once had together. Not that long ago, we were jumping hedges and tripping in the hills at the weekends. Now I had all this responsibility. It was what I had wanted, but reuniting with my old friends woke me up to the fact that I missed that freedom and adventure.

Just as I was looking at their life and thinking that I wanted to be part of that, Walshy and Ronnie were looking at my life and thinking that a bit of money and a warm place to stay might be nice for a while. When it came to me convincing them to join me in London, it didn't take much. Of course, Walshy moaned for a bit, predicting doom and gloom.

'What if you get into trouble with Brian? What if he turns against you?' he asked.

'Walshy, Brian and I are friends. You will get on with him too.' Despite his moans and predictions of doom and gloom, Walshy was happy to come back to London. He was a speed freak and needed money for that. There wasn't much of it living on a bus in Wales. Ronnie didn't need any convincing. He liked the lifestyle that came with dealing and was happy to be able to come and do it in London. With them came Sprog. Sprog had joined them in

142

Wales and was a proper New Age traveller – except for the fact that he was more of the Brew Crew than the peace convoy. That was helpful to me, because Sprog was heavy, rough, and didn't think twice about knocking somebody out. That was exactly the kind of muscle I needed around.

With my friends back with me and protection for the business, I could see the whole operation laid out before me. Walshy was great with the customers and Sprog kept them all in line. Despite Walshy's moaning and worrying about Brian, they ended up getting on like two brothers. The biggest problem I had was the supply – all of which came from Brian. Collecting the drugs from Brian wasn't always easy. One of the two old guys working for Brian – Jerry or Marty – would deliver it. They looked like they were granddads, so weren't likely to be stopped and searched. The rest of the time, I was going back and forth to the antique shop in a taxi.

I thought I was independent, running my own business. After I paid Walshy, Sprog, and Ronnie, I was still banking between one and two grand a week. Brian must have been taking at least fifty grand a week from me and the various other dealers – the ones that I knew about.

I began to wonder how much money Brian really made, let alone *his* supplier. Unless the drug supply comes from the source – where it is grown - there's always someone making more money, someone else that the dealer is dependent on. Dealers are not dependent on the customers. The customers needed me as much as I needed Brian and so it went, right back up the ladder. Customers were always at the bottom, slaves to our product. I thought we were big time, but soon found out we were an outpost compared to others that Brian supplied.

Chapter 11

Why do you need a fucking cage for a door?

I had gone to Declan's – another of Brian's dealers – to hang out. The minute I got there, I realised his operation was much more sophisticated than mine. We didn't have any bars on our door. We didn't even have a good lock. I was waiting by the cage while Declan was struggling up the stairs with a big suitcase.

'Hey, Mark, I just got back from holiday,' he laughed.

I knew what kind of holiday he had been on; it wasn't to top up his tan. I was hoping that he had some of that new acid on the streets, Blackcat. That was a great trip and everyone was trying to get their hands on it. The cage door swung open. Behind it there was a skinhead staring at me. He looked like he was built to break me with one hand. He was hyper-manic and chattering fast.

'Hey, man, hey, look, look at this fucking gun, man, look at it.' The skinhead was waving a shotgun in my face and it was the first time I had seen a real shotgun. I had carried ammunition but this was the real thing, loaded with bullets and ready to shoot.

'Yeah, man, fucking easy to load, look at this, pull it out, load the bullets, snap it shut and cock - ready - bang, bang, bang.'

Fuck, fuck, fuck.

'Don't worry about Charlie, Mark, he likes angel dust. A bit manic – Charlie, put that fucking thing away.' Declan unzipped the suitcase to reveal sheets of LSD. Inside the case there was more hash and grass than I sold in a week. I thought I was the big man, but these guys - man, these guys had guns and cage doors. They were older than I was, and it was then that I saw the truth.

These guys work for Brian.

They knew they worked for Brian. They didn't think they were independent like I did. They were owned by him.

Fuck, I'm owned by Brian.

BANG, BANG, BANG on the door and I was no longer thinking, I was shitting. Charlie was by the door, gun cocked, and Declan was closing the suitcase.

Nunchakus to the ready.

Two guys walked in as if they were expected. One of them picked up the nunchakus and started whizzing them around his head with skill. Charlie was still by the door, shotgun cocked. Declan was standing by the suitcase with piles of drugs.

'How much you guys say you want?' Declan asked.

'Five kilos.'

I could feel the tension in the room. These were the big guys dealing to big guys and it could have gone bad at any moment.

With those nunchakus, the guy could take me and Declan out and the other one probably has a gun to deal with Charlie.

Charlie was so wired on angel dust that I was worried he might mistake any movement as an attack and blow someone's head off.

I'm going to get shot and all I wanted was a Blackcat trip.

Declan was counting the money - lots of fifty notes. The two guys were bagging up blocks of hash, and Charlie was still manically eyeballing everybody with the shotgun. Then they were gone and Declan looked at me like nothing had happened.

'So, mate, shall we do some Blackcat?' he asked.

I was freaked enough.

There's no way I'm doing acid in this place.

We smoked a few joints and I went back to my pitiful drug squat with no metal cage, a queue of smaller customers buying smaller quantities. I was feeling lower than a chess pawn. Brian was the king. Or at least a rook or a bishop.

Chapter 12

I thought that getting my supply of drugs, independent of Brian, would be easy. I knew it was a step I needed to take to get my business to the place I wanted it: dealing in bigger quantities and taking more of the profit. I had to buy a lot and buy it cheap. That was the difficult bit. I had to travel to do that.

Mickey, the dealer that I had met in India, was the first person I called on for help. He had his own drug production operation in Amsterdam. He was producing high quality LSD and selling it to dealers like me. The price was as low as I was going to find for LSD. I went back and forth for several months. Smuggling it back was easy, but time consuming. To avoid border searches, I posted the LSD to friends staying in squats across London. I spread the risk by separating five thousand trips a time into birthday cards – if one of them got busted, they could just say it had nothing to do with them. To avoid further suspicion, with a postmark from Amsterdam, I travelled to Zandam and posted them from there. It was a significant profit. The only cost was the stamp for the card and a few LSD trips for the recipient of the card. But it wasn't enough. I needed more.

Smuggling the LSD back from Amsterdam took thought, planning, and effort. The next stage was to smuggle some hash back to London. I had experienced the risk of smuggling hash. To avoid the possibility of prison, I had to take the time to think, plan, and put some effort into this smuggling venture. But I was drinking all the time and snorting lines of coke from morning to night. I was wired every minute of every day and my mind started to see all the days as one. I was never quite sure from one to the other what was before or next. I was running about, picking up the drugs from Brian, and meeting all our customers' needs. I was looking after Walshy and the other guys, making sure they were happy and doing what they were supposed to. I worked all day – every day. Running a drug business was a twenty-four hour a day, seven day a week job. I wanted a break. In my addled state of mind I thought that I could combine a break with smuggling hash back into London. I planned to go to Morocco to do just that.

* * *

I flew to Malaga, Spain, bussed to Algeciras and took a boat the rest of the way to Morocco. I thought that getting a flight might raise suspicion about me being a smuggler if I then got a boat back. Consistency was the best idea. As soon as I got to Chefchaouen, I found a campsite where I could stay for the night. All I could hear around me were the chants of locals trying to sell me hash.

'Chocolat, chocolata, chocolat.'

I don't want any fucking chocolat.

It was years since I had got any kind of high off hash. I still smoked it, but for the same effect as a cup of coffee to other people. Opium, though – I had become obsessed with opium. I wanted to search for some opium, but needed to get a drink inside me first. I was starting to feel sick – it had been a few hours since I'd had a drink and I didn't want to be seeing snakes, spiders, and dead Grandma.

I was searching the campsite for some beer. There wasn't any. I searched for some whiskey. There wasn't any. I search for any kind of alcohol. There wasn't anything but hash and fruit and veg at the market stalls. I was just about to accept an orange juice that had been in the sun for too long when I saw someone selling dried poppies.

If I boil them I can down the liquid - that will take the edge off until I can get a drink.

The only problem with that idea was that I didn't have a camp stove or anything to boil it in. That's when I heard a loud voice shouting over the hustle and bustle of the camp.

'Anybody want to travel to Toga? We've got this bus and we've got space for a few people; we're going right through Morocco.'

This guy was standing in front of a Benz bus, the kind of luxury rock stars travel in.

They'll have a cooker inside.

Suddenly, it didn't matter that I was there on a mission for good dope. I had to get something inside me. Cravings were starting. Besides, I could just get off at Ketama on their way to Toga. I bought the dried poppies and jumped on the bus.

The bus was sent from a God I didn't believe in. It was stripped of seats but had beds to sleep on, a kitchen, and Sarah.

My beautiful English rose, Sarah.

Sarah's skin was blessed by the sun and her breasts were blessed by Mother Nature. I was blessing whoever had put her in front of me. The minute I saw Sarah, I had to have her. I had to know everything about her at once, I had to kiss her that minute, I had to have sex with her. But, as blessed as I was by Sarah, the first thing I had to do was boil the poppies and get something inside me, quick.

Sarah will still be here to kiss and have sex with when I get these poppies down me.

I begged the guy driving to let me use the kitchen, but he was anti-opiates. The whole lot of them stuck their stoned noses up at opiates. It was like that with drug dealers. We were all in the gutter as far as 'society' saw, yet the gutter still had a hierarchy. Opiate users were near *the* bottom – heroin, which is an opiate, was the bottom. They were called junkies. Brian and his crew were completely against junkies - noses falling off with the amount of coke they stuffed up there - but 'We don't touch that fucking smack – junkies' fucking drug.' The problem for the driver of the bus was that I really needed to use his kitchen – and not much gets in the way of me when I need a drug or a drink. So I begged him until he got bored of hearing me and let me use it.

I offered Sarah a sip of the poppy juice. She declined. She was smoking hash. I took my first sip. After the first sip of juice, I had ascertained that Sarah - my future girlfriend - was living in Spain, just off the Costa Brava.

Oh, I fucking love Spain.

A few more sips and I had discovered her work address – the Cottage Inn, where she served drunk tourists.

Oh, I fucking love the Cottage Inn.

Another sip and I had discovered that Sarah and I had more in common than our impending relationship: she sold speed and made a pretty good mark-up compared to what I made in London.

Oh, I fucking love speed.

The conversation with Sarah was going so well. She could see that I loved everything she loved. We had so much in common. As I sipped and she smoked, we locked eyes. I was definitely getting in Sarah's knickers.

We are going to have sex. If I can get an erection after all the opiate I've been drinking, I'm going to fuck you into next week.

A few more sips and a fantasy of me and Sarah took over in my head. We were off together, round the racetrack – the same racetrack I had been on in my head in India. Sarah was racing beside me on the track - no car - just Sarah and I zooming round the track. Then we were on a speed boat. I don't know where the speed boat came from, but we were lying on it. Sarah was next to me, naked, and we were whizzing around the Canaries on a speed boat. Having sex on the deck.

150

Everybody can see us having sex.

Sarah was bouncing up and down on top of me, and I was pounding in and out, and she was screaming and I was pounding and…

Where the fuck is everybody?

After a few more sips, we must have stopped somewhere, because I wasn't on a boat in the Canaries having sex. I was looking out of my tent, with a night gone. Sarah and the van were nowhere in sight.

That bitch, she's left me already.

I couldn't believe that they could just dump me in the middle of Morocco. I knew it wasn't Sarah's fault because she had given me her address. She wouldn't have done that if she didn't like me.

It was that fucking driver. Jealous, most likely. At least they left me the rest of the opiate juice.

I drank my breakfast and looked around. I considered my next move.

Fuck it, let's go to Ketama. Forget about Sarah and those selfish hippies.

By the time I got to Ketama, I was out of my head on opiate juice. There were now various states of 'out of my head' in my life. There was the slightly out of my head – that was the default setting. Then there was buzzing – that was the next stage up, after a few more beers and a few lines of coke. Then there was mashed – after half a bottle of whiskey, some trips, some hash, and some more coke. Right at the top was completely out of it, which could be because of a bad or good trip, too much of a new drug, or just a combination of many drugs and alcohol. This time I was completely out of it because I had drunk too much opiate juice – which was strong. Not the weak quality poppies I was used to in England.

Ketama turned out not to be a great place to be completely out of it. It was a dusty little market town. The heat was bearable, but only if I hadn't been sweating poppies. The worst thing about being in Ketama in this state was the locals surrounding me, trying to sell me something. I was a parrot, saying the same thing over and over again, regardless of what I was asked.

'Want to buy some woman?'

'Fuck off.'

'Want to buy food?'

'Fuck off.'

'Need hotel?'

'Fuck off.'

'Need taxi?'

Fuck off, fuck off, fuck off.

Eventually I heard something I did want.

'Do you want me to take you to where hash grows? I'll show you how we make it. And you can buy some too.'

I was definitely out of it because, with all those people around me, I couldn't see where the voice had come from. Everything was set in a yellow haze of dust.

'Yeah, great man, let's do it,' I shouted and hoped the voice would find me.

The voice must have found me. I don't how we got to the hut he took me to, because my memory takes me directly to the hut. There is no in between. One minute I was in the market; the next I was sitting, cross-legged, in a small hut that looked like it was made of dry mud. There were two guys sitting with me – I could tell they were locals by the colour of their skin and their dusty white robes.

Where did these guys come from? Where did the voice go?

I could see out of the hut door, which was open. We were surrounded by fields of crop. It was hash crop. In front of the two guys sat a big sieve – centre stage - and they were talking as they made hash pollen from the crop, using the sieve. I didn't know what they were saying. I couldn't keep track of what they were doing. All I saw was the pollen from the hash crop trickling down into powder. I knew from *The Great Book of Hashish* that the powder could be used for oil. I just couldn't remember what kind of oil. I still couldn't work out if I was in a dream or not.

One of the guys gave me about a hundred grams of golden brown, hand-pressed pollen. I started smoking a bit of it. The hash tasted just as good as when I sat and smoked at Siteram's in Malana.

If this is a dream, then I want to stay in it for as long as possible.

I realised it wasn't a dream, that this was real, when he asked me for money. He took thirty dollars. It was a rip-off, but I didn't have the energy to argue.

'Be careful,' he said. 'There's a police check about ten miles up the road.'

I looked ahead at the road. It stretched out for miles. The guy that had been standing with me, only moments earlier, had gone. I was alone.

Where the fuck am I?

I put my finger out to hitch.

Suddenly I was with some German tourists in the back of their Volkswagen. We passed the police check. There were no police. I realised that I didn't know how I got in the car or where they were taking me.

'Did you get some nice hash?' one of the Germans asked, with a manic grin only Eastern Europeans can pull off.

'Yeah, yeah, man.'

I remembered that at some point I would have to cross a border. I didn't know when, but I started to panic.

'Listen, guys, I need to stop. I need to stop now,' I said.

I've got to cling film the hash, get it inside me before we get to the border.

'Stop here,' I shouted. 'Let's stop at these woods.'

They stopped.

'You got cling film?' one of them asked.

They must have seen my thoughts. Or did I say all that out loud. I don't know. I don't care.

'Yeah, yeah,' I said. I left the Germans at the car, walked into the woods, and sat down. I had three ounces, maybe more, maybe less. One of the German guys came with me into the woods to wrap his hash.

I don't care.

153

I got the cling film, wound it round, got the lighter, and burnt the cling film at the ends of the hash pieces – it was a long, boring process.

Got to make it solid, got to seal it up.

I began to teach him how to wrap. He started copying me.

Why is he wrapping up twenty grams? What's the point in swallowing twenty grams?

He was wrapping and sealing; I was wrapping and sealing.

CRACK.

Shit. What was that?

CRACK.

Another branch broke behind me. I looked up.

Freeze.

There was a soldier standing in front of me with a gun. A big gun. A rifle. The rifle was older than he was. Shit, I was older than he was. I lost interest, mainly because I was running into the woods. I was just running and running.

Got to get away from the soldier, escape the rifle.

I was running and then I was out the other side of the woods. But I couldn't understand it because they were right in front of me, maybe fifty yards away.

That doesn't make sense: I was running and running and now I'm back where I started. Got to stash the hash.

The soldier was pushing the German guy to the car with the rifle, where the other German was. I put the hash behind the tree and buried it, like a dog hiding his bone for later retrieval.

Got to remember where the tree is. Pace back ten steps, forward ten, mark my spot, nearest location big tree to the left, ten steps from the road. Hash stashed, location memorised, back to the car to help Germans.

The Germans were standing with their backs against the car. I could smell their fear. I walked over to them.

'Problem, problem,' the soldier was repeating over and over. He had the small lumps of the Germans' hash in his hands. The lumps of hash were smaller than the bullets of the rifle.

He's on his own. It would be easy to hit him. I could just bash him on his head with a rock, take his gun, and drive off. Nobody else is here. We could get away with it.

The soldier was pointing for the Germans to open the boot. The Germans were doing it.

Fucking idiots. Why didn't they just fling the hash and run like I did?

The soldier put his head in the open boot. He was rustling through their bags.

I could just whack him from behind and stuff him in the boot.

He pulled out some magazines and held them up. He was smiling and leafing through the pages. I could see closer – it was German porn from their rucksacks. The soldier was leafing through the porn page by page saying 'Oh' over and over, each time deeper, until the 'Oh' was turning into moans and groans. Eventually, he looked up at me.

'Problem, problem,' he said.

I understand. He wants money. Maybe we can just pay him thirty quid and he will let us go.

'Come, come, over there,' he pointed us over to the tree with his gun. We walked back out of the clearing, away from the car, away from the road, away from sight.

He's going to shoot us, take the car, take the hash, take the money, take the porn.

He nudged us over to a big tree.

I'm not budging this time. I'm not turning around so he can shoot me in the head.

The soldier began to unzip his trousers.

Why is he taking a piss?

He was unzipping and unbolting and putting his hand in there and smiling and motioning me to bend over a branch sticking out from the tree...

Oh fuck, he's going to fuck us!

'NO!' I shouted. 'No, no, no, no,' I repeated, running over and waving my hands in manic protest. The soldier was smiling yes, yes and pointing to the tree, motioning for me to bend over.

'No, you fucking don't, man. I can't do that. I'm Scottish. I'M

155

FUCKING SCOTTISH.' He didn't understand my Scottish defence, so I pointed to the German.

'He'll do it. He'll fucking do it.'

Fuck it. It's their porn. That's what got this soldier horny. Besides, if the Germans had thrown their hash, or at least kept look out, we wouldn't be in this mess.

'He'll do it,' I pointed vigorously at the German, but not vigorously enough, because the soldier was still looking at me, smiling and edging closer.

I turned to the German in desperation.

'Listen - he wants to fuck us up the arse. It's simple. It was your porn, your hash. You've got to bend over and just do it…' The German looked confused. 'You've got to take it up the fucking arse, man.' He understood that.

'No, no, no, no, no, not up the arse, not up the arse,' he edged back.

'You can do it, man,' I encouraged with the voice of a mother, edging her son into school for the first time. 'You can do this! It's simple, it will be over very quickly, and he's so horny already from the porn.' He's listening. 'I'll never mention this to anybody again…'

'No, you do it, you do it and I won't mention it,' he shouted.

'I can't do it, man, I'm Scottish. I'm fucking Scottish. I can't take it up the arse.' My Scottish defiance wasn't making any difference to him, either. I looked back at the soldier with his gun pointing at me, his trouser zip open, his belt unbuckled, and lust in his eyes. I considered again whether we could take him out, but he had the gun and we had nothing. Nothing except arses he wanted to rape. I had to try to plead one last time with the German to take it up the arse.

'Listen. It's really simple.' I could already see from his face that my pleadings were falling on ears deaf to English. But I had to try. 'Simple. Bend.' I bent. 'Arse.' I pointed to my arse. 'Bum – in, out – quick. Nobody knows.' I put my hand over my mouth to signal a vow of silence. This last attempt to convince the German to take one for the team lasted several excruciating minutes.

Eventually the soldier got tired of our debating and sent us back to the car, while he sat by the tree looking at porn. He was leaving us to decide who was going to be taking it up the arse. It was dark by this point and I was starting to think none of us were going to end up leaving there alive.

He's either going to bugger us up the arse, shoot us, or both.

If I had to choose, I would have rather got a buggering than shot.

Fuck it, I'm not doing it, I'm not fucking doing it.

'Listen, guys. We're gonna have to decide who's doing this. I can't, I'm Scottish. And it's your porn, your hash. You need to decide who it is. One of you has to or he's gonna get us all nicked.'

They argued with each other for a while, getting nowhere. I sat back, exasperated and exhausted - the opiates and hash long worn off.

'Okay, okay, if you're not going to do this, we'll have to take him out. We'll have to hit him on the head or something, and go. We can shoot across the border and by the time they find him, we'll be gone.'

'No, no, no,' they both said.

If they're not going to take it up the arse and they're not going to hit him, what's left?

'Money. Okay, okay, money, we'll have to give him some money. How much money do you have?'

They searched their pockets. Between us we cobbled together thirty dollars. This time I had no qualms about sacrificing thirty dollars for freedom. At least it wasn't to buy a fucking goat. I offered it to the soldier and he looked at the notes as poor compensation for the lack of buggering.

'You can keep the hash,' I said, quickly. He held up the porn. 'Yes, yes, keep the porn,' I said. He shrugged his shoulders and motioned for us to drive him. The Germans spent another ten minutes trying to barter the hash back, but by this point I was ready to bash the Germans over the head and let the soldier take his fancy with both of them. I had done everything to get them out of this mess, a mess they had created, and now they wanted the fucking hash back! Eventually they gave up and we got in the car and drove.

We didn't know where we were going. We just followed the directions that the soldier was issuing, like we were part of his platoon. We arrived outside the police station.

After all this, he's going to lock us up, and maybe there's a dozen of these guys in there, horny as fuck, going to bugger us one by one.

But he was getting out of the car and leaving us there.

'No, no, we gave you money – now give us our passports,' I said. He smiled and started walking away. I bashed on the window and shouted.

'Give us our fucking passports.'

He popped his head through the window, threw the passports down, and then fled into the police station as if he was never here. We all sat, spent of emotion, spent of fear, spent of argument. I could hear a communal exhale, as if we were coming up for first air, almost drowned. We felt like we had been held under water for the last four hours. Now we got to breathe. Now we got to live. Free from rape, we sat in silence.

'Right,' I said, eventually. 'Let's go back and get my hash.'

Chapter 13

I didn't smuggle much hash back from Morocco beyond a little for personal use. It wasn't a profitable trip. It was a trip that almost cost my anal virginity. I had failed in my efforts to get my own supply of hash and bypass Brian, but the business was still growing. We started to sell thousands of trips a week and several kilos of hash a day. I had to shape up the business. I had to make sure my operation ran as smoothly as it could.

The first thing I did was divide the labour. I got Ronnie to sell the speed, Walshy to sell the LSD, and I sold the hash and dealt with the bigger customers. Sprog handled the security.

With more customers than we had ever had, I didn't want the drugs kept in one house. It became too much of a risk to keep all of our supply in one location. So I split the operation into three locations. The small squat was used for the small fry customers, who bought an eighth or a few pills at a time. I got a second squat for the bigger customers. These were the guys buying thousands of trips at a time and a kilo or more of hash. We then paid another friend to keep the bulk of the supply that we didn't need to sell during that day. We paid him in hash, which was an effective trade for labour.

The main benefit of splitting the operation this way was reducing the risk of getting busted. If one place got busted by the police then the others would still be able to function. We wouldn't lose all our supply in one bust and the other locations could just step right back in to serve our customers. The flats were like terrorist cells, each immune from the other. Also, two separate locations serving customers meant fewer people coming and going from any one squat. I was getting paranoid about the Drug Squad watching us. Whenever I went to pick up supplies from Brian, I caught a black taxicab and wore a suit. I thought that dressing and travelling like a city businessman was less suspicious. I was getting clever.

Having the three-squat operation didn't keep us safe from robbery. We were robbed by one of our own kind. Magoo was a black guy everyone knew. He was a dealer and a pimp. The difference between me and Magoo was that he cut out the supplier and stole what he needed from dealers like me. I knew about Magoo, but thought that my association with Brian would keep him away. I was wrong.

Dave was supposed to be covering the small fry house while I went out with the lads. I was taking everybody out for a 'staff night out' on the town. I left Dave three ounces of hash with instructions of what to sell and what to charge. I returned a few hours later to find Dave panicked in the corner. He had been robbed by Magoo and his gang. They had taken the lot. This was a big test of my authority, my credibility as a respected drug dealer. I had to go around to beat and slash Magoo.

'Sprog, get your nunchakus. We're going to sort this Magoo out.' Sprog was drooling at the prospect. I downed half a bottle of whiskey to calm myself. I was shaking at the prospect.

We went round to Magoo's house and stood at his door. Sprog looked at me for directions on what to do next. He was still drooling. I knew he wanted me to give the nod to break down the door and then nunchaku Magoo into pieces.

I'll check if he's in first. No need to go crazy yet.

I banged on the door.

I shouted through the letter box: 'Fucking open this door, I know you're in there.' The only noise I could hear from inside was a baby crying.

What is this fucking world where a baby's in a drug den?

I didn't want to break down the door, with a baby inside.

I can't just let him get away with it.

I looked back at Sprog, who was looking back at me. He wanted me to let him off the leash to nunchaku Magoo.

'Let's get him another time, Sprog. Keep him waiting for his punishment. The wait will be worse for him.' Sprog reluctantly lowered the nunchakus and we went home. I could afford the loss of the hash and the money.

* * *

As a big time drug dealer, with three flats, and a crew, I was getting enough sex. Our squat became a temporary home for any female hippy traveller visiting London. I sold them their drugs and then did my best to coax them upstairs with the promise of seeing my snake.

'Would you like to see my snake upstairs?' I would say.

'You cheeky bastard,' they would say.

'No, I mean an actual snake. I have a ten foot python upstairs.' Sometimes that would be all that I needed to say. That would get them upstairs. It didn't matter that it was my friend's snake. If that didn't work, I had other things to lure them upstairs with.

'I could read you your Tarot cards. I know all about Tarot. I could see your future for you.' It didn't matter what their future was. By the end of reading their Tarot cards, their future was bouncing up and down on my cock. If that didn't work, though, I had one last temptation up my sleeve.

'Would you like to come upstairs and see my Viking ruins?' If they came upstairs for that, I treated them with the full works. I would get on the helmet, the armour, and the robe. If that wasn't enough to get them into bed, I would just get them stoned

161

enough where sleeping with me was a great idea.

I woke up most mornings with a random girl lying naked next to me.

What the hell are you doing in my bed?

I was drinking so much that I blacked out at the end of the night and couldn't remember anything about who I was with or what I had done. I was drinking so much I was surprised I could even get it up. Before, I was drinking for confidence. Now, I was drinking because I had to. I drank as soon as I opened my eyes, naked girl lying next to me or not. I reached over to the side of the bed for the emergency can as soon as I woke up. I downed the can and then sent Alan out for more. Alan was my gopher, just as Jerry and Marty were Brian's. He came round to the house every day and worked for free hash, drink, and food. The only task I used him for were trips to the off licence to stock up on beer and liquor. In the morning he picked up my day's supply: twelve cans of Crucial Brew. He returned throughout the day to stock up if I needed more. Most days I needed more.

Getting the drink inside me was tough by this point. My body and head had different ideas about whether more beer and liquor was a good idea.

My body was saying: *Get this shit out of me.*

My head was saying: *I need it. I can't do anything without it.*

They always fought and my head always won. Not without the body shaking, sweating, and dry retching itself to victory. Then, throughout the day, it was a constant battle to top up and keep at my baseline. My baseline was how drunk I needed to be in order to get up in the morning, stay up during the day, and do my job. That was what the twelve cans of Crucial Brew did. When big customers came round or I was dealing with Brian, I would need a boost to my confidence. Half a bottle of brandy or Thunderbird wine was the perfect boost.

I drank or took anything that gave me a buzz, kept me numb, or sent me high – anything that stopped me thinking about the world

162

I was in and whether I could handle it. I drank the cheap, strong beer and I walked down the street glugging from champagne bottles like they were pop. They both did the same thing. The champagne just had the added benefit of making me look rich and powerful. It probably just made me look strange, though – walking down the street in Brixton, glugging from a bottle of Don Perignon. I needed drink more now than I had ever needed it. If I was drunk I could deal with the customers. I could handle Brian and his henchmen. The drink gave me the confidence. The drugs gave me everything else I needed. I smoked heroin, snorted coke, and drank from morning to night. The drugs provided the party; the drink meant I could turn up to it.

Everybody I knew, everybody around me, drank as much as I did. There were always a few travellers staying in our squat for short spells. Then there were my crew: Walshy, Ronnie, and Sprog. Lastly, we had the hangers-on and the freeloaders. They came for the party – to smoke our hash and drink our beer. That didn't bother me. Those guys provided extra muscle and entertainment. Just like my friends at school, whom I owned with the threat of a box or a shot with the air rifle. I paid them with kebabs, beer, and drugs. They weren't all a great help to have around, even for muscle. There was one particular guy who was more of a liability than help. He was a thief and helped himself to anything that wasn't his. He tried to turn over one of our top customers once, demanding their money until Ronnie intervened. I had to take him to the side and tell him not to do it again. I should have chucked him out, but I needed the hangers-on around as much as I needed my crew, the women, the drink and the drugs.

* * *

I took the time to get to know the bigger customers. These were the customers who bought thousands of pounds' worth of drugs at a time. I always made sure I had what they wanted, when they wanted it, and that they got the full service. They didn't want to be waiting in line behind a guy looking to score an eighth for his first house party.

With Clive, I got my job completely wrong. I didn't have what he wanted, when he wanted it – and it was all Brian's fault. Clive had been buying from me for about six months, each time increasing his purchases of hash from one kilo upwards. This time he wanted five kilos. I didn't have five kilos of hash to sell him that day, but I didn't turn away business like that. I paged Brian from the phone box outside Brixton police station. He called me back and I could tell he was coked out of his mind.

'Look, Clive's already here and he's got the cash for five kilos. When can we get the stuff over?'

'I'll be there in ten, max, just get the money off him and count it, I can't wait around.' He was definitely fucked. Brian never made deliveries.

Better keep Brian away from Clive. He will shoot him in the head or steal him from me as a customer.

Brian arrived with the hash and I hid him upstairs while I counted the money downstairs. It took time to count eleven grand, but Brian didn't want to wait. I didn't want him around for long either. If the Terrorist Squad were following him, they could be outside. I was ready to get Clive out of the door with the hash, but he wanted to try it and started rolling a joint. Brian was going nuts at me upstairs.

'I want my FUCKING MONEY,' he was raging. 'You go downstairs, get me my money, I gotta fucking go.'

I went downstairs to help Clive get out of the door. I stopped by the kitchen to down some whiskey.

If we get busted now, I'm fucked.

Clive puffed and left happy. Brian got his cash and left happy. Finally, my heart could relax. We hadn't been turned over, Brian hadn't shot anybody in the head, and the Terrorist Squad hadn't busted down the door.

164

This is a good fucking day.

I had a bottle to celebrate. Then another. And another.

Clive came back a few days later, unhappy about the hash he had bought from me.

'Look, it's all shit. I've offloaded two kilos of it, but I'm left with three kilos I can't move. I want a replacement or my money back,' he said

Fuck, how am I going to tell Brian?

'Brian, look mate, this guy Clive says the stuff is shit and he wants to return three kilos and get a replacement.'

'What you trying to say, Mark?'

'I'm not saying anything. It's the guy, it's Clive. He says it's a re-press, that it's bad stuff and he can't move it.'

'That is decent shit. I don't sell bad anything, right?'

'I know, I know, Brian, but he's not happy.'

'Tell him to fuck off.' He hung up the phone.

I downed half a bottle of Thunderbird and told Clive.

'Look, do you know who I am?' he said. I knew he was a biker, but not much else. 'I'm the president of the All England chapter of Hell's Angels. If I go back to my guys and say that you've screwed us, what do you think we are going to do to you?'

I knew what they did to the heroin dealers at the festivals: beat them to hospital and torched their vans.

Fuck, fuck, fuck.

I went back and reported this to Brian as delicately as I could.

'He fucking said what? Who the fuck does this cunt think he is?'

'Maybe we should just give him some new hash, Brian?'

'Listen, Mark, these fuckers, they're children. They fuck around on their bikes like they're hard men, but they're just playing around in the woods like cowboys, taking it up the arse the lot of 'em. You tell them to fuck off now or I'll shoot them in their fucking heads.'

I didn't know what to do. 'When all else fails,' Mum always said, 'honesty is the best policy.' Honesty was the only option left. I had to tell Clive the truth.

165

I downed some whiskey and told Clive the truth.

'Look, Clive, I called Brian and I couldn't get hold of him. Leave it with me and I'll sort it out for you.'

Clive left, but I knew he'd be back.

Brian was getting more unreliable the more cocaine he took. I had become restless. I could work hard and fast for long periods. Then I would need a break. That was what the trip to Morocco had been about – a break from London and the pressure cooker of the drug business. After the incident with Clive and with the problems I was having with Brian, I decided to go to India for a few months. Ronnie, Walshy, and Sprog would keep the business going. Nick had been released from prison so he was back in the business and would help.

Not long after I left for India, Clive turned up at the squat looking for me. Nick was left to deal with him.

'Mark is not here; he's out of the country,' he told Clive.

'Oh, very convenient, very lucky for him,' Clive said. 'A very lucky guy.' Nothing happened for a few months after that. No beatings, no shootings – no trouble. Nick was at his parents' house in Kent walking to the pub when a van pulled up. Clive called out of the window:

'Hey there, Nick, how's it going?'

'Yeah, yeah, man, all good.'

'That's good for you. How about we take you for a drink?' Nick couldn't turn down a vanload of Hell's Angels. One minute he was in the pub, drinking his pint, and the next he was coming to in a field, locked in a hut. He spent two days as a prisoner. He had no idea where he was, no idea what they were going to do with him. Eventually they started the interrogation:

'Where does this guy live?'

'What guy?'

'You know what fucking guy. The guy that Mark gets his gear from. Tell us where he lives and we'll let you go.' If Nick told them that information, Brian would shoot him in the head. Nick knew that, so he didn't. They slapped him, they beat him, they threatened

166

to kill him, but still Nick stayed silent. He knew that whatever they did to him, Brian would do worse. Then they carried him to the side of the motorway, cars roaring by at breakneck speed.

'Where the fuck does he live?'

Nick screamed that he didn't know. They grabbed his arms and legs and swung him from side to side.

'You're fucking going under the next lorry unless you tell us.' Nick was going to die whether under a lorry or by a bullet through the head from Brian. At least choosing the bullet gave him a chance of fleeing.

'Okay, okay – I'll tell you. It's number fifty-six Samerson Road.'

'Fifty-six?'

'Fifty-six, fifty-six, now put me down, I told you where.' They put him down. Nick was safe, but not for long. Brian would definitely shoot him.

Brian never found out. Through the noise, the chaos, the fear of death, the starvation of several days locked in a hut Nick got the address wrong. After that day, Nick left the drug business. I didn't see him or hear about what had happened with Clive until a few years later. He blamed me and I blamed Brian. I never once thought:

Maybe I should quit this life. Maybe this isn't for me.

* * *

My third trip to India was brief. It wasn't a profitable trip in terms of smuggling. I did meet Lesley. We met on the beach and spent hours talking. She smoked hash and I ate opium. She was searching for her ex-boyfriend who had disappeared before she left prison. It was crazy she was still looking for him when it was his fault she had gone to prison. She had smuggled heroin from India to Britain for him. He was probably dead. Her suspicion was that he had been murdered by her gangster dad in revenge for leading her astray. She was just holding out hope she might find him here alive.

167

I wanted to have sex with Lesley. I didn't have my friend's snake with me or my Viking ruins. I had my Tarot cards, but Lesley needed more work than that to get into bed with me. I put the hours into talking with her well into the night and then snuggling up to her. I didn't even try to put my hand down her knickers while we slept. Eventually, my hard work and patience paid off. We had sex one night. Then the next. Then another night. We spent the next few months having sex on the beach, sex in the hotel, sex wherever we could.

She returned to London before I did. Before then, we agreed that we were a couple. The problem was that I had been eyeing a hot Swedish girl in our hotel for the last few days. As much as I wanted to be in a couple with Lesley - as much I said I wished she didn't have to go - as soon as she did I was back at the hotel, reading the Swedish girl's Tarot cards and getting her into bed. I knew it had been a mistake as soon as I woke up. It wasn't even good sex. I told Lesley what had happened as soon as I got back to London. She was upset, but forgave me.

I got back to my life and Lesley fit in perfectly. She kept to her life working in the real world as a personal assistant and I kept to my life dealing drugs. We met up at weekends and I stayed with her when I could get to Tonbridge to visit. The only thing that had changed in my life was that I couldn't have sex with random girls any more. That didn't matter. It was a big enough job to keep up with everything as it was, without adding more girls to the mix.

Even with Lesley in my life, it was the same daily routine that had got me bored before I had gone to India. It was the same grind: up at eight, drink, stock up Crucial Brew, deal, opium, drink, deal, smoke hash, deal, line of coke, deal, line of coke, Brian, bottle of wine, Sprog, fight, opium, drink, sex with Lesley, drink, drink, drink, drink – pass out. That was it – days into weeks into months until a whole year had vanished.

I could see it was a wasted year. The business was staying the same – its growth had peaked, or maybe it was just that my ambitions were waning. It probably had more to do with the new drug I had started using shortly after I got back from India: heroin.

I was eating opium with Luke, the hanger-on that I'd had to reprimand for trying to steal from my customers.

'Mark – you have a proper habit.'

'What with?' I asked.

'With opium. You need to get yourself some proper stuff to keep you going. That's not going to touch the sides after a while. I can take you to a dealer who sells heroin.'

I'd never wanted to touch heroin. I had tried it once with Ronnie. He only did it once a month and me and Walshy would take the piss out of him about it as he slouched down the wall, to the ground, after the first hit. One day I thought I would try it to see what Ronnie got from it. It had no effect on me; I couldn't understand what all the fuss was about.

'I'll show you how to do it properly, Mark,' Luke promised.

He took me to a South African heroin dealer called Tox. I couldn't get it from any of the dealers I knew. They didn't touch heroin. As soon as we bought it, Luke got the foil and started burning it up. He held it for me to inhale the smoke up a straw.

'Chase the dragon,' he said. I chased the smoke as fast as I could. As soon as I'd got as much smoke down into me as possible I opened my mouth for air. Then I slumped down the wall. I had to sit down. My head, my body, went numb. I could feel tingles on every bit of my skin. I could see exactly what the fuss was about. This was the most magical feeling I had ever had.

I've got to do this all the time.

The problem with doing it all the time was that Lesley was starting to hassle me. We had been together for over a year and she wanted me to think about what I was doing with my life. She wanted me to cut down on the drink and the drugs. She was right – I knew that – my life was going nowhere at this point. My plans to become a drug dealer had been fulfilled. I didn't know what was next. I wanted something

169

to happen, but going a different direction with my life wasn't it.

Sprog and I talked about the traveller days a lot. He had been a proper traveller and had done the convoy for several years. I wanted to recapture that freedom of spirit from the traveller days in '84. I decided to head to Spain for a few weeks with Sprog. We took two friends with us – Alan and Rabid. Spain had two things going for it: a retirement campsite for travellers and my English rose, Sarah, whom I remembered worked in the Cottage Inn, dealing speed.

I thought that a break away with the lads would give me a chance to refresh and think about new plans for the business. I would be back to London in a few weeks with a couple of kilos of hash we could sell. Lesley and I were not as connected by this point, so that I didn't even bother to tell her I was going away. I thought she would be pissed off.

I loved her, but opium wanes at your groin, slowing it bit by bit. It steals your heart and your mind first. Then it takes the capacity to feel anything except numb. Numb was fine with me.

Chapter 14

We drank all the way to the campsite, downing Montea, the local 'special' hooch. We arrived steaming drunk. It wasn't like the traveller campsites that we had visited in the early eighties - full of tepees, caravans, and horse-drawn carts. There were a few of those types of dwelling, but there were mostly houses on this campsite - houses without the luxury of electricity. They were permanent dwellings for English travellers who had 'retired' in their mid-thirties to a permanent camp. These retired travellers just wanted to be amongst their kind, free from politicians or heroin dealers trying to destroy their way of life. They had created their own society. It was a peaceful society. Until we got there. We arrived expecting the campsite of the early eighties – drug tents, open-air music, campfires, random sex and free love. What we found was a calm and serene community in a field. We caused so much chaos with our boisterous noise and drunken antics that we were driven off the site within two days.

We abandoned the idea of rekindling our traveller days and headed for a club called The Cave. The Cave was well known amongst the travellers who still liked to party. The club was underground. It was a grimy, sweaty place, with a big screen overlooking the dance floor. The DJ was shooting tunes against a backdrop of moving images of The Clash. We were drinking and dancing. Every few minutes Sprog was buying bottles of beer.

'I'm fucking going mad,' he said. 'Is there someone taking our beers? I've been buying every few minutes.'

I agreed. Someone was definitely nicking our beers.

'Here. Give me a load of them trips.' I had about five hundred LSD trips on me. I give Sprog fifty of them and he popped a few into the bottles of drink he had just bought. I wasn't shocked that Sprog spiked the drinks. I had seen him do it many times before. A lot of people spiked drinks back then, for no other reason than it was funny to watch people, who didn't know they were tripping, trip out. He left the spiked bottles on the side while we danced. They were gone a few minutes later.

Suddenly Sprog wasn't on the dance floor. I could see him in the corner, where he had left the spiked drinks. He was facing up to three guys. I was drunk and tripping so I didn't know if the three guys were pissed off at having their drinks spiked or if Sprog was on them about taking our drinks. All I could make out across the darkened, sweaty room was Sprog's fists rapidly flaring. His hands were covered with tattoos - one with a big anarchy sign and another with a pentagram. I could always see where Sprog was. I just looked for the big fists and bare knuckles made for fighting.

Sprog went out of the door with them and I followed for backup. When I got outside, the scene made me freeze, unsure of what to do. Sprog was on the floor with the three guys laying kicks into him like crazy men.

I have to do something. I can't just stand here watching Sprog get beaten to death.

I knew I couldn't do much to help – there were too many of them. I tried to pull one of them off and got smacked. I lost it and started kicking and punching back. I pulled a mental face and screamed like a maniac to try to scare them into submission. It was chaos with fists flying, and legs booting. Rabid turned up. I thought he was there to help us, but he had the three guys' leather jackets and was

172

busy stashing them out of sight. Then there was loud shouting.

'STOP. You go, you go.' The landlord was shouting at us. It was then that I noticed the people surrounding us, watching the fight.

We better get out of here.

As me and Sprog were walking away, Rabid appeared, carrying three leather jackets. That's when Alan appeared again too. It was typical of Alan not to turn up until the chaos had passed.

'Fuck them wankers. I've got their jackets,' Rabid said.

We were laughing and slapping each other's backs as if we were all victors. We were oblivious to our cuts and bruises. We were oblivious to the police cars screeching up the road. We were oblivious to anything but our victory until we were shoved against the wall with our arms behind our backs. They put me, Sprog, and Rabid in one car. They put Alan in a separate car. By the time we were in the cars we had more cuts and bruises. This time we felt them. The Spanish police were brutal.

I knew that being caught with drugs on me by the Spanish police would be bad news. I stuffed the LSD down the back of the car seat. I had a Gold MasterCard and Visa in my top pocket that weren't mine. I pulled them out to hide them with the LSD. One of the police officers turned around and barked at me so I put them back in my pocket.

At least I've got rid of the LSD.

I hadn't used the cards in Spain yet. I had stolen them in England.

I could just say I found them.

By the time we arrived at the police station the guards had found Alan's LSD. He hadn't had the foresight to hide it like I had. The police had us all standing in a line. They stood around us saying, 'Oh, LSD, trippy, trippy.' Then they searched Rabid. They found his sheet of LSD too, but it looked like plain cardboard. He hadn't marked them or put any stickers on top of the LSD sheets to define individual trips yet.

Lucky bastard.

They couldn't see the cardboard was LSD so they chucked them in the bin. I started laughing. Rabid told me to fucking shut up, which got him a smack in the head from one of the guards. Any time one of us tried to talk back we got smacked in the head. So we all shut up. They searched Sprog and found nothing.

He must still have the fifty trips. Lucky bastard.

Then they searched me and found the credit cards. By the smile on the guard's faces it didn't look like they believed me when I told them that I had just found them.

Fuck, fuck, fuck.

The guards put us in a large jail cell together and left us there for a week. Nobody told us how long we would be locked up. Our only trips were to the toilet. Sprog had other trips. They hadn't found the rest of the LSD I had given him so he spent the week tripping on those. It was all Sprog's fault. Alan didn't speak to any of us because he thought it was all our fault. Not that he would say anything – to say anything would mean a slap from Sprog. I was scared of Sprog in the cell, too, because he always got into a fight when he was tripping. There was nobody but Alan, Rabid, and me to beat up in the cell. He kept seeing things that we couldn't and laughing manically. He was the only one laughing.

I couldn't drink and I decided not to take any of Sprog's LSD. For the first time in years I was in a situation where I had nothing inside of me to stop the pain. The pain wasn't so bad. I had only been drinking every day for a few years, so it was nothing more than a few days of sicking and sweating. The biggest problem I had without a drink or drug were the people around me. I hadn't been around anyone without a drink or drug inside of me since I was fifteen. My cell mates were sudden strangers. After the sickness, I had constant butterflies in my stomach. Most people talk about having butterflies in their stomach in relation to good things, like being in love. In truth it feels like having caterpillars wriggling about inside you, slowly eating your stomach. To top that feeling, I was paranoid about everything.

174

Don't look at Sprog that way, he might kill you.

Alan really doesn't like me. I can see by the way he looks at me.

Rabid is much better looking than I am. How did I become so ugly and smelly?

I could have tripped with Sprog to get my head back into line, but all the times I had tripped before were mostly bad ones. Having a bad trip in a jail cell with Sprog, who could flip at anything, was something I feared more than my sober head. I did a lot of worrying about the future in that jail cell. I knew this situation was bad and that it was likely I was going to do time. I had heard stories of people who had been arrested abroad and were held without trial for years. I still had hope that it would turn out okay – it always had done before. My biggest concern was the business.

Who was going to look after my customers?

Walshy would be okay for a few weeks in charge, maybe a few months. I wasn't sure about a few years.

All that hard work and it's gone for the price of a fight.

Lesley didn't know where I was. I hadn't told her I was leaving for Spain. I had only expected it to be a few weeks. If I was put in prison in Spain for a long time all she would know is that I had just disappeared. I couldn't remember her address so I had no way of writing to her. Despite our problems in recent months, while sitting in that jail cell, I loved her more than I had ever loved her.

Things are going to be different when I get out of here.

I was going to shape up, knuckle down, and make sure I never got into fights with Sprog again. Things were definitely going to have to be different when I got out of that cell.

The first thing I need to do when I get out of here is get a drink.

* * *

Our interpreter was the only one allowed in court to hear of our fate. We had to wait outside, not knowing if we were going back to the cells or if we were ever going to get out of Spain. The

175

interpreter came out of the court to tell us the verdict.

'Okay, this is the situation. You three,' he pointed at me, Sprog, and Rabid. 'You three can go. Alan, they will release you on bail, but you have to pay five hundred in English pounds.'

Okay. That's great – I'll just sell the bit of jewellery I have on me and that will cover the bail.

The interpreter went back into the court to sort out the release papers and bail money and then came back again.

'Okay, you two can go,' he pointed to Sprog and Rabid.

'And you two go to prison.' He pointed to Alan and me.

Hold on a fucking minute. What just happened?

One minute I was free to go, the next I was going to prison. Before I could protest, I was being led away. Alan told Sprog and Rabid to contact the Embassy and get us a solicitor.

'Just get us out of this place,' he begged.

Sprog wanted some money to do that, any money we had left, but I said no. We were going to need that in prison. Drugs cost money or favours in prison, and I didn't know how long I was going to be there. I wasn't going to be doing any favours for what I needed.

I'm Scottish.

* * *

Malaga prison was a zoo: full of caged animals in dorms as big as a warehouse. Alan and I were in dorm two with about a hundred other criminals. We were sharing a three-tier bunk with Tim. Tim had already been in prison for six months, awaiting sentencing for cheque fraud. His fraud was far bigger than my giro fraud a few years earlier. Tim's fraud went into the millions and spanned Britain, France, Germany, Spain and Italy. He was going to be in that prison for a long time and then extradited to Britain to face trial for more charges.

Tim wasn't what I expected to find greeting us when we arrived at the prison. He was posh, tall, and thin: a weakling in every respect.

176

That didn't matter, though. He had the blind confidence of a toff and the respect of a big time criminal. He also knew enough to induct his new bunkmates on the law of the land.

'There are two groups of people here,' he told us. 'At one end you have the Dons.' He pointed to the right side of our bunk and I looked at the Dons: shaved heads, pumped muscles covered with tattoos and so self-assured they didn't even notice me looking.

'These guys are the godfathers of the prison, the real deal. They are made up of terrorists, gang leaders, drug bosses, and kidnappers. They won't touch you if you just keep to yourself and treat them with respect. Don't suck up to them, but don't disrespect them. They will kill you for it.'

'At the other end you have the Dregs.' He pointed to the left side of the bunk. The Dregs looked like skinny chickens, pecking their heads up and down. They looked across at me in a threatening way. 'These guys are parasites, a complete nuisance - handbag thieves and small time dealers. They will demand your food and anything else you have. Don't give it to them. They will demand that you treat them like godfathers, but they are not and you shouldn't. They will poke and prod until you bow down and do what they want or fight them, and they'll probably kill you by accident. Stay away from them and if they come near you tell them to fuck off. If they mess with you and you don't deserve it then the Dons will sort it out – they don't like any kind of injustice and, when they have to, they'll step in and deliver a verdict.'

I was grateful for Tim's experience. Yet I was still unsure where Alan and I fit into Malaga prison.

'You don't. There are lots of us who just get on with it. We've done our crime and we do the time, even when we're innocent. We respect the Dons, stay away from the Dregs and we get on with it.'

I knew what he meant and I knew he was right. I was definitely not a Don. I rarely won fights, and compared to their scale of dealing, thousands of kilos a time, I was small fry. That didn't mean

I was ready to give up on wanting to be part of the Dons' family. If I couldn't be one of them, at least I could be accepted by them.

Before Tim's advice had the time to sink in, one of the Dregs already wanted to mess with me.

'Give me your fucking shirt,' the Dreg demanded. I was wearing the only clothes I had, and he wanted half of them. 'Give me the shirt.'

I was suddenly surrounded by Dregs watching. They were watching the new kid, watching to see if he could hold his own, whether the new kid would do as he was told. If he took the shirt off my back, anything else he wanted would be a breeze.

I can't give him my shirt.

'Fuck off. I'm not giving you my shirt,' I said.

Whispers and nudgings turned into shouts and shoving.

'Oh, Scottish! Gringo, Gringo,' they chanted.

The Dreg was waiting for me to give him my shirt and I had to fight or surrender. Either way would signal what was to come for the duration of my stay.

I have to fight.

'You're not fucking getting my shirt!' I made the John Wayne eyes and pulled a mental face. The Dreg called me bitch and other things I didn't understand in Spanish. Everybody around us was shouting and chanting.

'Just fucking hit him,' they were saying. I didn't know whether they were saying it to me or the Dreg. I circled him and snarled.

'Don't fucking ask me one more time,' I said as loud and as hard and as mean as I could.

He stared at me.

Stare back. Freak him out.

I stared at him.

It's working. Keep staring at him.

We stared at each other.

He looks freaked. Make the eyes.

I made the eyes.

178

Then he spat on the ground and flounced off.

I've fucking won.

I had won that time, but I knew that it wasn't over. The Dreg spent the next few days sharpening a coat hanger - embedded into a slab of wood, a makeshift murder stick - mimicking a jabbing of the ribs, which meant a straight sharp blade through my stomach, split of the second – *jab, jab* – then I would bleed to death. I couldn't sleep for three nights. I just watched and waited to get stabbed in the stomach. Just as Tim had said, though, when the Dreg realised I wasn't giving him an inch, he gave up threatening and I gave up watching.

Pepe and Raoul were top Dons, and came as a pair. Pepe didn't talk to anybody much. Raoul chatted to me every now and again. Our conversations had the intimacy of male strangers bonding over talk of women and football.

'Hey, Scotland,' he would call me. 'What are the Scotland women like then, eh?'

'Oh, feisty, very feisty,' I would say.

He told jokes and, even though I didn't understand them, I would laugh. If he was laughing, I was laughing. If he was rolling around the floor, I was rolling around the floor. I would do anything to make me one of his gang. Raoul, Pepe, and the rest of the Dons played dominoes and cards at night. They smoked hash and drank hooch. I watched them as they played and I imagined myself doing the same. They could get anything they wanted. The money from their crimes ran into the millions, which was enough money to bribe the guards for extra fruit to make the hooch, women, and cigarettes.

Raoul was doing time for smuggling hash. He hadn't done any of the smuggling himself. That was a runner's job - one of the many runners, gophers, and henchmen that worked for him. He was caught in his house with over a thousand kilos of hash. I was lucky to have sold thirty kilos a week. He had stores of guns and ammunition stacked to the roof. I only had the ammunition I stored for Brian. Raoul and Pepe and the other Dons were in a different

179

league to me. They were in a different league to Brian. I learnt more about the drug business in prison than I ever did with Brian.

In the seventies most of the hash was smuggled in from Lebanon. But in the eighties the hash started coming in from Morocco. Morocco was only twenty-six miles of ocean away from Spain. The hash was then driven to France and Britain. The drugs were smuggled in furniture, in the side panels of cars and lorries, and anything else they could hide it in. If they got the hash from Morocco into Spain, a thousand kilos would net a four hundred thousand pound profit. If they got it into Britain, it would net a two million pound profit.

I need to get into this business.

The problem was that I would need to have a million pounds to start. Most of the Dons had started at the bottom, selling more hash each time and ploughing the profits back into more hash. That sounded like hard work and I didn't want to wait around. In Malaga prison I was surrounded by big time smugglers. In Malaga prison I could make all the contacts I needed to get in at the top straight off, without all the groundwork the Dons had had to do.

All I have to do is make them like me and earn their respect.

I was suddenly in the best place I could be to further my own career and achieve my ambitions. So laughing at Raoul's jokes, whether they were funny or not, was the least I could do. I didn't bother with Pepe. He was unpredictable. His silence masked the rage of a lion. Tim had explained that the Dons were quiet because they already had authority. They didn't need to demand respect from everybody in the dorm like the Dregs. I witnessed with my own eyes what would happen if Pepe were provoked to anger:

There was a Spanish prisoner living a few bunks from me. Pepe passed him like normal, but things were being said in Spanish that I didn't understand. Without warning, Pepe picked the Spanish prisoner from the bed and threw him to the ground. He grabbed a chair and smashed it over his head, over and over again. The man's head was cracked and blood poured from it. Nobody went to help.

Even the guards took their time in coming to his rescue. By the time they did, they could do nothing but drag him away from the dorm. A trail of blood was the only evidence he was ever there.

The dorms we lived in were set around a courtyard overlooked by towers with turrets. We spent most of the day in the courtyard, the sun whipping our backs. The alarms woke us up as soon as the sun was up. It sounded like a nuclear warning siren and we were up and counted and cleaning the toilets before we could feel awake. There were three hours between breakfast and lunch, followed by another count, and then a siesta in the courtyard.

I spent my days pacing the inside perimeter with Tim, listening to his tales of adventure. I spent a lot of time with Roger and Dennis, too. They were Brits doing time for crazy crimes. Roger had been caught at the airport with a British Airways bag full of hash, and Dennis had botched up a kidnapping. Whatever our crime, whatever our story, it was all interesting - all relevant to our common objective: passing the time.

Sometimes we played with a tennis ball against the walls, but that was only when a ball was due over the fence. It was a ball stuffed with drugs. Mostly the guards wouldn't see or care, but sometimes they would make a stand and chase the ball. We would chuck it to each other until it reached its intended recipient: one of the Dons.

I bought my drugs from the Dons. I smoked hash, took occasional benzos, and drank hooch. Not as much as I did before prison, but that was mainly because of money. Mum was sending about twenty-five pounds a week – which was all the prison would let me have legally. It was enough to buy six joints a day, a few strong benzos, and a few drinks a month. My new regime of drugs was topped up with exercise. I was pumping for hours in the courtyard, doing press-ups, lifting makeshift weights, and running on the spot. The fact that I had cut down my drugs to six joints a day and a few benzos meant that I was the healthiest I had ever been.

Not many people back home knew where I was. Lesley had no

idea. I wanted to write to her, but I still couldn't remember her address. I'd never had to remember the address before. Sprog had told Walshy what had happened and he had written to say that the business was in safe hands until I got back. The only other person I wrote to was Mum. I told her that it had been a stitch-up and that I was innocent. She wrote back blaming the drugs and the drink and saying I needed to sort my life out.

Why can't she understand that these things happen to people all the time?

Malaga prison was full of English, Irish, and Scottish guys. I was hardly using anything, so I clearly didn't have a problem with drink or drugs. My problem had been that I was too small fry. The lessons and experiences from prison were making me more determined to follow my ambitions to be big time. As long as Mum sent me money every week I didn't care what she thought.

What does she know?

Alan blamed me for him being in prison. The others weren't with us for him to blame too. He was pissed off that I had brought Sprog and Rabid along, pissed off that I had given Sprog the trips, and pissed off that he had got caught for LSD when I hadn't. Alan knew that he would be doing at least four years with the amount of LSD they had found on him. After a few weeks in prison, already isolated from most of the other inmates, he distanced himself from me. He settled into prison life in his way. He got a hundred grams of hash smuggled in on a conjugal visit from one of his traveller girls. He sold it and used the money for hooch and food. He didn't respect the unspoken rules – the rules that Tim had outlined for us on day one. Pepe and Raoul wanted some of the hash and didn't like being refused by Alan. One day they followed Alan to the toilet, took all his hash, and left him with a black eye. After that, Alan got moved into dorm twelve with all the other Brits. I was pissed off at him after that. He had it easy in dorm twelve. There were no Dregs to bother *him* there.

I knew I had been lucky, getting away with hiding the LSD. The credit cards they found on me hadn't been used, so they couldn't keep me locked up for years. There was a moment shortly after I arrived where I thought that they were trying to catch me on an LSD charge. A new prisoner was put in my dorm and tried to make friends with me.

'What you in here for?' he asked.

'Plastic,' I said. That's what we called credit card fraud.

'What's your friend in for?' he said, pointing at Alan, across the courtyard. I didn't think it was strange that he knew Alan was my friend – or at least used to be my friend.

'LSD,' I said.

He nodded. 'Yeah, I got arrested the other night for drinking,' he said. 'They took me to the station and searched the car. They found a load of LSD. They got me on that too. Wasn't even mine.'

Fuck. Either this guy is really unlucky, or he's in here to get me - trap me with a confession.

'What was the design on your friend's LSD?' he asked. I wasn't telling him. He asked Alan, too. Alan did tell him.

Fucking idiot.

Alan even started drawing the design that was on his LSD for the guy. It was the same design that had been on mine.

'Oh – this was the design on the ones that got me put in here,' the guy said. Then he looked at us suspiciously. He was in prison because of me.

You poor bastard.

There was no way I was going to confess anything. I spent days worrying, but, shortly after, the unlucky guy must have got lucky, or, if he was undercover, been pulled, because he disappeared.

I knew he was probably undercover because all prisoners left the same way. They left by stretcher for the hospital wing or by their own grateful legs for the freedom outside the gates. It always happened at night while we ate dinner. I would be trying to keep the Dregs away from my pudding, and one of the guards would enter.

Silence.

183

The guard would shout someone's name and then 'LIBERATOR,' which we all knew as 'Get your bags, you're going home.' My heart raced at the sight of the guard, then sank at the sound of someone else's name. The rest of the prisoners would explode into cheers, celebrating the freed prisoner as a hero. They clapped, they bashed their trays on the tables and everybody chanted 'LIBERATOR'. My sadness at not being named the liberated one would be overwhelmed with cheers and claps and banging of trays. I would eventually join them. We all shared the joy of the freed one, whether we liked him or not. It would be one of us one day that would be walking out of those doors. Some of the prisoners knew they would never see freedom. They would grow old and die in prison. Others didn't know when they would leave. Yet we all shared the same dream that one day it would be us walking out of that door to the sound of cheers, claps, and banging of trays.

I wanted to go home. I wanted to return to my business and put my new knowledge, my new contacts into action. I couldn't understand why I was still locked up. I had spent five months without any idea of when I was getting out.

I shouldn't fucking be here.

The Consul was visiting, but she didn't seem interested in anything I said. The fact that I was pleading my innocence didn't hold sway with her. Even if it did, she couldn't have done much. After five months in prison, she dropped a bombshell on me. I could have kissed her and then killed her.

'You do know if you pay five hundred pounds you can go?' she said.

'What?'

'It says in your papers – pay the bail and you can leave.' I couldn't believe it.

'I've been here for five fucking months – how long ago could I have bought my way out?'

'Quite a while. I thought you knew.'

184

No, I didn't fucking know.

Mum sent the bail money. I didn't know when I was leaving and I was starting to give up hope. A few weeks later, a guard entered as we ate dinner. My heart raced. He mentioned a name, but I didn't hear it and my heart sank. I could hear the claps, the cheers, and the banging of the trays, but I no longer had the heart to join them. Then I started to get pats on the back. I looked up and saw the clapping prisoners looking at me.

It's me. I'm free.

I cried. It was the first time I had cried since being in prison, and the only time it was okay for me to cry. I would miss Roger and Tim and Dennis and Raoul. I didn't see Alan before I left. He wasn't in my dorm, so wouldn't have known I had left until the next day. He had to spend another four years in prison being pissed off at me. I didn't think about that. I was free.

I got given my passport back, and had no plans to return for any trial or hearing. As soon as I got more money, I was going back home. I slept on a park bench that night - thousands of pounds to my name in England, but not a penny in Spain. I may have been on a park bench, but it was warm under the stars. I was free - free from murderers and terrorists and petty criminals. I thought about what I would do with my freedom. How I would turn my business into an empire over the next few years. I thought about what I had learnt in prison and I felt the excitement of the opportunity those lessons had given me.

I slept like a baby.

Chapter 15

Walshy had fucked the business. What had started as a two-week trip had turned into a six-month absence. I had left him in charge and he had managed to lose almost all of my customers. The loss of my customers meant the loss of my business. The loss of my business felt like the death of who I thought I was. My identity came from the three houses, my customers, and drugs. I never saw me for who I had become – a junkie/alcoholic with three squats. I was going to use the business as a foundation for building a bigger empire where I could become a drug king, a Don. Because of Walshy I was now just an unemployed ex con.

If only I hadn't left the business with Walshy.

Walshy, despite his moaning, had become my oldest – my best friend. We had been best friends since we were fourteen and I loved him – despite all the moaning he did. But he was a speed junkie and spiralling fast. He had left Ronnie to handle the customers and Ronnie had decided to take them for himself. Walshy had been too wired on speed or too scared of Ronnie to stop it all from happening. Ronnie had left Walshy with just enough to fund *his* habit. It wasn't enough to fund both Walshy and me.

I was pissed off at Walshy for letting this happen. I had let him in on the action, and this was how I got paid. I should have cast him out right then. I couldn't do it. It was difficult to be mad at Walshy for long. I knew he couldn't have done much. He had never been a leader. That had always been my job. Besides, he was so sensitive I thought that he might kill himself if I stayed mad at him forever.

This is all Ronnie's fault.

I wanted to kill Ronnie for stealing my customers. I couldn't understand why he had done this to me. He had helped me get down to London. We had been friends back in Glasgow. I'd looked up to him – until my business had increased. It was inevitable I was going to end up doing better than Ronnie once we moved to London. While he was swanning off with Walshy, travelling on a bus, I was working the contacts and building the business from scratch. Now he was doing better than I had ever done, selling hundreds of kilos a week. I tried to have it out with him for stealing my customers. He just didn't see it that way. He hadn't thought I would be out of prison any time soon and said that it hadn't been fair to expect him to wait around.

Let's see you handle Brian. He owns you now.

None of it mattered – what I thought or what Ronnie thought. The fact was that Ronnie was in the game and I was on the sidelines, sniffing around for scraps. Although I wanted to kill him for it, Ronnie had always been a better fighter and I would probably end up losing. I was also in no state to do anything about it. Since returning to London I was using more drugs than I had ever used before. I was too loaded to do anything about Ronnie.

I had left the prison gates planning to continue with the healthy regime – exercise and no more than a few joints a day. I didn't have the money to return straight to London and didn't want to wait a week for a money transfer from Mum. I spent four days helping a busker in Spain. I was passing around his hat, which gave me enough for the return home as well as some drugs and drink. Busking on the streets was hard work. I needed the drink and drugs to get through the day, to break through the boredom. By the time I

187

got to London, I was back to the same routine, waking up downing beer straight away. The exercise was gone and, with it, all of my ambitions. My plans to write to people in prison, develop new links with international gang leaders, and invest in serious quantities of drugs from across the borders were gone. I needed alcohol and drugs more than ever.

I was starting out again. Walshy and I moved in with Dave, the guy whose house we had used as a safe place to keep our drugs. I still sold drugs, but the customer base was much smaller. I was still able to smuggle LSD back from Amsterdam. I visited Lesley, but she no longer lived there. Even if I had seen her she may not have understood that I hadn't been able to write. I just didn't have the energy to bother. I struggled to do much else than scramble together cash for drugs. I didn't miss Lesley. I missed being a big time dealer. I missed being popular.

It was my twenty-fifth birthday and I decided to hold a party. I thought that a party would help me to reclaim some popularity and some credibility. I invited all the serious dealers and players – Brian and his henchmen, Brian's dealers, my old crew. I didn't have much to celebrate, but I thought that if they could all see that I was still in the game - still someone they could trust - then maybe I could get it all back. A party was the best place to do that. Considering the different characters I had invited, I had to make sure there were separate rooms to keep some of them apart. Especially as Tox was going to be there. Tox had enemies amongst my friends.

I had been scoring heroin from Tox for several years. Just before I had gone to Spain I'd taken Sprog with me to score. Tox's house was like a doctor's surgery from the seventies - a flat upstairs, office and waiting room downstairs. We were waiting for longer than I had ever waited for a doctor. I knew why we were waiting. I had waited for Tox many times before. He kept us waiting because he was hitting up combinations of coke and heroin in his upstairs flat. He was more of a junkie than the people he was dealing to, which was why he had no more veins left and had to inject in his groin. I only wanted an eighth, but there was no 'fast drug' service. We had to wait whether we were buying two hundred or twenty pounds' worth. It infuriated me.

You don't keep me waiting. I'm not one of your fucking small time customers. But I was and he did.

Sprog was different. He was still a small time customer like me, but he didn't tolerate waiting. He didn't need a reason to fight either. It was getting late and we were waiting with Posh Bill - an actor with a raging heroin habit. Sprog was pacing up and down and Bill was keeping me entertained with stories of his acting adventures. Sprog was still pacing when Bill spoke to him, like a father to a child.

'Why don't you just sit down here, Sprog? Tox will be here when he can. I'm sure he has our best interests at heart, young chap.'

'Why don't you SHUT THE FUCK UP, YOU CUNT,' Sprog spat at Bill. Bill tumbled back into his seat, and Sprog continued pacing.

'There's no need to shout. I'm just trying to—'

No, no, no, Bill. Don't carry on.

Sprog punched Bill in the face and went back to pacing. I could see Bill was going in again, so I whispered to him.

'Listen, mate - best not saying anything else.'

Tox appeared in the midst of this at the door of the waiting lounge. He stood there, his eyes still rolling from the needle he had just stuck into his groin. His belt was still unbuckled.

'What's going on here?' Tox asked. 'Always the fucking small time ones, isn't it? Always the ones who buy small bits at a time that cause the fucking noise—'

Before Tox could finish, Sprog grabbed him by the neck and started slapping him round the head.

'Who the FUCK do you think you're talking to, cunt?' Sprog said to Tox. Slap after slap. Tox couldn't do anything but take it.

'Go up those fucking stairs and get that fucking heroin now,' Sprog said.

Tox ran up the stairs faster than I had seen anybody run.

I don't think I'm going to need to be giving Tox any money tonight.

Bill had introduced a game changer. The game was now turning over Tox. He brought down the heroin, shaped in cling film like bullets, and Sprog took four of them - about ten grams.

'Now fucking go back upstairs,' he told Tox and waited as he scuttled up the stairs again like a scared mouse. As we were leaving I could hear Bill starting to speak.

'But that's a bit—' but, before Sprog killed Bill, I said: 'No, Bill, not now – just don't say anything.'

Tox felt he had a reason to hate Sprog and Sprog felt he had a reason to hate Tox. The only reason I had invited Tox to my party was because he would bring a load of heroin. The party was full of dealers, most of them working for Brian in some way. As a result, none of them had any heroin *except* for Tox. Brian hated Tox, but Brian hated anybody that did smack. I made sure there was a smack room and a coke room. I didn't want Brian to start shooting people who were shooting up. I filled the house with alcohol and cut up seven grams of coke - enough to keep me wired and still share. I gave out free pipes and coke and alcohol and anything else I had – if I couldn't be a big time dealer, I could at least give a big time party.

There was smoke flowing through the house. The smoke had a smell of chemicals and burnt plastic. It was the smell of heroin and crack. It was mixed in with the smell of sweet hash. There were bottles of whiskey and wine and beers. I had coke lined up in front of me and was leaning down to hoover up my tenth line of the night. I was already drunk and high. The party was going well.

I could hear Walshy downstairs, shouting at Tox.

'Come on, Tox, let me try some heroin.'

Walshy doesn't do heroin. What is he playing at?

'No, man. I don't share,' Tox said. Tox had a high tolerance to heroin, he had been using for so long. The filters he used to take out the impurities and dirt from the heroin, before injecting himself in the groin, were lethal. An hour later Walshy decided to try to get a hit from Tox's filters.

'Fuck,' Tox was shouting from downstairs. 'Walshy's fucking OD'd.'

We ran down the stairs. Walshy was going blue. We dragged him outside doing the only thing we knew to do in this situation: slap him round the face, shake him, and dump him in the bath to cool down. I was out of it on tequila and coke and a bit pissed off for being pulled away from the fun I was having to clean up Walshy. As soon as he looked alive, I went back upstairs to drink.

He just needs to sleep it off.

I had left some of the guys to check on Walshy. For some reason there was a voice in my head that told me to go back.

Maybe go back and check on Walshy.

I was still passing out from all the tequila as the voice continued to echo in my head.

Go back. Don't let Walshy sleep. Keep him awake. Go back.

I knew I should go back. I could hear the voice, but I couldn't move, like in a dream where you need to run but can't or need to speak but nobody can hear you. I was drifting away and the voice was getting quieter, until it was nothing. I was out.

Shit. It's morning. Where is everybody?

I woke up with a raging head and a throat that felt like it had been sliced with razor blades. I was surrounded by empty bottles and everywhere I looked there was the carnage of the night before. Mirrors, bottles, cans, and some needles. The place was trashed.

That was a great fucking party.

I went downstairs to the bedroom Walshy was staying in. He was in the bed asleep. His Alsatian, Nessie, was lying next to him, keeping guard.

I knew he would be okay.

The dog looked sad. He didn't bark and didn't move. Walshy was lying on his back, was covered fully with the blanket. I pulled the blanket back. His face was blue and his mouth was caked in crusty vomit.

191

'Walshy, wake up.'

I shook him.

'Walshy, wake up, for fuck sake.'

I shook him again.

'WALSHY.'

I kept shaking him but he was a piece of meat in my arms.

'Fucking wake up, Walshy, just wake up, man, you silly cunt, you silly, silly cunt, wake up.'

Walshy wasn't waking up. He was dead.

Fuck. What do I do? Walshy's dead and I don't know what to fucking do.

I stood still, frozen in momentary hell where I wanted to die, too. I didn't want to be left to deal with this.

You fucking cunt, Walshy, how could you be so stupid?

I ran out of the room and ran up the stairs as fast as I could. I was running to get something inside of me. I made a crack pipe. I smoked it as quickly as I could but I was still shaking. The pipe did nothing. Walshy was still downstairs, still dead. The pipe didn't change that.

Got to handle this, Mark.

I had a pile of coke powder left on the mirror under my bed. I took one, two, three, four lines of coke. Then another crack pipe. I was raping the house for alcohol – anything would do, anything that would anaesthetise me. I found a bottle of wine, a full bottle. I opened it, glugged it – the red liquid shot through my body, like new blood, numbing me inch by inch.

I can't feel anything now.

I went back downstairs and sat with Walshy. He was lying on the bed, lifeless, blue in the face. Dead. My thoughts flipped from what I had to do next to handle the situation to rage at Walshy for dying like this.

Okay, Mark, what are you going to do?

How could you do this, Walshy?

How could you be so fucking inconsiderate?

192

I didn't know what to do. The house was full of drugs. There was half a kilo of hash and two thousand of Walshy's Es in the room. I had five hundred black microdots and a couple of ounces of speed upstairs.

Think, Mark, think. What the fuck are you going to do?

I couldn't call the police. If I called the police, I would get busted for all these drugs. I'd be in prison and Walshy would still be dead. I sat watching him for hours, sat with him dead, crusty vomit at the sides of his mouth, looking like a drowned rat. He had drowned in his own vomit.

You fucking idiot, Walshy.

The dog still hadn't moved. I was too scared to touch the dog. His mum had bought it for Walshy to keep him safe.

At least the dog will be something to console her.

Do something, Mark. You can't just sit here.

I phoned Tox.

It's his filters that Walshy smoked. It's all Tox's fault.

'Tox, Walshy's fucking dead. You better get your arse here now. Walshy's dead and you're responsible.'

'What do you mean I'm—'

'No, Tox, don't deny it. He's fucking dead and it's your fault. You gave him the filters. He's dead from your filters.'

'I'm coming round – don't do anything.'

'Bring some heroin. Bring me some fucking heroin, Tox.'

He owed me for this. He needed to bring me something, something to keep me under, keep any feelings away. He arrived and gave me a gram.

'No charge, mate,' he said like he was doing me some favour.

'No charge? You fucking wanker,' I said. Then he started to cry, but all I could see were crocodile tears.

He doesn't give a fuck about Walshy. He doesn't give a fuck about anybody but himself and his fucking heroin.

'Stop those fucking crocodile tears or I'm gonna fucking slap

193

you,' I said. He looked at me and he could see I was serious, so just stood there doing nothing. I started to pace.

'Listen, we need to work out - I need to work out what to do.' We talked for a bit, but I couldn't hear anything he said; none of it was of any use. He wanted to get out of the door quickly. The truth was I didn't want him there either. I had just called him for the heroin and to let him know it was his fault. I knew he wouldn't do anything, I knew he couldn't help. He was a useless junkie.

A useless junkie who got my best friend killed.

Tox left. Then Brendan was at the door. I hadn't expected Brendan to come round. He was an old pal of Walshy and was coming round to score some hash. I gave him the hash.

'Brendan, Walshy's...'

How do you tell a man his friend is lying dead in the next room?

I didn't know. I started to cry.

'Walshy's dead. He OD'd man, he's dead. I just found him.' Now my tears were crocodile. I couldn't feel a thing.

Brendan didn't cry. He just stood there. We were interrupted by the door before he could say anything. It was Leo. He was an old dealer friend that I trusted. I must have called him earlier that day to stash the drugs away from the police. I couldn't remember. Everything was turning into one long dream sequence. None of it felt like it was real. I paid Leo in hash and sent him off to stash the rest of the drugs. It had been six hours since I had found Walshy dead, and Dave was back.

It's his house. He can deal with it.

'What the fuck happened here?' Dave asked as he came through the door.

'Look, Dave, I have to go. Walshy – he's in the other room. He's dead.'

He stumbled out his words: 'Dead? What? Why? How is he dead?'

'He overdosed, man. Just phone the police and tell them you came back and found him like this. I have to get out of here.'

194

Dave wasn't happy, but realised he had no choice. I was leaving whether he wanted me to or not. He could see I was in no state to do anything. I fled the scene. I fled so fast that I left my driving licence. The police found it and started asking questions about me. Dave answered them.

'Does this man live here?'

'Yes, he lives here sometimes.'

'Does he sell drugs?'

'Yes, he deals a bit of hash.'

'Did he give the guy that died the drugs that killed him?'

'No, he didn't give Walshy the drugs that killed him.'

I wanted to beat Dave up for telling the police about me. He was lucky that I had bigger worries. I had Brian to deal with. I told him about Walshy before anybody else did. Brian loved Walshy like a brother. I couldn't bear to see him face to face to tell him.

'Who fucking gave him the heroin? Who the fuck was the dirty smackhead?' he screamed down the phone.

I couldn't tell him.

'It's that fucking Tox – that cunt Tox. Right? I'm gonna kneecap him, he's a dead man.'

I told him it wasn't Tox, that Walshy just didn't do it properly. He didn't believe me. The fact that Brian wanted Tox on a plate and I was standing in between them, saving Tox's arse, helped me get what I wanted, what I needed.

'I'm under pressure here, Tox,' I said. 'These fucking Irish nutters - they want your name. I'm protecting you. I think you owe me some gear, no charge.'

There were no depths I wouldn't sink to. I needed a fix and if I had to use my best friend's death, I would. I spent the next week using it, hiding out in squats, keeping out of sight. In the end everybody was looking for me – I had heard the police were asking people about me. I spoke to a lawyer who arranged for me to surrender to the police for a no comment interview. If I said nothing, they could do nothing. They had no evidence against me, no evidence that I was involved with Walshy's death. They didn't even have evidence that I was dealing hash except Dave's word. He wouldn't testify. I wouldn't let him.

Murder Squad were in front of me, shouting in my face this time. They shouted closer to my face and a bit louder with every 'No comment' I gave.

'Do you know we've had your friend on a fucking slab of concrete?'

No comment.

'How do you think his family feel, looking at their dead son on a slab of concrete?'

No comment.

'We know you didn't give him the drugs; tell us who gave him the drugs.'

No comment.

'Tell us who killed your friend.'

No comment.

'Why are you protecting this guy? What does he have on you?'

No fucking comment.

Now I had the Murder Squad and Brian asking me to give up Tox for Walshy's death. Sometimes I wanted to, but it was my free pass for heroin. Deep down I knew it wasn't Tox's fault. I had heard Walshy trying to get some heroin from Tox that night.

No, it isn't his fault. It's mine. I'm the junkie that let my best friend die.

The police let me go, and I went to Tox to demand more heroin. I wanted to be as numb as possible. This time I wanted two hundred pounds' worth and I wanted it immediately. But Tox had got wise after Sprog turned him over, so he didn't keep it in the house. That's what he said, but I knew it was a lie. He would make out that he had to go out to get it just so he wouldn't get turned over with it upstairs. I waited with Metal Mickey, who had HIV, Cathy, a big black prostitute from Kilburn, and a couple of other characters whom I didn't recognise. I looked around the room in the same way

196

I had done a hundred times before. The faces of the people sitting there with me were different. I had always seen myself as a different kind of junkie before. I was better than them. Yet, sitting there with them waiting for Tox to return, I could see my future in those faces. I felt like they looked. I wondered how long it would be before I looked how they looked too.

It was about three hours later that Tox finally returned.

'It's only me,' he shouted through the letter box at us, which I thought was strange. I answered the door. Then, in a flash, the room was full of police and I was up against the wall being searched. Tox had got pulled over for a broken brake light and the police had found heroin on him. They decided to search the house and found larger quantities upstairs in his room - enough to put him away for seven years. They found none on me, though. They asked my name. I gave them a fake one. They let us go and I never saw Tox again.

For the first time in my life, I knew how Dad must have felt when he drove the van that killed his friend. I wasn't driving a van, but I was at the steering wheel: Walshy died at my party.

The police are right. I did this.

Walshy was lying on that slab while I was too gutless to show up. So gutless, so scared for my own freedom that I made his parents wait to bury their son. I knew it was my fault.

If only I had stopped Walshy using the filters.

I knew how lethal those filters were. If I hadn't been coked out of my head I could have done something.

If only I hadn't fallen asleep while he was downstairs dying.

I could have got him help. I could have saved him.

Fuck, my head needed shutting up.

I was on the bus with Prostitute Cathy. I needed to score as I had got nothing from my trip to Tox's. Cathy knew where we could get heroin – but it was the other side of London. She was the kind of prostitute that fulfilled the seediest of men's desires - desires they dared not tell anyone. It felt right that that was whom I was with. Someone who knew the dark secrets of man, me holding the darkest of them all - that I was the junkie who killed my best friend. I had been reduced to using the dealing contacts of a street prostitute. I scored, smoked, silenced my head and set my mind to what was next.

There was no next. I was out of options. People blamed me for Walshy's death. Brian wouldn't deal with me any more. He held me responsible for a debt that Walshy had to him − I had paid him some, but was hiding from him for the rest. I had lost what friends I had in London and I couldn't deal. Not like I did before. I had lost all my avenues of supply. Word had spread amongst the travellers and throughout the campsites. The word was that I was to blame. I couldn't show my face on a campsite again and no traveller would have anything to do with me. Walshy's parents hated me. His brothers said that if I showed my face I would be the next one in a coffin. I didn't even know how long I could fund my own heroin habit. The habit was raging while my savings haemorrhaged.

The only place I could think to go - where I knew people that didn't know what had happened or didn't care - was India. India held some hope of freedom and rehabilitation. It would be freedom from London and rehabilitation with time away. It would give people time to forget, if not forgive. It would give me time to regroup and plan what I was going to do next.

Before I made my plans to head to India, I went to Gordon's to get back the only thing I had of Walshy. It was a dancing Sheba statue he had got me in Glastonbury. I didn't want to leave London without it. When I got there, though, Gordon had given it to Ronnie who had said I didn't deserve it. Not after killing Walshy. Gordon didn't disagree.

'What the fuck, Gordon? Who do you think you are talking to me like that?' I said.

'Well, you know, you were there - you could have done something.'

There's no way I'm taking this from Gordon.

'Where's your fucking hash, Gordon?'

198

'What hash? I don't have any.' That was a lie. I knew Gordon had hash because he was dealing. Not very well, not very much, but he was dealing and definitely had hash in the house. I slapped him round the face.

'Go and get me your fucking hash.' I slapped him again. 'Listen, Gordon, I'm not fucking messing around, I know you're selling hash, I know you've got it here. Don't make me beat you. Where's your fucking hash?'

He could see that I was serious - he could see that one more denial would release the rage I felt. One more denial and everything I wanted to do to myself - every fucking punch and kick I wanted to lay into my face, my rabid body – I would lay on Gordon. He could see in my eyes I wanted to kill. He just didn't know I wanted to kill myself.

'Okay, okay, it's in the letter box.'

I went to the letterbox, pulled the flap above the post box open, and found six or seven ounces.

Not much, but enough.

'Right,' I turned back to Gordon. 'Have you got any money?' Gordon played at denial again. 'Yes you fucking have, Gordon. Fucking go get your money and hand it over.'

He handed over sixty pounds. I knew it was all he had, because he was such a crap dealer. Just at that moment, Gordon's friend came chiming down the stairs.

'Hey, you can't do that,' he said. I slapped him round the head.

'Don't fucking tell me I can't. I can do what I want. You're lucky, Gordon, I'm not taking you down to the cash machine, making you withdraw all your fucking money.'

I left Gordon, never to return again. I spent the next month in hiding while I actually got around to getting to India. I smoked heroin and drank from the moment I woke up to passing out at night, mostly sitting on park benches, feeling miserable about myself. It was a self-pity party for one and I was doing half a gram of heroin a day and drinking eight cans of Special Brew. It was enough to make the party bearable. But only just.

The only person that was talking to me was Mum, but I couldn't bear to talk to her. If she could have just told me I was a rotten bastard of a son - if she could say she hated me for this - it would have been easier. She blamed herself – though that maybe if she had done something different with me as a child this wouldn't have happened. I knew that wasn't true. I think she did, too - she just couldn't allow herself to blame anybody else. If it wasn't her fault, it meant that I was a low-life piece of scum who had been passing out on drink and heroin while my friend choked on his own vomit.

Maybe Mum is right - maybe the drugs are the problem.

If I hadn't been on drugs that night - if I hadn't been drunk - I would have checked on Walshy. I would have got him to a hospital. The party might not have even happened.

Maybe I do need help.

But I still had money. I had about twenty grand I had saved from the drug business. With twenty grand in the bank, it gave me a few more options and *help* dropped to the bottom of the list. India was at the top.

I can live like a king on that money in India.

Chapter 16

It didn't take me long to learn how to live as a local in Delhi. At first, all I had was the knowledge from my previous trips to India. The scams I had learnt on those trips helped me make some money for a while. I partnered with some locals who knew how to scam better than I did. I needed those partnerships to navigate the black market. Anything I stole, I sold through those channels. I bought traveller's cheques from tourists – who could then claim on the insurance – then sold them on the black market. I used stolen credit cards and chequebooks to buy luxury items in the Western shops and sold them on the black market. It was enough money to get me the alcohol and drugs I needed. For the other living costs, I got Mum to send me over money from my savings.

I lived cheaply on a campsite opposite the slums of Delhi. The rows and rows of shacks and sheds that made up the homes of the poorest families in India were also where I bought my heroin. On the way through the slum, to my dealer's tin shed, the locals would smother me with pleas of desperation and offers of cheap goods and services. I only wanted one thing and I wanted it cheap. There was no cheaper place to score than a slum in India.

I waited in the dealer's home with his wife and children sitting watching me. I was sitting in a slum, yet, as I waited for the dealer to return with my heroin, I felt a greater desperation than this family in a tin hut. I felt sicker than the slums looked and looked sicker than they smelt.

I knew that using heroin was my problem. I thought that if I could kick that then things would be different for me. I was desperate for things to be different. I tried to detox when I first got to India. I met a man at the campsite who helped tourists detox in huts on the mountains. I went with him, but was so sick after the first day that I told him I wasn't that desperate. I was back scoring in the slum within hours. A few weeks later, I was set to detox again – except this time I was more motivated than I had been before.

My motivation to try to clean up from the heroin a second time came from Pippa. I met Pippa while I was selling hash to tourists in the markets. There was something about Pippa that jump-started me back to life for a while. She was slim, attractive, and younger than I was. She bought some hash and, within a few hours, we were back at her hotel room, smoking heroin together. She wasn't happy with her habit either. Her boyfriend was stuck in Thailand. That gave me an opportunity to try to seduce her.

If I get cleaned up with Pippa, then maybe we can start a life together.

She was keen to go through a detox with me. Before I could plan the inevitable partnership, which would follow a successful detox, her boyfriend got in from Thailand and decided he wanted to get clean too. By this point I thought I might as well go through with it, even with the boyfriend tagging along.

She will see the comparison and dump him in no time.

We got a little hut near Manali to stay in for a few days while we detoxed from the gear. We smoked up the last of it and set ourselves up in the same room, in our sleeping bags, ready to cluck. We were in the middle of the mountains with nobody around. It was the perfect place to be reborn and shed off the old skin for the new, emerging for a clean life.

With a little hash and a drink once in a while.

Heroin was my only problem. I never planned on giving up *everything*. I thought that if I could kick heroin and get by on smoking a little hash and drinking a little whiskey, then my life would be different. With the amount of heroin I had been smoking, I was shit sick within hours of stopping. I desperately needed something inside of me if I was going to see this through.

I just need a little whiskey.

If I could get a little whiskey it would take the edge off. Pippa and her boyfriend looked like they were as sick as I was.

'You guys need some whiskey? Just to take the edge off,' I said. They nodded. I took the rucksack.

I'll need the rucksack to bring the whiskey back.

I told them I would be back in no time and left the hut in search of whiskey. As soon as I got out of sight my head went straight to thoughts of opium.

Pippa isn't that great.

If I could have got some heroin in the middle of the mountains, I would have. I knew it was easier to get opium; that would do. I just needed to get something inside me. It needed to be quick. I asked at the village where I could get some opium and they pointed to the bus stop. I needed to head to Garca, which was miles away, up and down bumpy roads. It was two hours on a bus of sicking and sweating.

As I left the bus in Garca, I was sick again. It was dark and there was nobody in the village. The few shops they had were closed. It was just houses and huts. I needed something quick before I started to see spiders, snakes, and dead Grandma. I started to bang on doors. One after the other the doors opened, strangers staring back at me. Nobody spoke English. No tourist ever came there.

'Opium,' I said.

Nothing.

'Heroin,' I said.

Nothing.

I held my arm up and mimed injecting myself.

Nothing.

Eventually, after many doors, a little old lady pointed at the house opposite. I was like a man dying of thirst being offered water. I cried and ran to it.

I've been saved.

I knocked on the door. It didn't open. Somebody shouted the other side of the door.

'No speak English.'

I fell to my knees and cried: 'I need opium.'

The door opened. 'Ah, yes, yes, yes, come in.'

I gave him three hundred rupees. I didn't know how much I would get for that. I didn't care. I still had to wait until the morning when he could trek into the mountains to get me the opium. I was stuck in the basement of his house, the sound of cows mooing keeping me awake. It didn't matter because I couldn't sleep. I was occupied with sicking and sweating and shaking and holding my stomach to relieve the pain. Sanjay left as the sun came up. I knew he would return, because I was left with his wife. I kept being sick, but it was bearable now that I knew medication was on the way.

I waited five hours for the medication to arrive. He gave me about sixty grams of opium, rolled into balls. I went from being on my deathbed to kneeling at the feet of Santa.

This is fucking Christmas.

With the speed of a child unwrapping his first present on Christmas morning I unwrapped the first lump and ate it whole. Then, with the speed of Dad after his first bottle of whiskey, even before Christmas dinner was on the table, I slumped back into the chair.

Thank you, Santa.

I swallowed another lump. If one was too many, the second was lethal, but I was so sick by the time the medication arrived that my head was telling me to take as much as I could. I was like a camel storing water. Suddenly, my head and body were in different places.

204

My head was in the clouds, lying back, protected by them. The body was still in the hole. I could see, I could talk, I could hear. I just couldn't feel a thing.

Exactly how I like it.

I had an endless supply of opium, free board in the middle of the Himalayas, and home-cooked food. Sanjay and his wife offered me their basement for a while longer. I didn't want to go anywhere. I spent the next week, stuck in that hole, coming up only for water and food. I sank into a deep depression. I could feel Walshy in the basement with me. My head was bitching me about what had happened to Walshy. The voice sounded like Walshy.

Why did you leave me?

I took some more opium to block it out. It reappeared, louder.

You shouldn't have left me to die, Mark. You could have saved me.

No matter how much opium I took, I couldn't stop the voice in my head. I couldn't get the feeling of Walshy out of the room. All the time, I kept asking myself why I was here, why I was in India.

I could go home.

Then I remembered.

I can't go home. There's nothing left for me there.

I remembered and swallowed more opium.

I spent days going through that cycle of voices. Eventually I had a visitor to the basement. It was Sanjay's younger cousin. Word had spread that a Scottish guy was in the basement. He wanted me to teach him boxing. After a while, he turned it into a wrestling match - until I could feel his hard-on poking at me. He was fifteen. I'm sure he had never had sex. It wasn't his fault. He was just a horny dog that needed a leg. But not mine.

'No, no, no,' I said. 'I'm Scottish.'

I was grateful, though. He gave me the impetus I needed to get my stuff and leave Sanjay's basement. If it wasn't for Sanjay's fifteen-year-old cousin's hard-on, I might have just stayed in the hole forever, eating opium and wallowing in self-pity.

205

* * *

After my failed attempt at kicking the heroin habit I decided to get a break from Delhi. I thought that visiting Thailand would give me a new landscape and a new outlook. It was a different country that turned out to have the same landscape, the same people, and the same routines. It had become the same everywhere I went. The minute I got to a new place, I had to sniff out a dealer and secure a constant, reliable, and quality supply of drugs. If it couldn't be a reliable or quality supply, I would settle for constant – at least in the short term. I had found a supply of heroin from the cleaners in my hotel. It wasn't the best stuff, but it was cheap.

I also found other people to use the heroin with. That was the other thing about getting to a new place. It never took long to find people like me – people who used drugs. We would see each other in the corridor and within minutes of striking up a conversation we would be sharing a puff or a line. Sometimes you could spot another junkie by their eyes. Other times you would know by their walk. The junkie walk had two paces – going to score and just scored. Going to score was a manic, nervous, and agitated walk - with a look of purpose. Just scored was a manic, nervous, and agitated walk – with a look of fulfilment.

Once we met, it never mattered about our backgrounds or where we were heading. We all had different names and faces, but after a while all the faces looked the same to me. That was what happened to me in Thailand. I scored from the cleaners in my hotel and then met two new faces to smoke with on the roof.

'Mark,' the face said, 'why do you waste this stuff by smoking? This isn't meant for smoking. It's meant for injecting.'

'No, no, don't – this is bad,' the face's girlfriend said. She said it while preparing her own needle.

'Seriously, Mark, you're wasting it, wasting good stuff – you need to inject. Would you like me to show you?'

His girlfriend frowned on us while she sunk the needle she had prepared moments earlier into her arm. I had never wanted to inject. I had been injected by someone else a few times with coke and speed, but never with heroin. I had seen what it had done to Tox. He couldn't find any veins and had had to inject into his groin. I never wanted to get to that stage. I always got enough of a hit smoking it.

I might as well give it a go.

'Will you - will you show me?' I said like an eager child.

'Yes, I will show you how to inject, Mark.'

'Ah, that's great. Let's do it. Let's inject,' I raved.

I had good veins and the needle delivered the liquid to my blood easy. Then...

Fuck.

This feeling was different to the high from chasing the dragon. The heroin was pulsing through my veins like blood. My eyelids fluttered and my eyeballs danced. I felt completely at peace.

I'm never doing anything else but this.

Why would I? This beat any amount of opium, speed, coke, hash, alcohol – *everything*. This was it for me. With the prick of a needle, my habit became a horrid, torrid, nasty affair with the Grim Reaper. It was an affair that I couldn't stop. It was an affair that I didn't want to stop.

Injecting heroin took my habit to a new level. I was now using more than I had ever used before. It was also more expensive. From that moment on, every scam, every bit of money I could get my hands on, I needed for heroin. I met a scammer who offered me a job as a switch passenger on an immigration racket. The scam worked like this: a guy and I would get on the plane to England via Delhi. I would be seated with the ticket for England and the other would be seated with the ticket to Delhi. He would check my luggage in and I would check his in so we could swap tickets on the plane. I would get off at Delhi and the other guy would continue with my ticket, luggage already destined for England. When he got there all he had to do was claim refugee status. The questions from immigration would take weeks to filter back to the airline. It was a massive loophole before anybody cared about closing it. The scam made me five hundred pounds per trip.

I used the trip to Delhi to renew my visa and visit Manala for some hash. I planned to sell the hash to tourists back in Thailand, which would make the trip even more profitable. I swallowed fifty grams of heroin to take to Delhi, which was more dangerous than the ticket scam. If I had been caught smuggling drugs out of Thailand I would have got the death penalty. I didn't get caught for the ticket scam or the heroin. I swapped tickets on the plane and got off in Delhi as the other guy continued to England.

Smuggling the hash back to Thailand was more complicated than getting the heroin into Delhi. Hash was bulkier. Somebody told me it was better to case it in beeswax. By the time I got off the return flight to Thailand I had three hundred grams of beeswax-covered hash I needed to shit out, but I needed a hit of heroin more. I delayed my trip to the chemist for laxatives, hit up, and slumped out.

Day one, gone. It can wait another day.

The next day I got some laxatives and took them. Before they could take effect I was starting to get sick and needed another hit.

Day two, gone. Must get it out tomorrow.

It was day three and I had one hundred and fifty lumps of beeswax hash in my stomach, but still no peek of shit. I had done my maths. Each coating of cling film had twenty-four hours for the stomach acids to break it down. I had three layers of cling film, so I needed to shit soon. I went to the toilet to take matters into my own hands. I sat and pushed.

Nothing, not a peek.

My arse was straining and I was going to pass out or burst a vein. I had heard other people went that way.

I don't want to die on a fucking toilet trying to take a shit. I'm not Elvis.

I saw a hose, stuck it up my arse, and put the tap on full. It was spurting up me like a hot poker. Before I could protest 'I'm Scottish'

I started to feel the shit breaking through.

POP.

One block of beeswax hash.

POP, POP, POP, and they were all out, on the floor, floating in shit. I was relieved the hash was out, but wasn't happy to be wading in shit.

What has my life come to? I'm on the floor, kneeling in my own shit.

That's when I saw a watch. It was a brand new, flashy Timex watch somebody had left by the sink.

I can sell that.

Then, in a moment, the realisation of the pain and shame of the experience vanished with the promise of cash for a watch.

Chapter 17

I had been staying at Mama's Guest House for three months. Mama's Guest House was really just a flop house in Delhi. Most of her guests were junkies. They stole from the big hotels to feed their habit. Mama was Sheik, round, and my mother's age. Her age was the only resemblance to my own 'mama'. She provided a place for junkies free from the police, whom she probably paid off. The Nigerians controlled the heroin supply, but Mama had a licence to deal to her guests. Every morning she laid the parcel at my door, like a nurse dispensing medication for the day. It had been two years since I'd seen London.

I still sold hash to tourists when I had it. That was how I met Debbie. She was just like Lesley. Debbie also had a criminal dad – she had spent her childhood trying to get away from him. Except Debbie was a raging heroin addict, so her Dad had got rid of her. She had her own room at Mama's, but we spent most of our time together. All we did was drink and inject. We fucked as much as I managed to get it up. I didn't get it up enough for Debbie - within weeks she was cheating on me with a Nigerian dealer. We spent several months going through an endless cycle of breaking up and getting back together.

It didn't matter whether Debbie was there or not. My routine for the day wouldn't change. It just varied with degrees of excitement and adventure. My day always had the same objective: to find money for the next hit. I woke up craving a drink, usually before the sun rose. After the drink I needed a hit - half a gram. The hit was as important as the first coffee to normal people. I had to dig around trying to find a vein. They were hiding like a tortoise under its shell, seeking protection. It took a while. Then it was straight to the shop to buy half a bottle of rum or whiskey, whatever I felt like, as long as it was high proof. I drank my breakfast and came alive. Before this, I was a dead man walking. I was sick, my stomach was in pain, and I was paralysed with fear for the day. I was scared of dying. Yet, some days, it was all I wished for. Then, halfway through breakfast, I'd start to sing for the new day.

I'm back, ready for action.

I had to juice up on more rum, more whiskey throughout the day, refuelling to stay on top, to stay alive. I had to juice up to keep the sickness away. After all that it was nearly lunchtime and my thoughts would shift.

How do I get the money for the drugs I need today?

Mostly it was an easy job. The easiest was selling hash to gullible tourists. When I didn't have hash to sell, I worked quick scams that made enough cash for the next hit. I bought passports from tourists and sold them on the black market. I had already sold mine and claimed a new one from the Embassy five times; I found it easy to convince others to do the same.

Another quick scam was selling counterfeit currency on the black market. Tourists could get twenty-five rupees to the dollar from the banks and thirty on the black market. Most tourists didn't have a clue, though, the exchange rate was changing that fast. I could get thirty to the dollar from most of the black market traders. I approached on a rickshaw with the skin colour of trust - nobody expects to be scammed by a white Scottish guy in India - and I made the trade. I sold the black market traders a fake hundred dollar bill, which I had bought for twenty dollars, for six hundred rupees. Before they could see that it was fake the rickshaw would be off. It was a good scam, easy work, and high returns. The only reason I stopped doing it was because some wise guy almost caught up with the rickshaw. Despite the adrenalin rush, I couldn't risk being caught by a crowd of people and stoned to death.

I had become a full-time scammer to buy the drugs I needed every day. My life was now a never-ending game. Every day was the same thing. It was different scams, different people, but the same reason I got up: stick a needle in my arm and down litres of hard liquor. The same reason I went out to scam: keep the sickness away and remain numb. The same reason I went to sleep: because I blacked out from the drink.

Most days I would be lucky to end the day breaking even. I was out of cash and running out of life.

* * *

I was coming back from my breakfast run one day with a bottle of whiskey and orange juice. The hotel was surrounded by police. There were uniformed and plain-clothed officers, guns at the belt of their jeans. Against the wall the cheap labour were sawing into pipes.

Where have I seen those pipes before?

There was a Nigerian guy sitting amongst a crowd of police. He was tied up like a dog with chains across his legs to his arms. Watching over everybody was Mama.

I've seen that guy before.

The Nigerian guy had been living in the room opposite me. He seemed like a nice guy - at least nicer than the rest of Mama's residents. He was a religious man and was in India to buy doorbells and ship them back to Nigeria.

What do the police want with a doorbell smuggler?

212

It was then that I smelt it. My nose was attuned to the smell of heroin better than a sniffer dog. The smell was coming from the pipes being welded open and the smell was burning the insides of my stomach. One of the pipes snapped, and the police pulled out two long sausages stuffed with heroin.

That's why Mama's watching over this.

The Nigerian guy was a heroin smuggler and Mama had shopped him to the police. I realised why Mama had had a sudden bout of social responsibility when they opened a suitcase full of cash, tens of thousands. I had never seen so much cash. That didn't interest me. I had never seen that much heroin. I wanted to swim in it. I was trying to get close to the smoke from the welding open of the pipes. I hadn't had my hit yet and thought the smoke would give me something.

It's wasted on the police.

When the police left and the crowd of onlookers had dispersed, I was like a pigeon at bread following the trail of crumbs left on the floor. I wasn't the only one who got lucky that day. There was no mention of the money in the press reports, but a big smile was left on the faces of Mama and the police. That was how it worked in my world now. Everybody was scamming, even Mama.

It gave a different light to the sweet old mother, always smiling, always looking out for me. When she delivered the heroin parcels in the morning it was with the kindness of someone who had just baked me cookies. Her husband was a Sheikh and, to the outsider, this was a traditional religious family. But Mama was also the lady that let the Nigerian build his smuggling up to a point where she could shop him and take all the profit: she was the best scammer of all. The only reason she never shopped us was because our business had no profit. After seeing Mama do that to the Nigerian smuggler, I started to question what I was doing. It was crazy. Mama's was an open prison without the guards.

Then it hit me. I was in my room with Debbie and two junkies:

a Kashmiri guy and his girlfriend. I had a needle stuck in my arm. The Kashmiri guy was smoking and his girlfriend was hitting up in the corner. I could hear him telling her that she had to go back out on the street and sell herself so they could get another hit. Debbie was sitting in front of me with her neck stuck out.

'Do me in the neck, Mark, do me first,' she begged. The neck was the only place she could inject. I was still in the process of hitting up and wondering what the fuck I was doing.

Why am I here?

Debbie put a tape on and I could hear the words of the Chris Rea song, 'Road to Hell'.

'This is the road to Hell.'

Those words spoke to me. They said what I couldn't. I was in a trashy sewer of a room, Debbie with her neck stuck out begging for a hit, a prostitute and her pimp boyfriend in the corner.

This is the road to Hell.

For the first time I was outside myself watching from above. I didn't recognise me. I wasn't a big time dealer. I wasn't a popular guy. I wasn't even a half decent petty criminal. I was a fucking junkie. A junkie with a needle in my arm and no friends who were any different.

What am I doing here?

I wasn't travelling, I wasn't smuggling. I had no reason to be in India. I had a full-blown disease that needed medication every minute of every day and what was cheap before was now becoming impossible even at these prices.

This isn't the road to Hell. This is Hell. What the fuck am I going to do?

The worst of it was I couldn't muster the energy to care. I accepted this as my life. I could see no way out. Nobody was coming to save me. It no longer mattered if it was India or London. I just had to do it until I died, which, by the look of me, wouldn't be long.

I cried for the me I watched below and then returned to stick a needle in Debbie's neck.

214

* * *

The next day I started to make plans to go back to London. I couldn't renew my visa again and I would be deported if I didn't go. I didn't have the energy to run and hustle in order to stay. Besides, Debbie had left me again and I didn't try to stop her. I wrote to the only person I could for flight money and Mum sent me enough to get a ticket, with enough left over to buy three hundred grams of heroin. The lies I told my mum to get the money didn't matter. I couldn't afford to score at London's prices. I wrapped it into twenty gram balls. I lay on my back, pulled my legs up, and popped them up my arse, cycling my legs like riding a bike. I could have just swallowed it, but I didn't want to risk them leaking in my stomach. I'd be dead in minutes. I didn't consider that the same would happen in my arse. There was no voice of concern, no doubt. Not even a protest of 'I'm Scottish'. I just needed to get my drugs back at whatever cost. Even at the cost of my life.

I had missed the plane because I had nodded out at the gate. I was left with three hundred grams of heroin stuck up my arse. It was already killing me. I'd been bouncing up and down on the rickshaw and the balls were juggling inside me. Now I was bouncing again and I was ready to blow; I arrived back with no minute to spare and POP, POP, POP one after the other and I was on the floor too relieved to care that I was wading in shit again. If that had happened at check-in or on the plane, I would be in an Indian prison for a long time. I stuffed them in again, this time leaving more of a gap in between each one and cycling like crazy until the balls were neatly in, like a mother's packed suitcase.

I was going home. To what, I had no idea.

215

Chapter 18

I had returned to London in a worse physical and financial state than I had left India – which was something I hadn't thought possible. I had flown via Amsterdam, because it was easier to smuggle my heroin back the final leg of the trip by ferry. I thought I would offload some heroin in Amsterdam to raise some money. I didn't want much. The guy whom I tried to sell some heroin to ended up trying to rob me. I received a blow to the head and had nearly lost ten grams of gear. A month after being back in London I didn't have any heroin left. With nowhere to live I squatted in a battered, abandoned van at the back of Stockwell station.

As I clucked at the back of Stockwell station, trying to muster the energy to get a methadone script, my mind wandered to other plans.

Maybe I could go to South America. I could go to the source – get some coke. Yeah, I'll become a big time coke dealer. It's this heroin that is the problem. As soon as I get my methadone, I'll kick this habit and start working on plans to South America. That would fix all these problems.

Debbie was the one to provide me with a plan of what to do next. She had returned to London a few weeks after I did and we had started seeing each other again. She was getting heroin sent from India from the Nigerian boyfriend and paying for it by sending Levi's and trainers. Except she didn't send him anything and he tipped off the police. Her barrister told her she was going down for a long time. He suggested she may like to go to Israel for a while. She was Jewish so Israel made sense to her. She wanted me to go with her and start a new life. Israel seemed a better place to start a new life than clucking in the back of a battered, abandoned van.

The new life lasted a few days. She left me for someone else a few weeks after we arrived in Tel Aviv. I was in Israel, alone, with no money. I didn't know the scams in Tel Aviv, so I couldn't steal to buy drugs. The only thing I could do was steal alcohol to stop me seeing snakes, spiders and dead Grandma. It was a hooch-type drink called Wodka - which tasted nothing like vodka - that they left on display outside the shops. I only got caught stealing it once and they slapped me around the head. They couldn't cause me any more pain than I was already in.

The cuts on my legs and arms had got infected because I wasn't washing. I started to squat in a derelict building, which made it worse. I had been asleep on a park bench, out of it on the Wodka, when somebody called an ambulance. I woke up in a Tel Aviv hospital on a drip, and I spotted a guy sitting in the corridor. He had heroin.

We can see and smell each other, junkies.

Hitting up in the toilet of a Tel Aviv hospital with a complete stranger was the best moment of my new life in Israel.

Debbie got in touch with me and wanted me to meet her new man. She thought we could be friends.

Fuck that.

I wasn't going to meet her new man. She was upset, but what did she expect? That we'd all sit around on the beach, holding hands and singing songs?

In fact, fuck this. What am I doing here?

I got some money from Mum and flew back to London where I could at least scam enough money for drink and drugs. Debbie never returned to London. Her new boyfriend didn't know she was a junkie. She'd fallen against a toilet door hitting up and he couldn't get to her.

It didn't matter. She was dead.

Chapter 19

To passers-by, the park benches were a place of quiet reflection. To us, the benches were home. We didn't notice the people walking past us. We didn't notice the world. We had our own world, our own laws, full of our own kind of people. Everybody else, the ones living normal lives with houses and jobs, we're just like extras on a soap. They didn't make an appearance unless we needed something from them. They didn't notice us either, even when we begged them for change.

On the street we traded on our stories, our adventures. All we had was our past, because we were currently in a waiting room for death. All we could do was look back, with the rose-tinted spectacles of an old man in a nursing home, our past being the best years of our life. I was now occupying the benches in Brixton and telling my stories of Tel Aviv, my junkie friends admiring my tan. It had been a nightmare, but I didn't tell them that.

The next four years just passed. I didn't travel anywhere except to the chemist to pick up my methadone script, the butchers to steal some meat, and the dealers to get some heroin. I downed the methadone, sold the meat, bought some cans, and hit up. There were no more lovers or friends, just people I spent time with to mask the loneliness. People I could drink or use drugs with.

'Nobody is leaving this place until I get my twenty back,' I told them. I had been sitting for hours, hitting up, and drinking. Somebody had stolen my last twenty. I had worked hard for that twenty, begging people to give me cash to fill up my petrol can for my non-existent car. One of the junkies I had been using with had stolen it.

'I'm going to fucking search you all,' I said. 'I'll strip search you if I have to, right?'

They said nothing. I searched their jackets, I searched their pockets. I could see two of them were squirming.

'Okay, you two, take your fucking trousers down.' I had them standing naked, but still no twenty. The only other one was Karen, but she was a girl and I couldn't strip search girls. Even at this level, I had boundaries. She passed my bench a few days later and gave me a can.

'What's this for?' I asked. Nobody bought me a drink for nothing, not without extensive negotiation and bartering.

'I'm buying you drink because it was me that took your money,' she said.

I fell in love with her right then. She was smelly, she was a drunk, she was a junkie. But so was I. We hung out and kissed when it was needed. Usually when I wanted some of her drink or she wanted some of mine. I couldn't have sex much any more. I had brewer's droop. Karen had emotional droop when it came to sex. Her ex-husband was killed in a fire with one of her children. She had been using drugs and drinking for years. Her three kids were mostly in care. She was in so much pain that it was impossible to be conscious without sedation. Being with me was just a bit of comfort, a bit of company. We were like two patients in a hospital bed, dying, side by side.

We protected each other, but I always ended up worse off for it. Irish Gary called Karen a pikey, which was harsh because Karen was a traveller, not a pikey. Call her a junkie, an alki but not a pikey.

I threatened to beat him up, but was glad when he walked off because I was too drunk to fight. Hours later, I was walking to the Tube and Gary was walking towards me. I saw the knife in his hand. I didn't know what had happened until I was visible to everyone around me. I looked down and my shirt was growing blood, seeping through the fabric.

He fucking stabbed me.

'Somebody phone an ambulance,' I heard.

I was lying on the floor, dying.

This is it. I'm finally dying. About time.

I didn't die. I was patched up and put out on the street to die slowly from something they couldn't patch up. We were all dying together. Some of us knew, some of us didn't, and none of us cared. All we cared about was getting the next drink, the next fix. I was sleeping between benches and junkie squats. Wherever I lay my bottle was home.

Sometimes a familiar face would pass me on the street. Somebody I knew from the old days. Selling used underground train tickets to scrape some money together for a hit, I would see them and try to hide so they didn't see me. My old life would flash before me. Big time dealer to beggar selling used tickets.

Where did it all go wrong? Where did all my plans and dreams go?

It was at these times that I felt the shame and I'd think about killing myself. It didn't seem like there was anything to live for any more. I'd only ever had my plans and ambitions in life. I'd always had tomorrow in my sights – tomorrow was going to be better, because I would be a better fighter, a better dealer, more popular, more loved. Tomorrow didn't seem possible any more. Suicide was possible.

Passing cars, I would think: I could jump in front of that. It would be over in a split second.

Crossing bridges I would think: *I could jump and splat and still not feel a thing. Who would care?*

Karen would cry for about an hour, hit up, and then forget. Even faster than I had done with Walshy. That was what it was like on the street. Our memories only extended to what was in front of us. When those in front of us were gone, it was like they were never there.

The truth was I didn't have the guts to kill myself, because, when the time came to die, I fought to live.

I was drinking and hitting up with Karen in a junkie friend's council flat. I was jealous of Dean and Sandra. They were like me: the same desperation, same battle for the next drink and fix. Except they had a council flat - a battle base. We were all in the gutter, but some of us had roofs. To make it worse, Dean fancied Karen. I wanted to beat him up, but was too out of it to put action to thoughts. I went to the other room alone and drank myself to sleep.

I woke up coughing and couldn't see a thing. All I could see was smoke and all I could feel was burning.

I'm either dead and in Hell or the place is on fire.

I was feeling my way around the wall and trying to get to the window.

I can't see the window, I can't see anything.

I was feeling my way around, but was cooking and choking. I started banging the walls for help, banging and banging. All I could do was bang. I couldn't shout, no matter how much I tried.

I'm going to fucking die.

I must have been against the door because it opened suddenly and I collapsed through it, black from head to toe, but glad to be breathing. I was only in the hospital until morning and then was off to pick up my methadone script. Dean and Sandra were already there, waiting for me.

'We've got to get a new flat because you've burnt the fucking place down,' Sandra said. 'All the clothes have been burnt. We want some money to get some new clothes.'

Yeah, right. You want some money for drugs.

I asked how much she wanted. If it was a tenner I'd lump it.

'Well, we've worked it out. It will cost about three hundred to

221

replace those clothes. If you pay half it'll be fair.'

'No fucking way. You got those clothes for free from Crisis at Christmas. I was there. Don't be fucking trying to scam me over.'

'Look, if you don't pay up Dean's gonna have to fight you, make you pay up.' Dean was standing next to Sandra trembling.

He's not going to fight me. I'm not paying them for clothes they got for free.

'Fuck off,' I said.

I couldn't blame them for trying to scam me, even though I almost died the night before. We all went to any lengths, lengths and depths I never believed I would have gone to. We had no compassion for each other and even less for ourselves.

I rarely questioned the lengths and depths I went to on the streets. When I did it was a rude interruption from an old friend.

What are you doing? the old friend would ask.

The old friend was the voice of my spirit that had been forced into silent observation long ago. It was the silence of a loving mother forced to watch her son beaten by his father. Sometimes the voices would battle it out, but rarely – the old friend almost always lost.

I was walking down the road in Balham, desperate for a drink. Before I could drink, I needed a hit. Before I could get a hit, I needed some money.

There's a guy over there looking at me.

I could see he was a dirty old man, I could see from the way he was looking at me what he wanted. He wanted a hand job.

Whatever – what's a fucking hand job?

I could get twenty quid from a hand job. It would be over in five minutes and I could get some drink and a fix.

Being Scottish doesn't get me anything.

We went up an alley and he pulled his trousers down. His cock was in my hand. I looked up at him.

Go on, it's just a hand job.

I couldn't do it. I didn't like men. I had been brought up thinking gays were perverts and never knew anybody that taught me different.

222

The only gays I had met were the ones I used to sell drugs to. I was holding the cock and I was looking at his face and the old friend spoke to me.

You can't do this, Mark. You don't want to do this, you know you don't.

The voices are battling:

You need a drink, Mark. You just have to wank him off.

No, Mark, you're not a prostitute. Don't do this.

It was the only time the spirit voice won through.

'I want some money,' I said, dropping the cock. 'I can't do this. I want paying.'

He looked at me in disgust. The disgust he felt for me was nothing to what I felt for myself. He gave me a couple of pounds and walked off. I couldn't even cry.

* * *

It happened again, the battle of the voices. I was tramping around to get a fix with Dean. We started following a man walking in the street to mug him. I had mugged people before on the street and hadn't thought twice about it. Dean jumped to pull the man to the ground and the man screamed. The scream was shrill and loud. It sounded like the scream of a woman from this man. The scream hit me and I couldn't move. It was like all this time my body had been possessed, doing whatever the new occupant wanted, and that scream had brought Mark back to life, the Mark who loved his mother.

I couldn't see the man any more. I could just see my father screaming. This man we were mugging was somebody's father, somebody's son. I felt so much pain in my stomach, so much hurt in my heart. I felt hurt for the man we were mugging, hurt for his children, hurt for his father.

How can I do this to somebody's dad? What's wrong with me?

Dean was going through the man's pockets and, in a moment, the Junkie Mark repossessed my body, and I went through his pockets

223

too. Another two or three pounds and we left the man to cry on the ground while we went and got a fix.

After that day I thought about Mum. I only ever called her to get money. I called her about once a month and she was always good for a hundred pounds. I used to write all the time on my travels to get money, but she would get a story back then - something to justify the need. Now I just gave it straight: *I need money and if you don't I'm going to steal it*. She spent the rest of the time expecting a call from the police to say they had found me dead, overdosed like Walshy or shot and dumped in a bin.

She knew what the cash was for, but nothing about the life. I only told her what I wanted her to know. I wanted her to know it was crap enough to give me some money but not bad enough that she would hate me like I hated myself. She had watched my dad almost die with the drink and now she knew I was doing the same. I didn't want her to watch me too.

Maybe I should call her.

I couldn't call Mum then even if I could scramble together some money for the phone box. I was just half in, half out on my own park bench. I had given up thinking about killing myself or scamming. I didn't know what to do, so I just lay back on the bench, hoping the cold would take me.

'Mark?' I heard the voice, but didn't look. I knew it wasn't meant for me. 'Mark? Is that you?' The voice was over me. I looked up and saw my old street friend Joe.

Joe!

It sounded like Joe, but it didn't look like him. Nobody had seen Joe for a year so I'd guessed he was dead. People did that. They disappeared and died, like a fox sloping off to die out of sight so others don't have to see. But Joe wasn't dead. He looked like a new man and there was something in his eyes. I couldn't quite make out what it was. It was a spark I had long forgotten.

Then I remembered: that was life in his eyes.

'Mark, how much are you getting scripted?' he asked.

'About forty five mills…'

…and the ten cans of Special Brew and as much heroin as I can scam.

I didn't need to add that bit, he had been me a year before. He knew it. He sat down and looked me straight in my eyes.

'Mark. There's nothing you could get that would be enough.' He moved closer. 'Mark,' he spoke as if talking me out of a coma. 'Listen to me. You can give this up. You don't ever have to do this again. You can go into detox or rehab. You can get clean and you can change your life.'

I nodded. But I knew that wasn't possible. People didn't get clean. I'd never met anybody who had got clean. The only detox I had heard of were the Phoenix centres with dark tales of inmates scrubbing floors with toothbrushes, standing on tables with placards around their necks saying 'I'm an idiot'. Just when you're broken, they break you some more to make sure you're fully broke. That's the way they put you back together. I wasn't going to go through that.

But Joe was sitting in front of me clean. He had been clean for twelve months.

A whole year of no drink, no script, no drugs.

For a moment I felt a flicker of hope. Maybe I didn't feel it; I just saw it in someone else who had it.

'You don't have to do this any more,' he said.

Then he was gone, like he was never there. Whether he was or not, those words stayed with me.

I don't have to do this any more.

I just didn't know how to stop.

* * *

I spent the rest of the day trying to muster the courage to jump under a bus when I bumped into David. David had HIV and had to

225

go to the hospital for his diamorphine amps. The diamorphine was like a shot of pure heroin. I went with him to blag a free shot.

I was in the toilet at St Thomas's, hitting up my free shot. Then I was sloping down the wall.

I woke up. I didn't know how long I had been out, but I woke up and I couldn't see anything.

I'm fucking blind.

I was panicking. It was the worst thing that could have happened. This is the last fucking straw.

Then I saw a light from under the door as my eyes adjusted. I could see that I had just fallen asleep. Nobody had checked on me for hours and the lights had been turned off. I wasn't blind, which was worse, as the thought hit me.

I've overdosed. I'm passed out, and I'm fucking dying alone.

Even in a hospital I was dying in the toilet and nobody came to save me. Yet I was still alive.

Why am I still here? Why can't I die? Why can't I stop fucking killing myself?

Tears were shaking down my face.

I just can't do this any more, I can't do it.

I was crying and I was shaking and I was begging. I was on my knees and I was praying.

If there's anything out there, if there's anything fucking out there, please help me. Take me from this miserable fuck of a life or save me. I know I'm a cunt with a cunt fucking life, but please do something. Give me a fucking life. Give me life.

PART THREE

Chapter 20

I sat forward in my chair, expecting praise. My drug counsellor was opposite me, reading through the crumpled sheets of ruled paper, squinting to decipher my bad handwriting. I hadn't had much reason to write since school, except for the letters to Mum begging for money. Tony was used to people's bad handwriting, having been a counsellor in the rehab for years. His face had as many wrinkles as the detective had when I was seventeen. Except Tony's wrinkles represented hard years spent grafting on the street. Each one represented the names of the people that he had helped out of the gutter. It was the same gutter that he and I had been in. Tony looked up at me:

'What's this?' he asked.

'It's my Step One. It's mad crazy, isn't it?' I said. Step One was what we had to write in our first month of rehab. The rehab facility I was in was a Twelve Step-based recovery programme. I didn't understand what the Steps were then. Step One was supposed to be about all the things I had done during my using. I had done a lot of exciting things, and I couldn't wait to share it with everybody in group therapy. Tony didn't look as impressed as I had thought he would have been.

'It's like a brochure for going on holiday to India, Mark,' he said.

'What do you mean? You asked me to write about my life. I travelled to India a lot.'

'If I wanted a guide to failing at smuggling, this would be perfect. But Step One is supposed to be the start of your recovery from drug and alcohol addiction. This is supposed to help you see what that chaos led to. Where are you powerless? This makes the life you had sound attractive.'

I wanted to hit him. If it was anybody else I would have. But Tony was just like me. He was Scottish and from a hard family from my home town. He would have hit me back. He had also used drugs for most of his life. Tony was me. The difference was that Tony had been clean for eight and a half years. That's the only reason I listened to him – even when I didn't know what he was talking about.

'What am I supposed to write, then?' I asked.

'Where were you powerless? Like the time you failed to smuggle hash back from India and your friend Rossie got caught. How were you powerless then?'

I didn't like the way he used the word 'failed'. We had almost succeeded in smuggling the hash back. It was my choice to smuggle drugs back from India – and it was Rossie's choice to come with me. I didn't say any of this, but Tony had an annoying habit of knowing what I was thinking. He continued talking, just as if I had said it.

'You didn't choose to go and smuggle. You *had* to. There was something inside of you driving you to it. The same thing that was driving Rossie to come with you.'

I still didn't know what he was talking about. He could see that by my confused eyebrows.

'What do you want me to do, then?'

'I want you to think about all the times using drugs or getting drugs got you or others around you into trouble. I want you to write about all the times you tried to stop but couldn't. I want you to write about the chaos of this life – and how it felt. This has to be solid foundations – you aren't going to stay clean for long with this.'

I thought I had written the truth. I didn't want to do it again.

But Tony had said I wasn't going to stay clean for long with what I had written. I wanted to stay clean.

'Okay,' I said. 'I'll do it.'

* * *

I had gone from my knees, begging for salvation or death, to standing outside the hospital, wondering if three weeks in detox and then six months in rehab were really necessary. I would have done anything to stop taking drugs. Yet, waiting outside the hospital, mustering up the courage to walk in, I wondered if I could really stop drinking and using drugs forever. I didn't have to worry about that yet. The first ten days would be staged withdrawal. I would be given Librium to safely withdraw from the alcohol. The methadone was for heroin withdrawal. They would wean me off the methadone over ten days. I could handle that. I just didn't know if I would be able to handle nothing in my body after the ten days.

Stopping drinking and using drugs completely was the only thing I hadn't tried. I'd been kicked out of a detox before. I'd tried to get into this one in order to prevent a prison sentence. But I'd never actually *planned* on detoxing and staying clean. After the withdrawal from methadone, it would be three weeks in the detox before going to rehab. I didn't think I could manage an hour, let alone three weeks. I had drunk lager and popped Valium all the way to the detox. I was still drinking my last can as I got into the hospital grounds. I wanted to walk out the minute I went through the door, but I still had Joe's voice in my head:

You can do this, Mark. You never have to use drugs again.

I don't remember much about the first ten days. I took my medication, drank my methadone, and kept my head down. I had been drinking so much for so long that stopping drinking without the medication could be fatal. The methadone script was different to what I had been getting from the chemist because it was a 'blind withdrawal'. That meant that I didn't know the quantity of the dose.

I knew when the methadone dose was zero, though, because I was shit sick. I couldn't move from my bed; it was the first day where I was actually clean – not a drop of drink or any kind of drug in my body. I was shivering cold one minute and sweating hot the next. I didn't think I would get through it. I never slept that night. I didn't sleep much for a long time in detox. As I shuffled to morning group, I had one thought:

I've got through one day. Maybe I can get two.

There were a dozen other people like me sitting in morning group. Some of them looked as bad as I did. Others looked like they had some colour back in their face and life back in their step. I looked at those people and saw hope.

If they can do it, I can do it.

At the end of group, we had to say how clean we were. Somebody said 'twenty days' and everybody clapped and cheered. It went down like that – eighteen days, seventeen days, and sixteen days, until it got to me. I dreaded saying it:

'One day.'

I whispered so they would just miss me out completely and not feel like they needed to clap to save my embarrassment. They heard me. They clapped. It was the loudest clap of the morning, with some wolf whistles thrown in. I felt a bolt of energy to my system.

These guys are cheering for me.

It didn't take the desire to use drugs away, but it did give me hope that I could get another day.

I wanted to drink and take drugs the second day even more than I had the first. I was craving badly. I was still sick, still sweating.

If I just don't move. Stay in this spot right here and don't move.

When I made it to day three, the sicking and the stomach cramps started to get better. The cravings were still there. The cravings were talking to me.

231

You can't do this. You've tried it before. You're going to pick up again, so why put yourself through this pain?

Before detox, people who endorsed that voice surrounded me. The voice would say *drink* and there was always somebody nearby who had a can. The voice would say *rob somebody for some drug money* and there was somebody in front of me that looked ready to rob. The difference in detox was that I was surrounded by other people battling that voice. They were shitting and sicking. Some of them had a few days more than I did, others had almost three weeks and were preparing to leave or go on to rehab. At night, I would see the guys who were one day ahead of me and think *if they go one more day, I can go one more day*. In the morning they were still fighting, so I did the same. The voice telling me to use – that I couldn't do it, that I wouldn't do it - didn't go away. I just looked to other people for something else to listen to.

After a few days I started to emerge from my room. I was trying to do things that I hadn't done before. I was making cups of tea and going to the get the newspaper from the shop. Everywhere I went, the voice in my head was bitching me. I had never even done the simplest of things without the benefit of hard liquor and drugs.

I can't make tea. What am I playing at house for? Who do I think I am? I'm a street rat. That's where I belong.

It wasn't a counsellor who helped me see that I wasn't a street rat. It was another patient in the detox. John had already been in the detox for three days by the time I arrived. He had been a counsellor in a rehab facility for many years and had been clean for longer. Then he slipped up and was back where he started. He was a stocky guy from the East End – a proper cockney. He had a big smile. I never asked how old he was. He had grey hair and wrinkles and I looked up to him like a father.

We spent most of our time chatting about our adventures on the streets. John loved listening to mine and I loved listening to his. He was called Five Hundred Mills on the street on account of his

232

second name, Mills, and that he could handle five hundred mills of methadone. Except, with John's stories, there always seemed to be a message at the end of them. Despite John being as messed up as I was, he had some experience of how to get better. He wanted me to get better.

'You need something to believe in other than yourself, Mark. You needed a higher power – it doesn't have to be God. It just can't be you.'

I was starting to think that my mum was my higher power. She had always had faith in me, even when I didn't deserve it from her. She had never abandoned me. Mum was my cheerleader. She called me at the end of every day in detox.

'How are you doing, son?' she would say.

'I'm doing shit, Mum.' I would say.

'Keep on going – you can get through this, Mark. I'm proud of you.'

'I love you, son.'

'I love you, Mum.'

She always told me she loved me. She visited me after I had got through my first week without the methadone. I went to make her a cup of tea – mostly to show off that I was making cups of tea - while she sat with John. When I came back, I could tell that they had been talking about me. The room was hushed. John made his excuses and left.

'What's going on, Mum?'

'John was telling me about rehab. He said your social worker said that you might not get funding for it.'

I needed funding from the local council for rehab. Detox was just the start of recovery from addiction. John said that once I got the drink and the chemicals out of my system I had to learn how to live. The way I knew how to live, he said, wasn't going to keep me clean for long. There was a funding crisis, and my social worker had already warned me that I might not get funding for rehab. My head had been planning to start using drugs again if that happened.

I would have had a good reason. I could blame the detox for putting me back out on the street. Now Mum knew about the funding, she was looking at me as if she knew all about my plans.

'Mark – you need to get funding. If you don't, John says we have to appeal. He doesn't think you should go back to your old friends.' I was angry at John for telling Mum my business. I was angry at Mum for ruining my plans.

'Mum, I'm not going to go back to all that. I told you – I'm here to stay.'

I still wasn't sure if that was true. I was just planning on waiting until a decision came through on the funding. Then I would decide. I knew that John was right. My old friends were still out there, and they were dangerous for me. Just as Mum would call every night, so would Karen.

'Mark,' she would drone, 'I'm not using now.' I knew she was lying. She was as drunk and doped up as she ever was. 'I need you to come and get me.'

'I can't. I have to stay here – they won't let me out.' I lied. I could go to the shops. I went to the shops every day and stole things. I stole tennis rackets, goggles, and headbands from the sports shop. I hid them in the bushes around the detox. I wasn't sure why I stole them – maybe for the buzz, maybe to sell them later if I needed cash for drugs. I knew that if I went to see Karen, I would be one step closer to buying the drugs. And if I was one step closer to buying the drugs, then I would be one step closer to using the drugs, too.

'But you need to come get me, Mark,' she begged. 'I got arrested today, and they're saying they might section me. They're going to lock me up, Mark. I need your help.'

Now she was lying. There would have been some truth in it – no doubt she would have been stopped on the street by the police. But, just as I had done for years, she always added a bit extra on to the truth to get what she wanted. For two years on the street I had helped Karen. Even on a lie, I still wanted to help her. I told her I would think about it.

It was John that talked me out of it.

'What do you have to offer Karen, Mark?' he asked.

'I can help her,' I said.

'Mark, you can't help yourself. What can you give to her? What you're saying is you're going to put yourself at risk to change her life when you can't change it. If you go out of that door you will not stay clean.'

That was becoming a mantra for John. Everything I wanted to do, he used the 'you will not stay clean' line. It was as if everything I thought I should do was the wrong thing to do. I listened to John because he had been through it before. He was going through detox again, but he still had the experience of being clean and working in a rehab. I didn't trust the staff in the detox. For a long time I thought they were on a commission – getting paid more for every one of us they kept clean. I couldn't imagine why they would do the job for basic pay. Everybody was on a scam in my world. I trusted John because he was just like me. I didn't go to see Karen that night.

The detox had a routine. It was a similar routine to the one I had experienced in Malaga prison. We were woken up in the morning at eight, completed our cleaning duties, and ate breakfast. We didn't pace the courtyard all day. Instead, we had a heavy timetable of group sessions – group therapy, group meetings, and group activities. Some of the meetings were taken by people who didn't work in the detox. These people were addicts like me – except they had been clean for a long time. Some of them were clean for only a few years, but that still seemed a lifetime away for me. These were Twelve Step meetings.

The Twelve Steps were designed by people like me who couldn't stop drinking and taking drugs. *'The Steps are a process of awakening,'* I was told. I didn't know what that meant, so I asked what an awakening was. One of the addicts who took the meeting in the detox explained it as accepting that I couldn't control my drinking or using, and that my life was in chaos when I did what I wanted to do.

'Trust God, clean house, and help others,' they said.

235

I had prayed to a God in that toilet when I thought I had gone blind. I didn't believe in Him, though. John had said that it didn't matter what I trusted – as long as it wasn't me and my obsessive ideas. Mostly, I trusted what he thought I should do. Cleaning house was doing my best to make amends for any harm I had caused. The bit I really couldn't understand was helping others. I was in no state to help anybody. John said I didn't need to worry about all that yet.

'That's why there are Twelve Steps and in numerical order,' he said. 'You do the other steps first. By the time you get to Step Twelve, you are free to help others.'

I liked going to the Twelve Step meetings in the detox. I got hope from seeing people who were a few years clean. I liked hearing their stories. They called them 'war stories' because they'd been through battle – sometimes with other people, sometimes with authority – but always with themselves and drugs. We had to attend a few meetings a week outside of the facility as well. Most of the guys pretended they had gone to the meeting, but didn't actually go. I wanted to get to as many meetings as possible. The main reason I went to the Twelve Step meetings, however, was because of girls.

It turned out that the meeting was not the best place to talk to girls – I was too scared. The first meeting I went to outside the detox was strange. They looked too happy to be clean. They kept laughing. Some of them were laughing manically. I thought they must be on hash. They passed a cup round the room for people to put their change in – they said it was for tea, rent, and literature, but I thought that was a cover story. I thought they were collecting the money to buy some hash at the end of the meeting. Why else would a bunch of addicts get together and be so happy about it?

There wasn't any hash at the end of the meeting. They put away the chairs, cleaned up the room, and washed up the cups. They hugged each other and went for coffee. It looked like the most boring way for people to live. But I kept going because I wanted to get out of the detox. The more I went to the meetings, the more I heard from people who sounded like me.

They didn't look like me. They were clean, well dressed, and physically healthy. They didn't feel like me. They smiled, they hugged each other, and they pretended they liked me. I knew they were like me, though, because they talked about how they were scared of everything. They talked about the way they felt safe, confident, and full of life when they drank and used drugs – then scared, shy, and suicidal without it. Their *stories* were different from mine. But their *feelings* were the same as mine. Their *thoughts* were the same as mine. They had loved drink and drugs the same way I had.

As I attended more meetings, I heard more of what they were saying. At first it was just bits and pieces I was hearing – mostly about the amount of drugs they took and the crazy things they did. Over time, my ears were getting unclogged and my head less clouded, and I could hear more. I started to think that if these guys could stay clean – and these guys were crazier than I was – then I could definitely stay clean.

I had almost made it to three weeks clean. It seemed like a lifetime just a month ago. Now I knew that I could do it - the only thing that was plaguing my mind was the question of whether I wanted to continue to do it. I was starting to look better physically. I was getting colour back, and I was getting some fat on to my skinny frame. I had arrived at detox on my knees and completely beaten. In just a few weeks I was looking in the mirror admiring how good-looking I was. I looked good enough to go to a party and meet some women. The problem was that the only parties I had ever been to had drink, drugs, and women. It was in that order – I couldn't get to the women without the first two. When John suggested we go to the party run by the people who took the Twelve Step meetings, I couldn't see how I would enjoy myself without being drunk or high.

As I expected, the party was different from any that I had attended in my life. There was no alcohol, no drugs – just a hundred addicts, like me, pretending they were having fun. I didn't even try to pretend. I knew that we were in a tatty church hall in the back end of Brixton. I watched them all dancing as if they were high. They looked like idiots; there was no way I was going to dance with them. There were attractive women dancing, too, but I didn't have the confidence to talk to them any more. I sat and watched everybody pretend to have fun. John was doing the same as I was. Then somebody entered the room that seemed to wake him up.

'That's Eric Clapton over there,' he said, pointing at the old man with the beard. I couldn't believe Eric Clapton – music legend that he was – what would he be doing in a tatty church hall in Brixton? 'Yeah, it is. It's Eric Clapton,' John confirmed.

I wanted to go over and ask for Eric's autograph. John was pushing me to do it. He didn't have the courage to go up and ask. Neither did I. I had held my own with hard gangsters – but that was with the benefit of hard liquor and drugs. Now I was back to the fifteen-year-old boy trying to muster up the courage to go over and ask Big Tits Dawn out on a date.

'What do you have to lose, Mark?' John said. I knew I had to do this or I would never be able to do anything without drugs.

If I can talk to Eric Clapton clean, I can talk to anybody clean.

I went over to Eric, my heart racing. I asked for his autograph - *for my friend*. He asked me how I was getting on and seemed like he genuinely cared about the answer. Then he wrote his autograph for me, too. As I skipped back to John, I was pumping like I had popped speed. I watched the band playing on stage. My head was in the clouds. Then something happened that amazed me. Eric got up at the side of the stage, picked up a guitar, and played along. The music legend wasn't a music legend in that moment. He was an addict, standing at the side, supporting the band. John was always talking about humility – I understood what he meant, but this was the first time that I had seen it.

I looked around the room and it was as if I had a new pair of glasses. The people that were dancing around me were the same people as before – except they looked genuinely happy. They were laughing with each other. There were some people flirting. Others were dancing badly and didn't care. They were having fun. They looked free – free to be who they were and still have fun.

That night I went back to the detox with the hope that living life without alcohol and drugs didn't have to be boring. If all those people in the hall could dance and have fun without anything inside them, then I could do it too. If Eric could do it, I could do it. The next day my social worker told me that I had got funding for rehab. John was happy. Mum was happy. I was happy. Yet, even after the experience at the dance the night before, I still had a lingering voice telling me that one last use-up might be a good idea.

The rehab was in Bournemouth. It was a good idea to move out of London so I could be away from my old playgrounds and play friends. I had to say goodbye to Karen before I left London. I got a day pass, which included a night stopover. It wasn't a good idea. If I had told somebody I was going to see her, they would have told me it wasn't a good idea. I had been clean for four weeks and was sure I could handle it. I agreed to meet her in a pub just around the corner from the hospital. When I saw her approaching me, I was shocked. She had changed from a month before. She looked like a haggard old woman. She had shrunk, too. I never liked small women, and Karen was the smallest woman I had ever seen.

'Hello, Mark,' she croaked.

'Karen,' I said, trying not to sound shocked to see her in that state. 'It's so good to see you.'

I kissed her on the cheek, missing her lips. She smelt of stale sweat and beer. She smiled up at me. I noticed her yellow stained teeth.

'Well, get the brandies in,' she said.

'No, I can get you a brandy, but I'm sober. I don't drink now, you know that.'

'Can you handle me drinking?' she asked. I hadn't thought about that. I didn't know if I could handle it. But I wanted to show her that I could. Karen had encouraged me to go into detox. She had also worried that the staff in detoxes brainwash you. I wanted to prove that they hadn't.

'Yeah. Of course I can.'

She drank her brandy. Then another. And another. I sat watching her drink each one. As the brandy touched her lips, I savoured the taste on my own. As it tippled down her throat, I could feel it down mine. Everything inside me was screaming to have a brandy. But I couldn't have just one brandy. I would need to have a brandy, then another, and another – just like Karen was doing. I sat, watching her, and drank my Coke. It was a miserable Coke.

She asked if I wanted to go and steal some meat with her in Tesco's. That was something I could still do. I didn't need the meat or the money, but I liked the rush I got from it. Nobody had said I needed to stop stealing things. We went into Tesco's and walked around the aisles trying to stuff as many steaks into my jacket as I could. We sold the meat in the pub and I bought Karen half a bottle of Mad Dog – fortified, strong wine. We went back to her council flat. She stood in front of me completely naked. It was like I was looking at the body of a grandma. Her skin was shrivelled, bruised, and pale.

'No, Karen, we can't do this,' I said.

'You don't want to fuck me? I want to fuck you, Mark. Please.' I wanted to make her happy. When we were together on the streets, I felt like I loved her. In reality, I needed her at times for company. Now I wanted to make her happy because I felt sorry for her. I was seeing Karen with a new pair of glasses – except these glasses were showing up a naked woman I no longer recognised.

'I can't, Karen. I don't want to.'

'You fucking wanker, Mark. Let's just pretend my ex is going to come through the door and catch us fucking. That used to turn you on.' It didn't now. Nothing could have; I was staring my past in the face, and it was the most unattractive thing I could've imagined.

'No. I have to go. I have to get back.'

'No, Mark, don't lie. You said you had an overnight pass. You said you would stay.'

'I have to get back. I can't handle this.'

'That's a pity,' she said. 'Because I'm going to buy a couple of rocks of crack. Sure you don't want some?' I ignored her. Then she started screaming: 'You fucking liar. You said you could handle me drinking. You think you're better than me. You're just like me. Don't fucking turn your back on me.'

I turned away and ran as fast as I could back to the detox. I played those words in my head – *'You're just like me.'* She was right. I was just like her. It wasn't Karen that was a different person. I was different. Karen was the same person. She was exactly who I had been with for those years. She was exactly who I had been for those years: a haggard old husk of a man, smelling of stale sweat and beer. I kept running. I was running away from Karen. I was running away from my old life, back to safety in the new. I saw the sign for the hospital – the detox was based in a psychiatric hospital. I laughed as I saw the sign. I was running to a psychiatric hospital in search of sanity.

Chapter 21

The rehab was split into three houses, where twenty of us shared a kitchen, a lounge, yet just two to a bedroom. Our routine was much like detox. Most of the day was spent in group sessions and with our drug counsellor. After completely failing to impress Tony with my Step One, I had to ask others to join me to form a mini group, which Tony hoped would help to break down my denial about my past. John had left detox and gone home. I didn't have him with me to help with this problem.

There were several of us with the same problem. The problem we had was denial. I had always believed that I had made a decision to do the things I had done. I had always believed that if I stopped using certain drugs, then my life would get better. Even in the early stages of detox, I was contemplating dealing drugs when I got clean and left rehab. I knew that there were some addicts who had done the same. Being a drug dealer clean would enable me to do a better job and be more successful, I figured. That idea, that everything would have been okay without the drink and drugs, was crushed when I had to answer the question in group:

'What was life like without alcohol and drugs?'

It was hard to think back that far. I took my first drink at twelve and my first puff of hash at fifteen. Before the drink, my life was like everybody else's on my estate. Some were richer and some were poorer, but we were all pretty much in the same boat with parents who were heavy drinkers.

'How did you feel without alcohol and drugs?'

Trying to think about how I felt as a child was difficult. I am not sure I could have done it on my own. In group, there were other addicts like me who were sharing how they had felt. Most of the time I zoned out of what was said by others in group and tried my best not to fall asleep. But this time somebody said something that shot my eyes open:

'From the moment I was born,' he said, 'it felt like I should have been left in the womb. I never felt comfortable living.'

At first I didn't know what he meant. I just felt something about what he had said – I felt that it was me he was talking about. I never felt comfortable as a child. I wasn't comfortable at home because Dad might be drunk or angry. I never felt comfortable at school because I had to act hard and fight to make friends. I never felt comfortable with my friends because I had to force them never to leave me. I never felt comfortable with girls because I never knew how to have sex or even what sex was.

'When did you feel comfortable?' Tony asked. I didn't realise I had said all that out loud in the group.

'I don't know,' I said. 'I just stopped feeling uncomfortable.'

'What was it like when you had your first drink?' he asked. That was an easy question that I knew the answer to.

'It was like I didn't need to worry about anything. I could talk with anybody; I could be anybody I wanted to be.'

'Were you comfortable?' That had never been something I'd looked for when I drank. I just drank to help myself do things that I couldn't do when I wasn't drunk.

'I was comfortable for a while…' I said, unsure of what I meant.

'Comfortable for a while?' Tony coaxed me.

'I was comfortable until I needed more.' It always stopped working.

Once I got that feeling of comfort in myself and the world around me, I didn't want it to stop – so I drank and drank and drank. When that stopped working, I found drugs. When that stopped working, I chased both of them – drink, drugs, drink, drugs. Eventually none of it was working. The very thing drink and drugs had done for me – made me comfortable – destroyed my world to the point where I needed drink and drugs to avoid seeing what was the truth. I was still as scared and as lost as the twelve-year-old boy who picked up his first drink – except now I was thirty-two and my world was more shattered than it had ever been.

'Is that what you had planned for yourself?' Tony asked.

'No,' I said. I put my head in my hands and cried. My life hadn't been an adventure. It had been a slow death from drink and drugs – and I hadn't had any power in me to do anything to stop that.

I had finished my Step One and my first month of rehab. It was Christmas. I sat with other addicts in our shared kitchen. We were eating Christmas dinner. I hadn't eaten sitting at the dinner table since I was a child. I had rarely eaten Christmas dinner. We had a coal fire burning and Christmas cards decorated its mantle. It was warm and we ate well. We gave each other presents. Everybody else handed out presents from the PoundShop. I gave them all sports gear from the bushes. We played charades and cards.

As I looked at all of us sitting, laughing, playing cards, and having fun, I felt a connection. It was a feeling of connection that I had not felt before. I felt like I belonged. It reminded me of the Dons in Malaga prison, playing cards, drinking hooch, and smoking hash with each other. It reminded me of my dad sitting in the pub getting slaps on the back from his laughing friends. I had longed for it then. I thought that drink would bring me to it. I'd never felt it beyond the first drink and the first high. I could only watch others who had it and wished it for me. For the first time, I was living the scene – not just watching it from the outside.

And these people didn't drink.

* * *

I was starting to see why I drank and used drugs. I became convinced I drank and used because of other people. No matter what I did, they always had a habit of ruining my day. Umis was an example of that in the rehab. He was my mentor – which meant that he was a bit further along than me and would show me the ropes. The problem was that he was lazy. Every morning I would get up to do my chores before morning group and Umis would still be in bed. I was fed up with having to do his work, so I told him.

'Fuck you, Mark,' he said.

'Who do you think you are talking to? If we were on the street, there is no way you would talk to me like that. I'd use your head as a mop,' I said.

'Fuck you,' he said. He knew I wouldn't hit him, because I would get thrown out of rehab. It infuriated me, yet I could do nothing about it. Then he had the cheek to challenge me in group:

'I think Mark is pretty dishonest about things,' he said.

Umis was an alcoholic and sex addict. He had been a serial stalker and had gone about the streets flashing his willy to women. Who was he to judge me? I stared him out, ready to pounce on him.

'Fucking shut up, Umis,' I warned. 'Fucking shut it or…' Even before I could finish my sentence, Tony was on his feet and in my face.

'No. That is not what we do here,' he said. 'You're not on the street now.'

I wanted to punch him too. I always wanted to punch Tony. I couldn't, though – Tony had the power. He was the counsellor.

'You are not on the street now, Mark. That is not who you are.'

He was wrong. I was a fighter. I always had been. That's what everybody did in Glasgow, that's what everybody did on the streets, and that's what I did.

I should fucking hit him.

Tony was still standing in my face, staring me down into my seat.

245

Everybody in the room was watching me. I was raging inside.

How dare you do that to me in front of the whole group?

In a few moments he was sitting back down and the group session was finishing. He didn't say anything to me afterwards. Neither did Umis. I went to my room and paced.

That fucking bastard. If he comes near me again I'll punch him.

They made the rules, though, and I was pretty sure punching wasn't allowed. I had to do something. I couldn't let it go.

It's not right embarrassing me in front of the whole group.

The group…

That was it! I could challenge Tony in the group. It was one of the first things they got us to do in group therapy. We had to share our 'feelings' about things that had happened in the house. If we had a concern about somebody, we shared it. We had a whole meeting dedicated to it – the monthly concerns group. They gave us pens and paper so that we could list anything we wanted to talk about. Mostly it was petty stuff – not washing the dishes, getting up too late, or being aggressive. Now I had a genuine grievance to bring to the table and Tony would have to apologise.

The next day I sat opposite Tony. Everybody in the group was looking from me to Tony, from Tony to me.

I stared.

Tony wrote on his clipboard.

I snarled.

Tony looked around the room, smiling.

'So, anybody got any concerns today?' he asked.

Fucking fanny.

'Yeah. Me actually.'

'Mark – of course. What is it you want to talk about today?'

Don't push me with your smart ways.

'You,' I said.

'Okay. What is it you want to say to me?' He was still smiling. But it was a welcoming smile. It wasn't a smile that said *'Fuck you.'* I was

246

disappointed. I could do something with a *fuck you* smile – I didn't have a clue what to do with a welcoming smile.

'I have a concern about the way you got in my face in front of everybody yesterday.'

'How did that make you feel, Mark?'

'Angry. I was angry at you,' I said, not realising I was falling into one of his word traps.

'Why are you angry, Mark?'

Why am I angry?

I looked down to the floor. 'I don't know,' I said.

Tony had defeated me again. This time with a question I didn't have the answer to. It was the same question my mum had asked me years ago when I'd boxed my friends. *Why are you angry, Mark?* I didn't know when I was a child and I didn't know when Tony asked me in group.

After a few months without alcohol and drugs, I was angry with everything and everyone. I was angry I still had to sit in group and talk to these idiots. These guys didn't know what it was like to be a drug dealer. They didn't know what it was like to live on the streets. Most of them had had jobs before this or lived off benefits. I came from a different world of drug dealing gangs and adventure. I didn't want to be around these people. They kept going on about me needing to hand my life over to something greater than I was – to accept I wasn't a good driver for my life. I couldn't see how me giving up on managing my life was going to get me where I wanted, even if I didn't really know where it was I wanted to go or who I wanted to be. I just knew I didn't want to be sitting in a group therapy session, day in and day out.

A short time after that altercation in group, I went to a Twelve Step convention of addicts. It had the same format as a meeting, except with lots of speakers throughout the weekend. Over a thousand addicts attended. I was listening to a woman on stage. I was still angry with the world and couldn't see how this woman had anything in common with me. She didn't look like she had been on the streets or running in drug gangs like I had. She was sharing the same story as everybody else of how she came into recovery – took too many drugs, life got bad, needed help. I was zoning out of what she was saying until something she said hit me.

'...after I came into recovery, I was so scared of whether I had got HIV that I didn't get tested for two years. Then I got tested and I got diagnosed with HIV...' She stopped what she was saying and started crying. She broke down on the stage, in front of everyone. I felt embarrassed for her. I cringed in my seat.

Why is nobody doing anything? Why is she still standing there?

Then somebody shouted from behind me.

'We love you!'

Then another person.

'We love you!'

Then another, and another, until the entire hall of addicts were shouting and whooping and clapping.

All the anger I felt about all these people - all the anger I felt having to be with these people - vanished.

This is where I am meant to be.

I could feel the love. I could feel the energy in the room. I had never seen anybody be so honest. I couldn't imagine anybody doing it in front of all these people. The woman on stage had done it and she had been accepted. I had been chasing gangsters all my life and had never been accepted - not without conditions of who I needed to be.

That's what I want. I want to be accepted. I want to belong.

I looked around the room at the claps, the cheers, the smiling faces. People were crying. I felt lifted out of my seat and carried to safety. For the first time in my life, I felt like I was accepted. I had found a home.

The next day, on the way back to the rehab, I sat at the train station. I thought about what had happened during the day and what I had felt. That woman was like me. She had the same fear about everything. Yet she had trusted that everything was going to be okay

248

– even when she got the news she feared the most. She was okay. She had more friends than I had ever had. They were friends who cared about her. She could cry on stage in front of them and she was still okay. It was then that I thought that maybe I didn't need to be so scared. Maybe things would be okay without me in charge.

I still felt the warmth from the convention. I felt connected with the world. I looked up at the sky and watched the stars. As I did, a Concorde shot past. The fastest plane in the world looked small and insignificant against the black mass of sky.

If that plane is insignificant, then what am I? A speck of sand.

I felt completely insignificant, like a grain of sand, yet completely significant and part of everything in the universe. I started repeating one of the Steps in my head – the Step about striving through prayer and meditation to improve our conscious contact with a power greater than ourselves - I realised then that I was praying. It wasn't like the time I was in the toilet, praying to something I didn't believe in, through desperation. This time I realised I felt conscious contact with something bigger than me.

At that moment a train shot past at maximum speed. I cried and cried as it did. I screamed tears. It was a moment of realisation. I felt the presence of something other than me. I had spent my life visiting ashrams in India, travelling to see spiritual gurus, and here I was at New Cross Gate station having a spiritual awakening.

I was insignificant in the greater scheme of things. Yet I was also connected to everything – I was part of the universe. That connection to the universe was my higher power.

That understanding gave me peace.

I don't need to be in charge.

Chapter 22

'You have to get a sponsor, Mark. You won't stay clean for long if you don't,' Tony said.

A sponsor was somebody like me – who had used drugs and didn't any more. My sponsor needed to be farther down the road than I was. We would be leaving rehab, and we each needed to make sure we carried on with the Twelve Steps once we did. They had kept us going to meetings and connecting with other addicts outside the rehab. I met my sponsor at a meeting. I heard him share his experience – and thought that if he could be the person he is today, after experiencing the same as I did, then maybe he could help me.

Jimmy and I continued on with the Steps whilst I was preparing to leave rehab. He was turning out to be a good sponsor, and we had finally reached the point where I had to list all the people I had harmed over the years. It was a difficult thing to do because I had spent so many years thinking that I had been let down by others. I had never seen the damage that I had caused to people through my actions. As I looked at what I had written about what I had done, I felt shame. I hated myself for it.

'Can you see what you did to the people around you?' Jimmy asked.

'I'm a bastard,' I said.

'No.'

'I'm like my father,' I said.

'No.

'We're sick, Mark. We have been sick for a very long time – and that sickness shows itself in self-centred. For me, I don't know when it started. But I know that the first time I took drugs, the world became a great place to be. I could talk to people just fine. I felt safe.'

Jimmy had a beautiful way of exposing me to the truth of what I felt without making me want to punch him. There were times I didn't like what he said. There were times I cursed him behind his back and to his face. He cared about me enough to tell me the truth anyway, and I cared about him enough to hear it, even if I didn't like it. As I worked through the list of harms I had caused, he sat with me that afternoon and he told me about what had happened to him. He told me how the drugs and drink had helped him for a time, and then one day they just stopped working. When they stopped working, he still couldn't stop taking them. He had tried to make it work. He'd spent most of his life trying to make it work. In the time that he had spent trying to make the drugs work, he destroyed his health, relationships, and sanity.

'The very thing I took drugs to cure – fear – brought about everything I was scared of. I had nobody left who cared about me, I had no money, and I was dying. You're not a bastard, Mark. Your father wasn't a bastard, either. You were sick.'

I sat and listened like I had never listened to anybody before. I listened to how he got better, Step by Step. How he had come into detox alone and almost dead, but had met other people just like him. How he felt he wasn't alone any more.

Jimmy had told me I would need to go back and clean up the mess that I had made. To be able to move on with my life, I needed to help others I had harmed move on with theirs. Where I had hurt someone, I had to try to make it right. It wasn't something I was keen to do. I could see many reasons why the people I had hurt were

251

either partly or fully responsible. We were all in the same game – doing anything we could to buy, sell, and take drugs.

What Jimmy had asked me to do only made sense after a group therapy session in the rehab. As usual, it took somebody else like me to share what had happened to them for me to see what I needed to do next. There was a woman sitting across from me who began describing a man who had betrayed her. He had left her one day and never come back. She cried as she told us how this man had been the love of her life. She told us how the man had cheated on her, yet she had forgiven him. She couldn't understand why he had left.

'I'm just a piece of shit. That's why he left,' she said and then wailed pain.

I looked at her and saw Lesley. The face was different, but what she said – she was describing me.

That is what I did to Lesley.

I started to fidget in my seat, as tears welled up in my eyes.

'What's wrong, Mark?' Tony asked. I couldn't reply. I didn't want to cry in front of everybody. If I opened my mouth, I would end up crying. I just shook my head.

'Did that affect you, Mark?' he asked. I cried.

That was the first time I could really see what Jimmy was saying. I needed to clean up the mess and make things right so I could be free. I couldn't be free of shame while Lesley was feeling like a piece of shit, not knowing why I had just left. Jimmy made me write a list of all the people I needed to make amends to. He got me to talk through what I had done and what the circumstances had been.

'Now, this is when we work out whether you are going to stay clean for long,' he said. 'Most people don't get past this bit – this is going to take courage to face up to these people.'

My mum was the first person we looked at. I read the letters I had written to her over the years. There were dozens of letters. They were all sent to beg for money. I remembered the rare times I had gone home to visit her. She had tried to help me stop drinking.

She had limited me to a few cans a day – then, when she'd slept, I had stolen her gin. I had begged her for money when she wouldn't give it to me. She knew it was going to be spent on drugs. Even as she'd cried, I'd told that if she didn't give me the money I would rob somebody. Out of everybody, my mum had suffered the most.

'You know, this isn't the most harmful thing you did, Mark,' Jimmy said.

'Seriously, that's everything I did. I have been completely honest,' I said.

'What about the worry you caused your mum? What was it like for her thinking that her son might die with a needle stuck in his arm? What was it like waiting for a call from the police?'

He didn't need to carry on. I understood. My mum had lost her son for all those years. That was the most harmful thing I had done to her.

I sat with Mum and my stepdad, Bill, outside a café. I had bought Mum some earrings and Bill a political book. I wanted them to have a present from me – something they had never had. I looked at Mum. She was old. Older than I ever remembered her. I had seen her over the years, but I'd been so lost in myself that I hadn't seen her. I had spent more time with her since I got clean, but I hadn't noticed how old she had got until she sat before me.

'Mum,' I said, 'I wanted to tell you something. Over the years I caused you pain. I caused you worry and stress. I have been a terrible son to you at times. There is nothing I can really do to change that. I love you. Thank you for being there for me. Thank you for having faith in me when I didn't. You never, ever gave up on me.'

I turned to Bill and told him the same. I told them both that if there was anything I could ever do to make things better, I would do it. There was silence for a few minutes.

'Mark. I have always loved you, son. Always. I just hated your behaviour.'

I looked down, ashamed of myself. Then she touched my hand.

'I still love you, Mark. But now I also always love your behaviour.'

She had tears in her eyes. I cried. Then we hugged and I felt at peace. As I sat watching her for the rest of the afternoon, I noticed her age again. I had Jimmy's voice in my head, *'Your job now is to continue to be a good son - sorry is just the start.'*

There were many amends that I couldn't make. Some of the people I had harmed, I couldn't find. I tried to search for Lesley every way I knew how. The problem was my memory – after years of abusing my mind with drugs, I didn't remember the minor details of addresses or phone numbers of people from those times. Jimmy said that it was important to clean up where I had harmed somebody – but the main thing was that I became willing to do that. If I couldn't find the person, then, as long as I was willing to if the opportunity ever came up, that was enough. There were others I had harmed for whom it would cause more harm to them – or to myself – to make amends.

When I worked through the list with Jimmy, there were amends that I didn't think would be possible to make. Walshy was dead. I didn't see how I could make things right with him. His mum was still alive, so I started with her. She had lost a son. I knew now that I hadn't killed Walshy. He had made the same choices as me and for the same reasons. He was an addict. I couldn't have encouraged him just as I couldn't have dissuaded him. Yet it was clear that I hadn't been the friend I'd thought I was to Walshy. I'd left him to deal with the business, and then blamed him when it went wrong. I hadn't got him to a hospital because I'd been passed out. I was as sick as Walshy had been – but I still needed to explain to Walshy's mum what had happened.

I wrote her a letter. I told her that I was sorry for what had happened to Walshy. I told her that I was sorry that my actions had contributed to the way Walshy had lived his life. I told her that if there was ever anything she would want me to do for her, then I would do it. I had read the letter to Jimmy first. It was important that I got the letter right – this was about how she felt, not me.

Jimmy warned me that I would probably never hear back.

Jimmy was right. I never did hear back. She died a few years later. I will never know what that letter meant to her, if it meant anything at all. I went and visited Walshy's grave. I hadn't been allowed at the funeral, because his brothers had threatened to kill me at the time. It was the first time I had visited the grave. I laid some flowers by the gravestone and sat talking with him for a while. I didn't talk about much. I just told him what I had been doing. I told him that I was sorry that he died. I told him that I wished we had both been able to get help.

The amends that I found most difficult to do were to my father. It took me several years to even see that I owed him amends. I had gone through the Steps and seen that my father had been as sick as I had been. I had seen that the things he'd done, he hadn't done to me - that he had been a bad father because he hadn't known how to be a good one. He hadn't even had the sanity to be a good one. I had kept in touch with Dad during my recovery, much more than I had ever spoken to him before. He had got sober again. But he only ever seemed to manage a few years. Two years into my own recovery I rang him and found him the other end of the phone, drunk. I wanted to give up on him.

'Where have you tried to stop drinking and failed?' Jimmy asked. There were many times I had tried and failed. Even at two years clean, I still had moments where I wondered whether I could make it another year – sometimes even another day. Yet I did what my Dad didn't do – I kept going to meetings, I kept in touch with my sponsor, I did the Steps. Dad did that for a while, got a bit better, and then dropped it.

'You can help him, Mark. You are not a child any more.'

'I don't know how to help him,' I said.

'Start by forgiving him. He was sick. He didn't set out to hurt you. Forgive him and see what happens.'

It was still something I didn't think I could do. But I could see

255

what Jimmy was saying. I knew how it felt to have people forgive me for the things I had done – my mum included. It helped me carry on without that guilt and shame hanging around my neck, weighing me down. I decided to try to do that for Dad. I asked him, if he was to go anywhere in the world, where would he most like to go. He said Egypt. We went on a trip with the intention of reconnecting and bonding. I watched him as he spent his time talking with strangers. He had a way of chatting to anybody. It amazed me that they would chat back, laugh at his jokes, and find him interesting. I had never seen that side of my dad. It was a mirror of me – sociable, likeable, yet at times very selfish. I couldn't chat with him, laugh at his jokes, or find him interesting. I was starting to see what these strangers saw in him more as the week went by.

I had planned on starting the amends by admitting to something I had done to my father years ago. I had once stolen his ring and pawned it for drugs. I bought him a new ring and gave it to him. He looked down at it. As he did, I felt a sudden burst of emotion inside me. I felt shame. It was difficult to admit to stealing his ring. I wanted to make it right between us. I just didn't know how.

'Look, Dad,' I said, 'this has been amazing that we are here together.' I looked at him looking at me. I noticed that he looked emotional. He looked vulnerable. He was just as vulnerable as I was. I didn't want to stay angry at my dad, who was now an old man.

'We are the same, Dad. You and I are the same. We've had our differences. We have both been lost to our addictions – you to alcohol and me to drugs. But you are my father. You're my only father. And I love you. I love you, Dad, and I'm sorry whatever pain I've caused you in your life.'

He sat opposite me, and I could see tears in his eyes. I knew his guard was down and that he was open and vulnerable. Hi sadness mirrored a deep wound and sense of sadness within me. I could see his pain. It felt like he was me himself as a little sad abandoned boy. I started to cry. He told me, 'I love you, son,' and I told him, 'I love you, Dad.' Then we hugged. As we did, I put my hand behind his head to support it, as a parent supports a child's head. I forgave him for what had happened in that moment. I felt like a parent of a child, holding him.

After starting to clean up the mess I had made, I felt ready to move forward with my life. Bournemouth was like a recovery theme park. Theme parks are fun, but they're states of perpetual childhood. I had to grow, and I knew that part of growing was moving forward. I had to get out of Bournemouth to stay moving forward. That was the aim – always moving forward. If I stayed still, I got bored. If I was bored, I would be using in no time. Shortly after I left rehab, I went to college. Jimmy had said that I needed to learn how to do a proper job.

'One day you have to start working and paying taxes. Giving back to the community, instead of taking from it,' he had said.

Jimmy was always telling me that I needed to give back. I knew what he meant – I hadn't paid taxes since I worked at the base when I was eighteen. Most of the other addicts out of rehab in Bournemouth were getting odd jobs on building sites. I didn't want to do that. I still had ambition, even without the drugs. Some of the guys who had left rehab were selling drugs or doing tobacco scams. I didn't need Tony to tell me that selling drugs wouldn't keep me clean for long. Jimmy said a lot of addicts become counsellors – it was a big cliché. Cliché or not, it seemed a good way to make money, pay taxes, and help others. Those were the things Jimmy said I had to start doing. I went to college and qualified to be a counsellor.

After I qualified, I realised that there was nothing left in Bournemouth – aside from the recovery meetings – that was keeping me there. Everybody I bumped into on the street, I knew from the rehab or the meetings. It was like a small village where everybody knows each other's business. I got a job in London. I was going to be a drug counsellor working in police stations. The last thing I did before I said goodbye to Bournemouth was hand in my benefits book. I could now be self-sufficient.

257

Chapter 23

I was sitting in a police cell again.

It had been five years since I had left rehab and six years since I had taken a drink or a drug. This time, drugs had nothing to do with it...

When I was over a year clean, I got a driving job in Bournemouth. I drove around girls who were selling roses in pubs for charity. The business that collected the money paid a percentage to charity and then took a profit. A friend in recovery, who was doing the same as I was, suggested that I do it for myself. If I sold the roses, I could donate a percentage to charity and keep the rest. The guys I was working for were donating ten per cent. I figured that if I donated twenty-five per cent, it would be a better deal for the charity.

Who is it harming anyway?

It was a bit of extra money to get me through college. I had told the charity that I was selling lollipops to raise money for them. I told them that I would take out money to pay the costs – petrol, lollipops...

...me.

I didn't add the last bit. Although I told myself it was completely legitimate, the fact that I was profiting from the scheme left me with an uncomfortable feeling. I ignored the feeling and decided that I would only do it for a few months. As nobody complained about what I was doing, I got used to the money – a few months turned into a few years. When I moved to London, I thought I would do it for a few more months to get myself settled. I employed a girl to work with me on Friday and Saturday nights, selling the lollipops in the pubs of London. She quit on the first night.

'It doesn't feel right,' she said.

'Come on,' I said. 'Who is it harming?'

It wasn't just the money. I got a rush with every sale I made. Sometimes I would get asked about where the money went. I told them the truth – most of the money went to charity, except for the costs of the lollipops, petrol…

…*and me.*

That's how I met Estee. I was selling lollipops in a pub in Guildford, and she was drinking with a friend.

'Mark – is that you?'

Fuck.

'It is you, isn't it?'

I didn't recognise the voice. There was something about the face I recognised, which gave me butterflies in panic. I always felt that way whenever I heard my name shouted out. It could be anybody from my past – and I had a past full of people I wanted to stay away from.

'I knew you at Wandsworth Road,' she said. We had got busted by police at that squat. I remembered a few women police officers from that time. I wondered if she was one of them. I wanted to sprint out of the pub. 'The last time I saw you, you were trying to swap twenty-five thousand trips for a barge in Amsterdam.'

As soon as she said that, I remembered who she was. Estee had lived next door to our squat. She was a law student and I supplied her and her friends with hash. There were many times back then that I had tried to get her into bed with me – the snake didn't work, the Tarot cards didn't work, not even the Viking ruins made a difference. I shared a bed with her once, but she pushed my hand away every time it moved in for a sneaky grope. She was sexy then and she was still sexy.

259

'Are you seeing anyone?' I said. She laughed.

'Still the same old opportunistic Mark. Well, actually I am. What are you doing at the moment?'

'I work at the police station. I'm a drug counsellor there. I've been clean for five years.' She looked down at my charity badge. I don't think she believed that I worked for the police or that I was clean. 'No, this is just a bit of charity work,' I lied.

We spent a lot of time together just chatting and getting to know each other in the weeks that followed. I decided, after meeting in the pub, that I was going to focus on getting to know her – not trying to sleep with her. It was a first for me. I liked her and there was something that seemed right about me when we were together. She was everything I had once thought I wasn't – smart, attractive, and funny. I was starting to get used to the idea that I had those qualities, too. I felt like we were a good match for each other. But she had a boyfriend. I decided to respect that and just be her friend. Then, one night, she phoned me, upset.

'Mark – my grandma's died,' she said.

'I'm sorry, Estee. Are you okay?'

'No, not really. My relationship is over, too.'

I jumped around the room, trying not to cheer.

'Oh, I'm sorry Estee,' I lied.

'Actually, to tell you the truth, Mark, I had a conversation with my friend about this. She said I'm in a relationship with you. We just haven't had sex yet.'

That's more than you have been telling me.

We waited another day. Then we got together. Within a few months, she was pregnant and we were living together. I was six years clean and my life was transformed. I had a flat that I owned, I lived with a woman I loved, I had a good job helping other people, and I was about to be a father.

Everything in my life, for the first time, was starting to feel right. That made what I was doing with the charity business more uncomfortable than it already was. I felt shame every time I went out to collect money and had two voices battling again.

One voice said: *Stop what you are doing, Mark. This path leads to trouble. This is not who you are.*

The other voice said: *Who is it harming? Just do it for a bit longer, make some more money – you are going to need it. I'll stop in a few more months.*

Jimmy always told me that sometimes we keep doing things we know are not right until it gets too painful that we can't do it any more or we will use again.

'Sometimes,' he said, 'God will do for you what you can't do for yourself.'

One night, I went out with two new helpers. Despite the voice of caution, I was getting greedier and had taken on two new people to sell more lollipops. We all got arrested that night outside St Paul's Cathedral. They found the badges and the pots in my car. If it had just been my badge I would have been okay. That was the badge that the charity had given me. I hadn't bothered registering the two new helpers with the charity, though, and had made their badges myself. That was what had got the police suspicious. That was what had got me stuck in a jail cell.

Back in a jail cell again. What the fuck have I done?

I had used my phone call in the police station to speak to Estee. She was organising a lawyer to come and help me. She had known all about the scam and would question me about why I was doing it. I always told her that I would stop soon. I told her it wasn't a problem. I told her I was in control of it. The truth was that I couldn't stop. It was just like with the drink and the drugs – I was too hooked into the easy money it provided. I sat against the cold concrete wall wondering how I had got here again. That was when I noticed a name scrawled across the wall.

Maria Dempster Was Here 2001.

I thought it was strange that my second name was on the wall of the cell I was in. I shouted out to one of my helpers stuck in the cell next to me: 'Hey, my name is here on this wall.'

'Well, you are obviously meant to be here,' she shouted back.

It was then that I saw the reality of my situation.

God will do for me what I can't do for myself.

I couldn't find the motivation to stop the charity scam. But, now I had been arrested, I would have to stop. I couldn't see how I kept doing this, how I kept ending back in trouble with my head in my hands. I'd thought it was the drugs. But I was clean and I still ended up back in jail. Jimmy always said it wasn't the drugs that were the problem. I always nodded. I'd thought I understood him, but I never did. Sitting in that jail cell, I finally understood him.

It's me that's the problem. It's me that keeps doing these mad things.

I had been doing these things before I sipped my first Special Brew or smoked my first bit of hash. I had found out in rehab that the reason I drank alcohol and took drugs was to change the way I had naturally felt. I had been clean for six years by the time I ended up back in a jail cell. I was as scared as I had been when I was a child, jumping the bins to make my friends like me. Just as alcohol and drugs had stopped making me less scared, so had the chase for money. I knew that things had to change.

As soon as the lawyer got me out, I went to see Estee. I had to tell her the news that I had been charged with fraud and suspended from work. She wasn't happy.

'Mark, what are you doing? You're going to be a dad. If you don't stop all this, I'm going to leave you.'

'What do you mean? I'm not going to do the charity thing any more,' I said.

I was still going to keep hold of the tobacco selling. I had been selling tobacco I smuggled back from Europe for years. Everybody did that. Surely that would be okay.

'No, Mark, I mean everything. Including the tobacco. You have to go completely legit. Nothing illegal! I am not going to let you be the influence to this child that your father was to you.'

She was right. There were still big contradictions in my life: on one hand I was a drug worker in a police station and on the other I had been arrested for breaking the law. I had never seen it that way until she had said it. My dad had been an alcoholic and a thief. He had neglected me as a child because he had known no better. He didn't get the help that I had got to recover. He stayed sick most of his life. I didn't want my child to have to go through what I had gone through. I didn't want my child to believe that I didn't like him. I didn't want my child to believe that the only way he could be at peace with himself was to fight, to drink, to take drugs, to run with gangs. I didn't want to be that father and I didn't want him to be that son. I had been faced with this choice several times in my life – somebody saying that I can choose this path or that path. I had always chosen the path that I wanted – the easier path. But the easier path had always turned out to be the hard one in the long run. It had always led me to pain. I decided to do the opposite of what I thought I should do this time.

'Okay, Estee. Completely legit,' I said.

This time I was going to try the other path. I would do everything it took to make it work.

The charges were dismissed from court a few months later. The fact that I had donated some of the money to charity – at least the percentage I had planned to – meant that I had done nothing illegal. I was allowed back to work. I did as much overtime as I could to make sure we had the money we needed for when the baby was born.

A few weeks before the charges were dismissed, my little boy was born. I held him in my arms in St Thomas's hospital. Some people say they worry they won't love their children when they're born. I never worried about that. I never thought about it. I was too excited about being a dad. I knew that love was doing nice things for the other person. I knew that love was making sure they were okay. I thought I had a pretty good idea of what love was. But, when I held Him in my arms for the first time, I felt a deep sense of belonging and purpose like never before. I had spent years looking for that purpose and belonging. It had taken me to dark places where people died around me and I had almost died with them. Now, in my arms, was my life's purpose. I didn't need to search any more.

I'm here to help someone else. That is my purpose.

The birth of my son had shown me life's purpose – to help him grow and learn and live – but it wasn't until I connected it to what Jimmy said that I realised that service didn't have to be limited to my baby boy. Trust God, clean house, and help others wasn't limited to my son or my Estee, or even those I counselled at the police station. *Help others* meant standing, ready to serve anyone that crosses my path. I had seen him do it. He had always helped me. He helped others like me, too. He helped us because we were like him. He helped us because somebody had helped him. But, mostly, he always said, he helped us because in doing that it helped him feel better – the way he thought drugs would help him feel better. I realised that I had something to give other people. I needed to help others to stay clean and be a good father.

That's the way to stay clean.

I went to the toilet. I found myself in the same cubicle that I had been in seven years before, the night I thought I had died or gone blind. I looked at my reflection in the mirror and compared my happiness and joy with the despair and dereliction of myself seven years before. I started to cry.

I thanked whatever higher power had given me life and fatherhood. I have never been more grateful to be alive than I was then. A higher power did for me what I couldn't do for myself – he gave me life.

Epilogue

At the time of writing this book I am sixteen years clean. Many people say that this is a miracle. It might seem that way from my journey. It would be poetic to attribute my recovery from drug and alcohol addiction to a mystical power. That isn't quite the truth for me. I do believe in a higher power – something greater than I am. I have had several incidences that I can only attribute to something greater than I am; I can't explain them rationally or logically. I was promised when I got into rehab that if I got a sponsor, did my Step work, continued to connect with other addicts staying clean, and helped others then I would stay clean. I have done that and I have stayed clean. Life takes work.

A lot of learning how to face life has been trying to do the next right thing. Sometimes I need help working out what that is. I know if I keep doing that, along with the suggestions that were given to me when I first came into recovery, then I will continue to stay clean, a day at a time, for the rest of my life.

Some of the people I have been in recovery with have relapsed and used drugs. Some of those people come back and get clean again. More of them have ended up missing or dead. I know that it doesn't have to be that way. I never have to use drugs again.

I also know that I have friends who have recovered from drug and alcohol addictions who are atheists and do not believe in the higher power concept. They still practise a programme of recovery and still stay clean.

In all those years of using drugs and, later, on the streets, I never imagined I would be a father. I know that I couldn't have been a father when I was using – not the kind of father that children can depend on for anything, let alone unconditional love. There was never a doubt, though, when He was born, that I could give him the unconditional love he needed. Two and a half years later our second child was born, Jess. Being a father to both my children has been the most rewarding thing I have done in my life. They have taught me how to love more than anybody else could. I have travelled the world; yet the most beautiful thing I have ever seen and experienced has been the birth of my two children. Watching them grow up and learn to make their way in this world brings me continued happiness and fulfilment.

I had many happy years with Estee. She taught me much about life that I didn't know. Although our relationship ended when I was ten years clean, we are still united in our commitment as Mother and Father to our two children. She is an exceptional mother.

After I went completely legit in all my dealings in life, I threw myself into work. I had as much drive and ambition to succeed as I ever had – except this time I put that into training and completing numerous qualifications. I progressed in my career from the front line to management positions working in detoxes, rehabs, and drug and alcohol services. I have worked with street homeless and millionaires alike, helping them get clean and change their lives. Of course, just as I chased bigger things in drugs, I chase bigger things in my career. When I was twelve years clean, I set up my own counselling practice on Harley Street. At the time of writing this book, my practice is thriving.

I am currently in a relationship with a woman who inspires me and encourages me to go forward in my life and career. We enjoy sharing that journey.

267

The people I wrote about in this story are only a few of those who were part of my journey. Not all of them have been able to get recovery. Not all of them have happy endings.

I kept in touch with John Mills for over ten years. He continued to give me praise during our many conversations and, in many ways, remained a father figure in my life. He struggled with his physical illnesses as a result of his drug addiction. To my knowledge, he never attempted to get clean again. A couple of years ago his phone was shut off, he no longer lived at the same address, and all my attempts to track him down failed. His health was deteriorating for some time and the prognosis was not good. My belief is John has died.

Rossie went to prison for smuggling drugs back from India with me. He was released from a French prison two years later. We spoke once, when I was still using, and he was angry that I had left him and only tried to visit once without success. I have not seen him since. He is somebody that I still owe amends to, and I hope one day to be able to make them.

Ronnie overdosed on heroin and got Parkinson's syndrome as a result of oxygen starvation to the brain. We talk every few months and I share my experience of recovery. He is still a using addict.

Rabid died two years after Walshy of a drug overdose.

Sprog has six children and is living in Wales. He still drinks and smokes dope.

Dave lives in Ireland and still travels back and forward to India regularly.

Magoo spent five years in prison for robbery and was released three years ago. The last time I spoke to him he was volunteering for a Christian-based outreach service.

I met Clare when I was eight years clean to make amends to her. She was a librarian and in a long-term relationship at the time. She was looking forward to having children one day.

Despite many attempts to track down Lesley to make amends, I have not been able to find her.

Tox was sentenced to seven years in prison for heroin dealing. I never saw him again.

Davey works as a school teacher in theology and works with children who have challenging behaviour.

Nick and I spoke once after the Hell's Angels incident. He is married with children and lives in Kent. We haven't spoken since. I still owe Nick amends for what happened.

I never saw Gordon again.

I saw Terrorist Brian and his henchmen once more. It was shortly before the birth of my son. I was shopping in a supermarket and I heard him shout across the aisle at me. He gave me his number and said that I could call him any time. I never did. I don't know what happened to him, his 'businesses', or his henchmen.

Tony has a private practice in Glasgow, Scotland, specialising in addiction. We are still close.

Jimmy is a representation of three different sponsors that I have had during my recovery. All three of my sponsors have given me good guidance and shared their experience of staying clean. The guidance they share comes from the Twelve Steps that are used by a number of recovery fellowships. My current sponsor is twenty-two years clean and still provides kind and loving support.

I have talked about my experience of the Twelve Step recovery programme in this book. However, there are many ways that people recover from drug and alcohol addictions. I have found that a Twelve Step programme worked for me. I have also gone through extensive counselling, group therapy, development workshops, and explored esoteric teachings. The Twelve Steps have always been my foundation – but that is just a beginning. I needed extra help and guidance to get to work on the other aspects of my character and life that I needed to repair or improve.

What helps me to stay clean, most of all, is service to other addicts. I sponsor people like me. I have continued throughout all my recovery to share my experience in prisons and detoxes. I have commitments to help make sure meetings are available for me and other addicts to attend.

My mum still lives in Scotland with Bill. I remain her loving son and do as much as I can to make sure she gets the support she sometimes needs from me. Most of all, she no longer needs to stay up at night, wondering if the police are going to call with the news that I was found dead in a skip.

My dad died on 13 April 2012. He died suddenly of a heart attack. He was seventy-two years old and had been sober for fourteen years – the longest period of his life. He wasn't a religious man, so I took his funeral service. I gave an honest eulogy and talked about my dad's alcoholism as well as his humour and the happy times we shared later in life. We had rebuilt the father and son relationship in our recovery from drug and alcohol addiction. We had moments of connection where we touched each other's soul and achieved a level of intimacy I never thought would be possible.

My father did the best job he could.

For most of his life he preferred to isolate, avoiding intimacy and social interaction, choosing to watch TV, drink tea and smoke cigarettes. He felt more content and at peace near the end of his life.

Alcoholism and drug addiction affect many lives – not just the underprivileged. I have witnessed many from privileged backgrounds suffer from addiction. It ravaged my community and my family when I was a child. It has killed most of my friends.

It is also a sickness that can be treated.

I have been able to recover.

I hope that this book shows somebody else that they can do the same.

I have travelled extensively in many countries where there is no treatment. In some, the form of treatment is being locked up in a mental institution. This is what used to happen in the UK about forty years ago. Other countries adopt a more barbaric approach where people are punished or beaten while detoxing. I am lucky to have had access to treatment and to live in a country where the government prioritise treatment for many addictions.

For this I am truly grateful. Treatment saved my life. I am committed to making sure that this option is available for future addicts seeking recovery.

I can only keep what I have by giving it away.

For more information about the author or this book visit
www.nothingtodeclarebook.com